"pioneer"

use of ∫ "aliyah"
        ⌊ "yishuv"

- easier to
  get passport (Russian) to Palestine

emigration
drama

- leave
  Palestine

- prison

U·S·=
ideology

labor
market

צריך לבדוק

An Unpromising Land

STANFORD STUDIES IN JEWISH HISTORY AND CULTURE

EDITED BY *Aron Rodrigue and Steven J. Zipperstein*

An Unpromising Land
Jewish Migration to Palestine
in the Early Twentieth Century

Gur Alroey

STANFORD UNIVERSITY PRESS

STANFORD, CALIFORNIA

Stanford University Press
Stanford, California

This book is published with the financial assistance of the Faculty of Humanities at
the University of Haifa.

Printed in the United States of America on acid-free, archival-quality paper

Library of Congress Cataloging-in-Publication Data

Alroey, Gur, author.
 An unpromising land : Jewish migration to Palestine in the early twentieth century /
Gur Alroey.
  pages cm -- (Stanford studies in Jewish history and culture)
"The skeleton of this book is my Hebrew publication Imigrantim: Ha-hagirah
ha-yehudit le Eretz Israel bereshit ha-meah ha-esrim (Immigrants: The Jewish
Immigration to Palestine in the Early Twentieth Century), which appeared in two
editions in 2004 ... The present book is an expansion of the previous Hebrew
editions."
 Includes bibliographical references and index.
 ISBN 978-0-8047-8932-5 (cloth : alk. paper)
 1. Palestine--Emigration and immigration--History--20th century. 2. Europe,
Eastern--Emigration and immigration--History--20th century. 3. Jews, East
European--Palestine--History--20th century. 4. Jews, East European--Migrations--
History--20th century. 5. Immigrants--Palestine--History--20th century.
 I. Title. II. Series: Stanford studies in Jewish history and culture.
 JV8749.A436 2014
 304.8'5694047089924--dc23

                              2013045877

ISBN 978-0-8047-9087-1 (electronic)

Typeset by Bruce Lundquist in 10.5/14 Galliard.

To the memory of
PAULA HYMAN
1946–2011

Contents

Illustrations

Figures

Tables

Preface
Two Grandfathers—Two Grandmothers

When I was a teenager in the late 1970s and 80s, I spent my summer holidays at Kibbutz Afikim with my grandfather, Moshe Belindman-Alroey, and my grandmother, Sarka Press-Alroey. Both of them were from small towns in Lithuania and had come to the land of Israel at the end of the 1920s and the beginning of the 1930s. My grandparents were among the founders of Kibbutz Afikim. They were Zionists, socialists, tillers of the soil. My grandfather worked for many years in the fields of the Jordan Valley. When he grew old and no longer had the strength, he became responsible for the kibbutz's assets, traveling once a week in a blue pickup truck to Tel Aviv to buy whatever was needed to sustain the kibbutz. My grandmother worked in the cooperative kitchen or the laundry. In their activities and way of life, my grandfather and grandmother took part in the Zionist revolution and became the new Jews. They were pioneers.

During festival days I traveled to see my other grandfather and grandmother, who lived in Tel Aviv. Emil Tadger and Ernesta Farhi-Tadger had emigrated from Bulgaria (Sofia and Varna). Grandfather came at the beginning of the "third aliyah" when he was 16 years old, and grandmother came in the late 1930s with a tourist visa. There was an age difference of eleven years between them. Grandfather worked in the family owned Avoda candy factory, and when it went bankrupt he became a plasterer. He spent all his life in the building industry, renovating and plastering the city of Tel Aviv. My grandmother was a housewife. My Tel Avivian grandparents were not the "new Jews" nor were they pioneers.

✳

Zionist historiography stressed the pioneer ethos and regarded cooperative-agricultural settlement as the glory of the Zionist endeavor and the source of its success. The movement began in the years 1904–1914 when young socialist immigrants arrived in the land of Israel and settled in its peripheral areas to establish these cooperative settlements. Members of the group totaled about 2,000 to 3,000 persons out of the 35,000 immigrants who reached the country from the beginning of the twentieth century until the outbreak of World War I. It was from this group of pioneers that the Zionist leadership emerged. All the heads of the Israeli government until 1969 arrived during this period of time, which is known in Zionist historiography as the "second aliyah." They laid the path and created the myth according to which my grandparents from Kibbutz Afikim immigrated to the land of Israel and became tillers of the soil. The focus of this book is not on this particular type of immigrant—but on immigrants like my Tel Aviv grandparents.

This book, *An Unpromising Land: Jewish Migration to Palestine in the Early Twentieth Century*, examines the majority population that arrived in Palestine (together with the pioneers) and settled in the cities and town settlements; this group became petite bourgeoisie in character. Since they were not part of the Zionist revolution and did not become the "New Jews," historiography devoted very little to researching their contribution to the Jewish Yishuv in Palestine. Doubt has led me to reexamine the period of the second aliyah—the one that is considered to have been the most ideological of all the aliyot to Palestine and the State of Israel from the late nineteenth century up to the present. Seeing the Jewish immigration to Palestine at the beginning of the twentieth century in a wider historical context had allowed me to detach myself from the ideological image of that period and focus on the complete sector of Eastern European migrants who arrived in the country. Immigrants in this wave were primarily small merchants and artisans, and they constituted the greater majority of the second aliyah immigrants.

The skeleton of this book is my Hebrew publication *Imigrantim: Ha-hagirah ha-yehudit le Eretz Israel bereshit ha-meah ha-esrim* (Immigrants: The Jewish Immigration to Palestine in the Early Twentieth Century), which appeared in two editions in 2004. During the ten years that have passed since that book's publication, I have published three other books that have deepened my knowledge of Eastern European Jewry in general and Jewish migration in particular. I found new sources and my perspective broadened, accompanied by development of a comparative viewpoint between migration to Palestine and migration to the United States. The present book is an expansion of the previous Hebrew editions. It includes a new introduction that attempts to examine how and why migration to Palestine became a unique and exceptional case in the history of Jewish migration in general and to the United States in particular. The first chapter examines the reasons for migration to Palestine in a much wider context and with a new conclusion. The other chapters have been updated and amplified, and they discuss new historical and sociological issues that were not dealt with in the Hebrew editions and are given expression in this new version.

A number of scholars and colleagues have assisted me and offered valuable advice. I would like to thank Steve Zipperstein for his help and support in publishing the book, and also Professor Hasia Diner, who read the manuscript and made important comments both on the content and structure. Special thanks are due to Philip Hollander, a friend and colleague who is thoroughly familiar with the period of the second aliyah and those who were active in it. Thanks also to the dean of the faculty of Humanities at the University of Haifa, Professor Reuven Snir, and also to the chair of the Department of Israel Studies, Dr. Yaron Perry, for their generous financial support. I wish to thank the Lucius N. Littauer Foundation that supported the book's translation, the translator, David Maisel, who translated selected parts of the manuscripts, and the staff members of the National and University Library in Jerusalem, the Central Zionist Archives (CZA), the Central Archives for the History of the Jewish People (CAHJP), and the Pinhas Lavon Institute for the Research of the Labor Movement. I want to express my gratitude to the editors with whom I worked at Stanford University Press in preparing this book for publication: Norris Pope, Stacey Wagner, Thein Lam, and Emily Smith.

The late Paula Hyman was one of the historians who most influenced me. As a bachelor's degree student at the Hebrew University of Jerusalem, I read her researches and was exposed to the importance of social history and the methodology that characterizes it. Professor Hyman was cognizant of the main thesis of migration in contrast to aliyah in the Palestine context and encouraged me to continue developing it, and she even drew my attention to gender issues. I owe her a great debt of gratitude. I dedicate this book to her.

An Unpromising Land

Introduction
Aliyah versus Migration

The great Jewish migration from Eastern Europe (1881–1914) was one of the formative events in the history of the Jewish people in modern times. During that period, more than two-and-a-half million Jews migrated abroad. Demographically, socially, and culturally, this wave of migration had an enormous impact on Jewish society. Those who reached their countries of destination integrated relatively quickly into their surroundings and gradually and persistently climbed up the socioeconomic ladder. This Jewish migration also led to the creation of new Jewish centers where there had been none before, while former sites gradually began to lose importance and influence until they finally disappeared during World War II.

Two outstanding centers of the Jewish world that came into existence as a result of this mass migration from Eastern Europe were located in the State of Israel and the United States. For the Jewish communities in these two countries, the years 1881–1914 were a formative period in which the foundations were laid for their growth. In Jewish communities in both Israel and the United States, new social elites developed in place of the former religious and economic elites. But despite the similarities that led to the creation of Jewish communities in Palestine and America, over time two different historiographies came into being, each dealing with the same historical phenomenon but interpreting it differently: one was the focus on Jewish immigration to the United States; the other was the process of aliyot to Palestine.   I

These two historiographies refused to recognize each other and were created independently without any points of contact. Although the immigrants who reached the United States and Palestine at the turn of the nineteenth and twentieth centuries came from the same countries of origin, spoke the same languages, and shared the same cultures, the two historiographies chose to emphasize the difference between the two groups of migrants. According to them, the immigrant to Palestine came because of his values and ideology, while the immigrant to the United States came for economic and other prosaic reasons. In Palestine the immigrants were said to have created a model society and laid the infrastructure for the evolving Jewish State, while in the United States they sought to improve their economic status, integrate into the surrounding society, and create roots in their new country. "The world of our fathers" evoked in Irving Howe's eponymous monumental book on Jewish immigration to the United States was not the same world as that of the Jewish immigrants who came to Palestine and sought to begin a new life there. Moreover, Zionist historiography has hardly touched on the history of Jews in America and almost completely neglected the period of the great immigration. This subject was relegated to the margins of historical research in Israeli universities without any regard for the importance of the phenomenon and the greatness of its influence. Almost nothing was written in Hebrew or translated into Hebrew about the great journey of the Jews of Eastern Europe westward, the life of Jews in the Lower East Side of Manhattan, sweatshops, the social and cultural life of Jews in the United States, or other important aspects of the subject.[1]

While Zionist historiography disregarded the great migration from Eastern Europe, it was fulsome in its praise of the immigration to Palestine. If the years 1881–1914 are considered "the period of the great migration," in Zionist historiography the period is divided into two parts: the first is called the "first aliyah" (1881–1903) and the second is called the "second aliyah" (1904–1914).

Zionist historiography generally emphasized the difference and special character of the immigration to Palestine and stressed the importance of Zionist ideology in this wave of immigration, seeing it as the chief motivation. The key criterion according to these historians was quality, not quantity. The small number of immigrants who preferred Palestine to America implied a special and exceptional wave of immigration. Why else did they choose from the beginning to come and settle in Palestine and not immigrate directly to the United States?

Thus, immigration to Palestine was taken out of its broader historical context and became disconnected from time and space.

The present work seeks to revise the picture of Jewish immigration to Palestine at the beginning of the twentieth century and to question the prevailing assumption that it was something special and unique in the history of Jewish immigration. My purpose is to examine the "second aliyah"—the most ideological among the waves of immigration to Palestine—in the broader historical context of the period of the great migration from Eastern Europe. I will do so by using accepted methods of research into immigration in general and Jewish immigration in particular. Stated more precisely, this book seeks to investigate the history and origins of immigration to Palestine from the beginning of the twentieth century until World War I through an examination of the three stages that are part of every immigration process: (1) factors in the land of origin that caused the emigrants to leave; (2) difficulties and obstacles that emigrants encountered until they reached the land of destination; and (3) the degree to which emigrants were absorbed into their new social framework. Thus this study seeks to envisage the history of immigration to Palestine as the history of the immigrants themselves, based on a view of their social, cultural and demographic backgrounds in their lands of origin as the starting point for their acclimatization in the Yishuv (the term used for *Jewish* residents in *Palestine*, before the establishment of the State of *Israel*) at the start of the twentieth century. Moreover, this work is not only a chapter in the study of Jewish settlement in Palestine at the end of the Ottoman period but also a chapter in the history of the great Jewish migration that began in the mid-1870s and ended with the outbreak of World War I.

This introduction is divided into three parts. The first part investigates how the terms "aliyah" and "migration" came to be adopted in Zionist historiography and examines the influence of these terms on research in the field. These terms not only created a distinction between immigrants to Palestine and immigrants to America but also determined that immigration to Palestine was investigated according to different criteria than those generally used in the study of migrations. In the first part of this chapter, there will also be an attempt to trace the point in time when the first waves of immigration to Palestine were taken out of their broader historical context and began to be treated as a special and exceptional phenomenon. The second part paints a general picture of the "second aliyah" as depicted in Israeli historiography and examines the influence of Zionist terminology on historical research into the history of immigration to Palestine. In the third part, I discuss the methodological problems and the primary sources that made possible the writing of this book.

Olim (Ascenders) and Immigrants

The terms "aliyah" and "migration" exemplify more than anything else the dichotomy between the two historiographies of the great Jewish migration from Eastern Europe at the end of the nineteenth century and beginning of the twentieth century. The sweeping and uncritical use of these terms was one of the main factors that led to two historiographies that dealt with the same historical phenomenon but treated it differently.

The meaning of the term "aliyah" in the Hebrew language is "going from a lower place to a higher place." The source of the word is ancient, and it already appears in the Bible in its primary sense of moving from a low level to a higher level: "And I have promised to *bring you up* out of your misery in Egypt into the land of the Canaanites, Hittites, Amorites, Perizzites, Hivites and Jebusites—a land flowing with milk and honey" (Exod. 3:17). Because Egypt was geographically lower than the land of Canaan, the children of Israel had to ascend from that low land to the land of hills and mountains that comprised the land of Israel. The same applied to the journey of the children of Israel from Babylon to Jerusalem in the time of Ezra: "Anyone of his people among you—may his God be with him, and let him *go up* to Jerusalem in Judah and build the temple of the Lord" (Ezra 1:3).

It was the biblical commentators who transformed the term "aliyah," giving it not only a sense of physical ascension but also a spiritual sense. Rabbi Solomon Yitzhaki (Rashi), for instance, claimed that, because of its sanctity, the land of Israel is more exalted than other countries, and therefore reaching entails ascension. Gradually, "aliyah" was taken out of its narrow context of entry into the land of Israel.

A much broader series of concepts came into being, including *aliyah la-regel* (going to Jerusalem to celebrate Passover, Shavuot [the Feast of Weeks], and Succot [the Feast of Booths]), *aliyah la-torah* (reciting blessings on the Torah when the portion of the week is read in synagogue), and *aliyat ha-neshamah* (the elevation of the soul in the upper world through its rectification in this world). At the same time, despite all these idioms, the commonest use of the term "aliyah" denotes the arrival of Jews in the land of Israel. This special Hebrew word has no equivalent in any other language. In the deepest sense, the process of aliyah to the land of Israel is not simply immigration or emigration but a very special kind of migration. Hence, "aliyah" refers to the realization of the desires of a Jew who, by coming to the promised land, both fulfills the divine promise in practical terms and exemplifies the concept of the Jewish longing for the land of Israel.

In the Zionist ethos, aliyah to the land of Israel is totally different from ordinary immigration, and this special type of migration is one of the foundations of Zionist thought. The aliyah of Jews to Palestine is not comparable to the emigration of Jews who left their lands of origin and reached other destinations. With the Jewish national awakening and the rise of the Zionist movement at the end of the nineteenth century, the waves of immigration to Palestine increased significantly. Zionism, which sought to create a "National Home for the Jews" in Palestine through international law, saw the immigration of Jews as a necessary condition to achieve this end.

Zionist historiography distinguished five waves of aliyah to Palestine, each of which had special characteristics of its own. These were the first aliyah during 1882–1903, colonists who founded the *moshavot* (agricultural colonies); the second aliyah, 1904–1914, socialist pioneers who came to Palestine alone or in pairs; the third aliyah, 1919–1923, socialist pioneers who came to Palestine in groups and founded the *Kibbutzim*; the fourth aliyah, 1924–1929, groups of Polish immigrants from the bourgeois class; and the fifth aliyah, 1933–1939, "Yekkes" (German Jews) who came from Germany. After World War II, the labeling of waves of immigration came to an end, although the number of immigrants who arrived before and after the founding of the State of Israel was greater than the total number of those who came in all the previous waves of immigration.

The ideological load carried by the term "aliyah" was so rooted in the Hebrew language that it was difficult to distinguish Jews who immigrated to Palestine from Jews who "made aliyah." Zionist historiography took it as an axiom that the Jews who came to Palestine in the first three "pioneering" waves of immigration were olim (ascenders) and not immigrants. The Zionist narrative differentiated itself from the general history of Jewish immigration and made aliyah into a unique phenomenon unparalleled in Jewish or world history. It must be pointed out that this narrative was also accepted unquestioningly by the Jewish American historians who dealt with Jewish immigration and who refrained from any comparison with Palestine.[2]

If one wants to locate the point in time when the first waves of immigration to Palestine were taken out of their broader historical context and treated as a unique and exceptional phenomenon, it would be difficult to locate within these waves of immigration themselves. During that period it was recognized that immigration to Palestine was an inseparable part of the general Jewish migration. In newspapers of the period and even in early memoirs of immigrants' experiences, there were articles, comments, and criticisms to the effect that those entering Palestine were not different from the masses going to America. This, for example, is what Moshe Smilansky wrote about the wave of immigration of the 1880s and 1890s:

> Every ship discharged hundreds. These people were divided into various groups. A small number were rich, well-to-do people. . . . Most of them were poor people who had nothing. Some were typical immigrants who only by mistake had made their way to Jaffa, and some were passing by Jaffa on their way to New York. Those who had some money continued on their way or returned to their beloved Russia. Those who had no money remained in the country with nothing and became laborers against their will. These became a burden on the [Zionist] executive committee.[3]

Menahem Sheinkin, head of the information bureau in Jaffa from 1906 to 1914, described those who entered the gates of the country as follows: "Miserable paupers, depressed and patched up, with bundles like rag-merchants, the poorest of the poor, who could not possibly be a blessing to the country." He added that as an official of the information bureau, he could "provide this information every week."[4] And indeed, as we shall see in chapter 3, analysis of the demographic profile of the immigrants who arrived in Palestine at the beginning of the twentieth century shows a great similarity to the composition of Jewish immigrants to America.

The immigration to Palestine was typified by its family character and the large proportion of women and children. Similar to immigrants to the United States, most of the immigrants to Palestine wanted to settle in the cities and continue in their old occupations in the new country. The term "aliyah" was known to the people and there was no doubt about its meaning, but those who entered Palestine chose to see themselves as immigrants, wanderers, or simply incomers—not as olim. When was the distinction made between olim and migrants, and between aliyah to Palestine and immigration to the United States? At what stage did the term "aliyah" become a common expression in academic discourse, uncritically accepted by all?

It seems that with the renewal of immigration to Palestine after World War I, the institutions of the Yishuv began to make a widespread use of the term "olim" in describing those entering the country. The neutral terms used at the beginning of the twentieth century were replaced by qualitative terms that gave expression to the strengthening of the Zionist-nationalist idea after the Balfour Declaration. In a few years, the terms "aliyah" and "olim" became expressions that were identified more than anything else with the Zionist enterprise in Palestine. Although it was obvious in the Yishuv that many of those entering the country came because of "push factors" in the countries of origin rather than "pull factors" in Palestine, they were nevertheless described as "making aliyah" rather than immigrating.

On the other hand, it seems that, in academic discourse, the use of the term "aliyah" as a typological expression with a different meaning from ordinary immigration began at the beginning of the 1930s with the publication of Arthur Ruppin's book *Ha-sotziologia shel ha-yehudim* (The Sociology of the Jews). This book was intended as a sequel to Ruppin's previous book, *Die Juden der Gegenwart—eine sozialwissenscaftliche Studie* (The Jews of Today), written in Berlin in 1904. In the light of changes that had taken place in Jewish society in the twenty-five years since the first book appeared, Ruppin wanted to reexamine

the social structures of the Jews as they were in 1930. In his introduction, Ruppin observed it was important "to state the facts in the
book in an objective way without omissions, and in this way to create
a scientific basis for sociology of the Jews."[5] At the same time, in the
chapter dealing with immigration, it was difficult for him to free himself from the Zionist terminology that was in general use during that
period. If Jewish immigration to the United States was due to natural
population increase, economic distress, and pogroms, those who came
to Palestine, according to Ruppin, were not immigrants but olim supported by the Hovevei Zion (Lovers of Zion) movement.[6]

In the 1940s and 1950s, demographers and sociologists like Jacob
Lestschinsky, Aryeh Tartakower, David Gurevich, Roberto Bachi, and
Shmuel Eisenstadt continued the line pursued by Ruppin in the 1930s.
They removed the term "aliyah" from its broader historical context
and placed it in the narrow Palestinian space of the Zionist endeavor.
Thus a Zionist narrative began to emerge that stressed the special na-
ture of aliyah and the Zionist enterprise in relation to Jewish immigra-
tion to other countries.

The researches of the demographer Jacob Lestschinsky represent
an interesting case of an expert on immigration who adopted Zionist
terminology in the 1940s, although he devoted most of his life to a
struggle—mainly intellectual—against the Zionist ideology.

Lestschinsky wrote many books and articles on Jewish society in
general and on immigration in particular, and by this means attempted
to understand the core problems of the Jewish people in his time.[7] He
began his research career as a Zionist with the publication of his article
"Statistika shel ayara ahat" (Statistics of One Town) in the newspaper
Ha-Shiloah. After the Uganda affair he left the Zionist movement, and
together with Ze'ev-Latski-Bertoldi and others founded the territorialist Socialist-Zionist Party (S''S) in January 1905. After World War I
he immigrated to Berlin, and joined with Boris Brutzkus and Jacob
Segall to edit the journal *Bletter far Yiddishe Demografia, Statistik un
Ekonomik* (Journal for Jewish Demography, Statistics, and Economy).
Five issues of the journal appeared in Berlin, including articles on subjects concerning the Jewish people: the development of various Jewish
communities throughout the world, movements of Jewish populations,
the number of Jews in the world, the economic situation of Eastern

European Jewry, and so on. In 1925 he assisted in the founding of YIVO (Yidisher Visnshaftlekher Institut) and organized the economic and statistical section of the institution.

From the mid-1920s until his death in 1966, Lestschinsky published many books and dozens of articles dealing with various aspects of Jewish migration.[8] In 1959, Lestschinsky immigrated to Israel. Upon his arrival, he donated his library, containing thousands of titles, and an archive built up during many years of research to the Hebrew University.[9]

An examination of his researches through the years shows that the closer Lestschinsky drew to the Zionist idea, the harder he found it to investigate immigration to Palestine using the same criteria as for investigating Jewish migration as a whole. The quantitative and qualitative methods that characterized this phase of his work were not used in his late researches into immigration in Palestine. Questions about the demographic composition of immigrants to Palestine, which were an inseparable part of his researches into Jewish immigration, were not asked at all in the context of the immigrants' chosen land of destination. He seems to have completely adopted the Zionist terminology and, like Ruppin, saw immigration to Palestine as something unique and a special case. In his book *Nedudei israel* (Israel Wandering), he wrote that aliyah to Palestine was an incomparable model of human migration:

> Aliyah to Palestine is a little current in the huge, broad sea of migration; a pure, clean current rooted in elevated, distant national and social goals; an organized, planned current that is all idea and vision, and therefore is limited in scope and has never attracted people who are fanatical about making money and getting rich; a current that has never thrilled the hearts of those who need to earn a living but rather self-controlled people who can see the future, pioneers of the nation and lovers of the homeland.[10]

This father of Jewish demography, who devoted his entire life to the investigation of Jewish society at the turn of the nineteenth and twentieth centuries, and who published scores of academic papers, edited important journals, and took part in pioneering research projects, saw immigration to Palestine in value-related and not critical terms, using phrases such as "lofty social objectives," "idea and vision," "seeing the future," "vanguard of the people," and "lovers of the homeland."

Lestschinsky's position is interesting and important because he was one of the outstanding researchers, if not the most outstanding, in the discipline of the demography and economics of Jewish society. His researches have served, and still do serve, as the basis of all research investigating the changes that have taken place in Jewish society in the last two hundred years.

The second generation of Zionist demographers in Palestine continued in the same vein as Lestschinsky. This generation made its appearance in the period of the Mandate, when the Zionist movement began to recognize the importance of quantitative, statistical research for constructing the National Home. The most outstanding of the demographers of the Yishuv in Palestine was David Gurevich, who headed the statistical department of the Jewish Agency for Palestine from its foundation in 1924 until his death in 1947. Gurevich, who came from Ludza in Latvia, immigrated to the United States and studied science and statistics. He settled in Palestine in 1921 and was secretary to the government's Department of Trade and Industry.[11] His quantitative researches on the Yishuv during his twenty years of activity made him an outstanding figure in the Yishuv in the area of demographic research. He left behind a large number of books, pamphlets, and research papers covering all aspects of the Yishuv and its economy, including immigration to Palestine.

His book *Ha-aliyah, ha-yishuv ve ha-tenua ha-tivit shel Ha-ukhlusiya be-eretz israel* (Aliyah, the Yishuv, and the Natural Movement of the Population in Palestine), which appeared in 1944, examined immigration to Palestine from a local, Zionist standpoint. Like Ruppin and Lestschinsky, Gurevich also stressed attraction to the country and especially to Zionist ideology as the main factors that drew immigrants to Palestine in the years 1881–1914. He described the first aliyah as the aliyah of the Biluim (the "Bilu pioneers") (the acronym is based on the *verse* "Beit Ya'akov Lekhu Venelkha" ["House of *Jacob*, let us go up," Isa. 2:5]). Gurevich saw the pioneering agricultural workers of the second Aliyah as representative of the aliyah as a whole because they left their imprint on the society of the Yishuv at the beginning of the twentieth century.[12] Gurevich disconnected the waves of immigration to Palestine at the turn of the twentieth century from the broader historical context of the great Jewish migration. "The path of the first olim was not strewn with roses," he wrote, "but in the land's book of life they will be recorded as pioneers who went before the camp and laid a path for those who came after them, and prepared the soil for the great Aliyah which began after the war."[13]

Moreover, Gurevich divided immigration to Palestine into five aliyot in his book, although he was not the first to do so. He placed the first aliyah in the years 1881–1903, and the second in the years 1904–1914. This periodization came to be accepted in the historiography of the Yishuv and few people questioned it. Although Gurevich as a demographer and statistician had the tools to examine aliyah to Palestine as a trend of immigration and to focus on the majority population that entered the country, he chose to emphasize the ideological olim unrepresentative of immigrants as a whole.

Roberto Bachi continued on the scientific path of Gurevich and accepted the same interpretations. Two years after the appearance of their joint book on aliyah and the Yishuv, Gurevich published an article in the newspaper *Ahdut Ha-Avodah*, in which he wrote:

> In the series of departures of the people of Israel with the ambition of building a new society in the land to which the people was morally and historically linked, its attraction to the land was not due to its lack of economic equilibrium. . . . In the case of the waves of Aliyah, unlike migration, their values and their composition were not dependent on the economic situation in Palestine but on the social and political situation in the lands of exile.[14]

From their way of looking at the first waves of immigration to Palestine, it would seem that a succession of leading demographers of the period avoided a demographic analysis of the profile of immigrants. They recognized the importance of Jewish migration at the end of the nineteenth century as an event that affected the Jewish people, but they did not succeed in connecting the great migration with the waves of immigration to Palestine. The point of view represented by these aliyot was totally contradictory to the usual methods of demographic research. Instead of examining all the components of aliyah to Palestine in a deductive manner, the demographers adopted an inductive approach.

The ideologically motivated handful who came to the country were taken as the particular case that represented the whole. If the history of the waves of aliyah to Palestine had been researched as a trend in immigration, and from a quantitative and not a qualitative viewpoint, the resulting statistical and demographic picture would not have differed from a similar analysis of Jewish immigrant society in America.

The approach of the demographers undoubtedly also influenced the Jewish sociologists of the generation after Ruppin. Aryeh Tartakower is an example of a sociologist who adopted the axiomatic distinction between aliyah and migration made by Ruppin and the demographers Jacob Lestschinsky, David Gurevich, and Roberto Bachi. Tartakower was born in Brody in Galicia in 1897. With the outbreak of World War I, his family left for the capital of the Austro-Hungarian Empire, and there he finished high school and was accepted in the law faculty at the University of Vienna. At the end of 1916 he was conscripted into the Austrian army and served until the end of the war. In 1920 he received a Doctor of Law degree, but instead of continuing his academic career Tartakower chose to undergo agricultural training and then immigrate to Palestine. In September 1920 he settled in Palestine and found employment working on road construction and draining marshes. But after contracting malaria he had to leave the country. He only returned in 1946, when he was appointed a lecturer in Jewish sociology at the Hebrew University to replace Arthur Ruppin, who had died three years earlier.

Like his predecessors, Tartakower devoted most of his research to an investigation of the Jewish people and Jewish immigration, continuing the line that distinguished aliyah to Palestine from general Jewish migration to various countries. In his book *Nedudei ha-yehudim ba-olam* (Jewish Wanderings in the World), Tartakower wrote that Jewish aliyah to Palestine was "a unique phenomenon in the history of Jewish immigration." According to him, the force that drove the Jews to Palestine came "from their desire to build a Jewish national home in the country. This national desire was in previous years almost the only cause of Aliyah. In recent years, other factors, political and economic, were added, but these did not succeed in changing the essential character of Aliyah to Palestine in the teachings of the national movement."[15] His conclusion was that "one cannot compare the immigration to Palestine before the war, with its modest scale, with the three million Jews from Eastern Europe who at the same period found a resting-place and a place of livelihood in countries overseas."[16] Tartakower's conclusions were aligned with those accepted by the Israeli academic world in the early stages of research, which distinguished aliyah from Jewish migration to other countries.

However, in the 1950s, Tartakower completely changed his assumptions. He retracted his earlier claim that "Aliyah is a phenomenon unique of its kind in the history of Jewish immigration," saying instead that it had parallels both in the Jewish world and the world-at-large. In his book *Ha-adam ha-noded* (Wandering Man), he discussed a number of basic concepts related to immigration and its influence on human society, and one of them was aliyah. The challenging definition he offered created new research possibilities that divested the case of Palestine of its unique status. According to Tartakower, aliyah was "immigration for the good of the community based on a certain idea, and involving a certain program and a certain organizational framework, as well as training for a new life."[17] The importance of this definition is that it does not make Palestine a necessary precondition for aliyah. He came to the far-reaching conclusion not only that aliyah does not have to be made by Jews to Palestine but also that it can be made by any people in any country if the right conditions exist: namely, it just needs an idea, a plan of action, and an organization to carry it out. Perhaps, added Tartakower, the concept of aliyah has not yet been formed among the peoples of the world, but "even if the concept was not clearly articulated in previous generations," that does not mean that the phenomenon did not exist.[18]

Tartakower's suggestion that there could be kinds of aliyah to places other than Palestine was a voice crying in the desert. The Holocaust, the founding of the State of Israel, and the mass immigration of the Jews of North Africa completely changed the face of the Jewish people and Israeli society, following which there were new sociological questions on the academic agenda of the State of Israel. In view of the challenges faced by Israeli society with the arrival of hundreds of thousands of new immigrants, different questions arose, with a stress on internal Israeli matters relating to the formation of Israeli society in its early stages.

In 1954, at the time of the great wave of immigration from North Africa, the sociologist Shmuel Eisenstadt published an article titled "Aliyah ve-hagirah: kavim le-tipologia sotziologit" (Aliyah and Hagirah:

The Outline of a Sociological Typology). The timing of the publication of the article was not accidental. In the five years from the foundation of the state to 1953, about 670,000 people arrived in Israel. The article summarized the views of current social scientists concerning aliyah to Israel. Considering this wave of hundreds of thousands of immigrants in such a short time, Eisenstadt drew a comparison between aliyah before the founding of the state and after. As a starting point, Eisenstadt declared that an oleh is a person who moves from one place to another for ideological or national reasons, while the immigrant "changes his place through a need to improve his economic situation."[19] At the same time, Eisenstadt suggested that although one should not be satisfied with seeing economic necessity as the chief cause of immigration, "the distinction between Aliyah and migration must necessarily begin with a comparison between the sociological reasons for the immigration of each of these types."[20] He claimed that the situation that drove the oleh to Israel was totally different from the experience of immigrants. According to him, immigration develops in societies experiencing processes that undermine the family structure and the social makeup. Factors such as a natural increase, resulting in fierce competition for employment opportunities, together with "the increased pressures of young men who do not find it possible to play their customary social roles" cause a real rupture in the societies of origin. Accordingly, immigration was a means of improving the economic status of the family, which sought "to continue its old way of life in the new country." In other words, the social crisis driving immigration "does not undermine the values pertaining to the initial identities of the immigrants and does not impel them to produce pioneering groups in the process of immigration. The immigrant carries with him and continues his former way of life, and from his point of view his new environment must be adapted to this purpose."[21]

As against this, he claimed that the type of crisis that caused aliyah, and especially pioneering aliyah, was different from that which led to immigration. The pioneering aliyah did not arise out of the impoverished socioeconomic strata of Eastern European society, and it was not a solution to the problem of demographic pressures on the Jewish population. A large part of the pioneering aliyah came from Jewish families that were enjoying economic growth, on the one hand, but on the other

were still close to traditional society. "The tension between the two po-
larities—the polarity of traditional life on the one hand, and the rise in
economic and political status in the society as a whole on the other—is
what caused the awakening of the movement of aliyah to Palestine."[22]
The motive-force of aliyah, according to Eisenstadt, was not a weakening in the economic basis but rather a weakening of the basic values of
identity in Jewish society. Another difference between the oleh and the
immigrant was their relationship to their society of origin. The oleh rejected the social values and institutional structure of the society he came
from: "While the immigrant is only interested in improving or changing
the existing society on functional points, the *oleh* comes to build a new
society with new values."[23] These differences, said Eisenstadt, largely determine the nature of the absorption of the oleh and the immigrant in
the new country. In the case of the immigrant, his previous connection
to his land of origin, its values and people, is evident for a long period in
the new country as well. For this reason, the immigrant has a strong tendency to live among his former countrymen, while the oleh has scarcely
any connection with his country of origin and its values. These considerations brought Eisenstadt to the conclusion that, until the foundation
of the state, those who came to Palestine could be described as olim, but
from the time the state was established, mass immigration changed the
essential character of the incomers, who were now immigrants.[24]

The importance of the article does not necessarily lie in the typological definition of the oleh and the immigrant but rather in Eisenstadt's
statement of principle that not all forms of entry of Jews into the land
of Israel is aliyah. This was the first time that a sociologist proposed
investigating immigration to the land of Israel in terms of immigration
itself. No longer were the incomers "a pure, clean current rooted in el-
evated, distant national and social goals," in the words of Lestschinsky;
instead these immigrants wanted to preserve their old culture in the
new country. Although Eisenstadt did not apply this criterion to the first
waves of immigration to Palestine at the end of the nineteenth century
and beginning of the twentieth— only to the mass immigration from
North Africa—the precedent he established was relevant also for the
years 1881–1914. If the immigration of North African Jewry was a wave
of immigration, not aliyah, the same criterion may be applied to the
olim who came to Palestine at the turn of the twentieth century.

At the same time, Eisenstadt's assertion that the emigration of people from Eastern Europe was a form of aliyah, while that from North Africa was emigration, continued the main line of the pioneers of sociological and demographic research who saw ideology as the motive-force of immigration to Palestine in the years 1881–1914. It was these scholars' studies of Jewish immigration to Palestine and elsewhere that gave academic authorization to the idea that the case of Palestine was different from any other case of Jewish immigration. It seems that the axiomatic rulings of Ruppin, Lestschinsky, Tartakower, Bachi, and Eisenstadt later influenced the historians who began to investigate the first waves of immigration to Palestine. These later researchers uncritically accepted the findings of their predecessors and quite naturally focused on the ideological nucleus that arose in Palestine in the period of the first and second aliyot. Thus, the Palestinian sphere was disconnected from the broader historical context of the great Jewish migration, and there was no comparative perspective.

The historian and third Minister of Education of the State of Israel, Ben-Zion Dinur, continued the tradition of these two separate historiographies with regard to the great migration. In 1955, in a lecture at the Jewish Theological Seminary in New York, he stressed the essential difference and contrasting principles between olim and immigrants. In this lecture, which was attended by descendants of immigrants to the United States, Dinur declared his intention to distinguish between the ideologically minded olim, who did not immigrate to Palestine in order to improve their situation, and those immigrants who went to America to further their lot. "The enormous human effort invested in this process [aliyah] was only possible because the individuals were to a large extent filled with a sense of mission on behalf of the nation as a whole," explained Dinur.[25] For this reason, he declared, "we stress the fact that the country was a country of Aliyah and not a country of immigration, a country to which one 'goes up' and does not immigrate, and it was this that brought it about that the man who built the Yishuv became in the course of history the one responsible for the independence of Israel."[26] We see here that Dinur adopted the claims of demographers and sociologists of his generation and failed to present an alternative historical interpretation to that of the social scientists.

When speaking to a Jewish American audience, Dinur could not focus on the similarity between the first waves of aliyah to Palestine and the immigration to the United States. "Aliyah," said Dinur, "meant that the people went to Palestine and were taken by it. Each person bore Jewish society and the Jewish State in his heart when he was still in exile."[27] Immigration, on the other hand, had no national purpose, and its moral level was undoubtedly lower than that of aliyah to Palestine. Dinur's claim is especially interesting in view of the fact that he emphasized in his lecture the far-reaching demographic changes that took place in the Yishuv from the beginning of the first aliyah to the founding of the State of Israel, especially the impressive increase in the number of Jews from 1881 to 1948.[28]

His statement to his audience that the Jewish community in Palestine grew significantly following aliyah was correct, of course, but he did not provide an explanation for the increase. It was not Zionist ideology or the attractiveness of Palestine that brought tens of thousands of Jews to immigrate there; rather, the cause of this growth was due to unrelated external factors. Mass immigration to Palestine only began when American immigration quotas came into effect, closing the gates of the United States to Eastern European immigrants in general and to Jews in particular. Despite the symbolic importance of each wave of immigration to Palestine for the development of the Yishuv, it seems that 1925 was the turning point in the history of the Zionist movement and the Yishuv. This dramatic shift in demographics became a point of no return. In that year, for the first time, the number of Jews who reached Palestine exceeded the number of Jews who entered the United States. In 1919 there were 60,000 Jews in the country; ten years later there were 175,000; and, by 1939, 450,000 Jews. It would not be an exaggeration to say that immigration quotas gave the Zionist movement an unexpected boost, thus creating an unalterable demographic reality in Palestine.

But, in a lecture given only seven years after the founding of the State of Israel, Minister of Education Dinur could not diminish the importance of ideology as a central factor in immigration to Palestine. Dinur put before his audience other reasons for the shift that were not necessarily connected with the Zionist idea. In this lecture, Dinur not only separated the Zionist enterprise and aliyah to the land of Israel from the great Jewish migration to countries overseas but also gave the oleh a higher moral standing than the immigrant. This approach, as we said, was in agreement with the conclusions of the sociologists and demographers of his generation, Lestschinsky, Gurevitch, Bachi, Tartakower, and Eisenstadt, and it was the scientific infrastructure for later historical studies dealing with the great Jewish migration and immigration to Palestine in the years 1881–1914.

Shmuel Ettinger, for example, in his book *Toldot yisrael ba-et ha-hadasha* (History of the Jewish People in Modern Time), stated that the Jewish migration from Eastern Europe was an event of decisive importance in the life of the Jewish people. He pointed out that, as a result, new centers came into being as Jews congregated in large cities, and there was a great change in Jews' economic situation and occupations.[29] At the same time, he saw aliyah to Palestine in those years as a special phenomenon totally unconnected with the great Jewish migration. According to Ettinger, the olim in the first aliyah were few in number, but they came to the country with a specific national purpose: "to found agricultural colonies [*moshavot*] which would serve as a basis for the rooting of the Jewish people in its historical homeland." In the ten years of the second aliyah, on the other hand, about 35,000 olim arrived in the country, the vast majority of whom, according to Ettinger, were young. When they reached the country, "they renewed the pioneering legacy of the initial members of the 'first aliyah,' the people of the Bilu, who were close to them in spirit."[30] So we see that the great historian Ettinger also adopted the Zionist periodization of the first waves of immigration and made a distinction between olim to Palestine and immigrants to the United States during the years 1881–1914.

This principle became generally accepted in Israeli historiography, although in later years historians recognized the fact that large numbers came to Palestine who did not engage in agricultural colonization and did not cherish the idea of cooperative living and working the land. Ettinger's statement that the vast majority of the immigrants of the second aliyah were young proved to be incorrect. For these reasons, Yehuda Slutzky, in his book *Mavo le-toldot tenu'at ha-avodah ha-israelit* (Introduction to the History of the Labour Movement in Israel), gave the concept "second aliyah" two different meanings. The first was chronological: It referred to the olim who came to Palestine in the years 1904–1914 as a whole. But the second meaning was sociological and ideological: It referred to a particular stratum of immigrants who brought with them a special national and social outlook.[31] In this way, Israeli historiography absolved itself from having to discuss the olim as a whole, focusing instead on the founders of the colonies in the first aliyah and on pioneers who built the land in the second aliyah.

This book questions the accepted Zionist narrative that sees immigration to Palestine as a special and exceptional phenomenon and points out the similarities in the waves of immigration to Palestine and the United States at the beginning of the twentieth century. It is not the pioneers who drained marshes and built roads, and who came to Palestine "to build and to be built," that are the center of this book. Rather, I focus on the average Eastern European immigrant who was light-years away from Zionist ideology and who came to Palestine for various prosaic reasons that will be discussed in detail later on.

Moreover, the book not only presents the story of the aliyot to Palestine in a different manner but also raises a number of questions about the way in which the State of Israel (with the help of Zionist historiography) "marketed" the Zionist narrative of pioneering, settlement, and self-sacrifice to Jews of the Diaspora in general and to those of the United States in particular. Through the glorification of the Zionist enterprise, migration to Palestine supposedly became of greater value than migration to other destinations. But in many senses—as we shall see in the chapters to follow—this migration did not differ in motivation and population profile from other migrant streams. Generations of Jews were nurtured by this "heroic" Zionist narrative, which regarded migration to the land of Israel as a unique and extraordinary phenomenon. The State of Israel took advantage of this narrative, both in conflating the ideals of Jewish *kibbutzim* with the State of Israel and by raising funds for the welfare of migrants and their descendants in Israel.

The Portrait of the Second Aliyah (1904–1914)
in Zionist Historiography

Zionist terminology largely determined the point of view of many scholars who dealt with the history of the waves of immigration to Palestine at the end of the nineteenth and beginning of the twentieth centuries. The abundant literature on the two waves of immigration during this period focused on a small, qualitative, but unrepresentational group of olim who came to Palestine on the strength of Zionist ideology and proclaimed a new national gospel. Other groups, not necessarily Zionist, who arrived in Palestine at the same time as the pioneers, disappeared from historical research as though they had never existed. The Zionist narrative was unquestioningly accepted, and the second aliyah came to be known as the most ideological of all the waves of immigration that reached Palestine.

The narrative of the Zionist endeavors of the pioneers of the second aliyah was didactic, somewhat simplistic, heroic, and full of pathos. These were the main lines of the story of the second aliyah in Zionist historiography:

At the beginning of the twentieth century, the new Yishuv in Palestine was in a state of distress. A stalemate had overtaken the Zionist movement after the Uganda crisis and the death of Herzl. At the height of this period, voices began to call for the realization of the Zionist enterprise. The most famous of these voices was that of Joseph Vitkin, a teacher in the colonies established by the first aliyah, who in March 1905 published *Kol kore el tze'irei yisrael asher libam le-amam u-le-tzion* (A Voice Calling Young Jews Who Have Their People and Zion at Heart), and entreated the young people to come to the country and revive "the days of the Biluim with renewed vigor, for otherwise we are about to perish."[32]

The new upsurge of the Zionist enterprise brought to Palestine members of the wave of immigration known as the "second aliyah." After the pogroms in Kishenev in Russia in 1903 and following the revolution of 1905, there began a new wave of aliyah to Palestine that lasted about ten years, until the outbreak of World War I. The number of immigrants in those years is estimated at between 35,000 and 40,000; the overwhelming majority were from Eastern Europe, with a minority from the Islamic countries. The number of *halutzim* (pioneers) who arrived in the country at that time was between about 1,500 and 2,500.[33] The pioneers brought with them new ideas that led to a reawakening of the Zionist idea in Palestine. They were strongly critical of their predecessors, members of the first aliyah, and they sought ways to change the reality in the colonies and forge new paths in settlement and organization of the Yishuv. These immigrants subscribed to a socialist ideology that became a source of new ideas in Palestine. The members of this group created a new concept—the Hebrew agricultural worker, tiller of the soil of the land of Israel—which they saw as a way of normalizing Jewish existence. The problems confronting those who had experienced the failed 1905 revolution in Russia when they reached Palestine were to a great extent similar to those that confronted immigrants to the United States: Both groups encountered institutions established and run by the generation of the 1880s. But unlike the immigrants to America, in Palestine the revolutionaries of 1905 succeeded in standing on their own feet and setting up, on a small scale, a political, cultural and economic system of their own.[34]

When the pioneers of the second aliyah arrived in Palestine, they encountered twenty Jewish colonies. The inhabitants of these colonies employed Arab workers who were used to the working conditions, accustomed to the climate, and satisfied with low wages. These colonists distanced themselves from the young immigrants. Against this background, the pioneers conceived the idea of the "conquest of labor" and the "conquest of guard," which became the slogan and chief objective of the group. The pioneers saw the idea of the conquest of labor as a supreme value and the basis for the healing of exilic Jewish society. In order to achieve this goal, they wanted to "conquer" labor in all sectors and improve the conditions of employment for Jewish workers. The resulting struggle for "Hebrew labor" led to a confrontation between the colonists of the first aliyah and the young people of the second aliyah.[35]

In order to realize the central idea of the "conquest of labor," the members of the second aliyah created unifying institutions: They created cooperative forms of work and forms of settlement, founded political parties and workers' organizations, and made contacts with the Zionist Federation in order to strengthen the workers' position. The main means of achieving this were organizations and associations. When they arrived in the country, it was hard for laborers to enter the local workforce, and therefore they set up contractual groups for certain jobs so that a worker would not have to struggle alone to penetrate one branch or another. The first cooperative settlement was founded by a group of workers from a Kinneret farm in the year 1909. A year earlier, the group had taken upon itself all the agricultural work at the farm, which had been set up by the Palestine Office.[36] After the Kinneret group had worked there for a year, it was given a piece of land in Umm Juni to create a new point of settlement. That is how Degania, the mother of the *kevutzot* (collective settlement), came into being.[37]

Another way of realizing these objectives was political organization in parties. This was already familiar to the pioneers from Eastern Europe from the experience they had gained in their countries of origin. The underlying assumption was that in Palestine the party framework would also help the lone worker in his struggle with farmers over low wages, as well as assisting him in confronting cultural difficulties in the workplace. The major organizations established in the period of the second aliyah were two parties: Ha-po'el Ha-Tza'ir (The Young Worker) and Po'alei Tzion (Workers of Zion). Ha-po'el Ha-tza'ir was founded in 1905, and was originally called Histadrut Ha-Po'alim Ha-Tze'irim. It was the first organization in the Yishuv founded on a countrywide, democratic basis, open to members and to ideological fellow-travelers.[38] It was the first political party established in the Yishuv, although its founders denied it was a party. As a precondition for the realization of Zionism, the founders of the party thought it necessary to throw off the shackles of the exile, increase the numbers of Hebrew workers, and strengthen workers in all branches of employment.

The Po'alei Tzion Party came into existence a short time after the founding of Ha-Po'el Ha-Tza'ir, and to a certain extent as a reaction to it. The founders of the party had taken part in the revolution of 1905 and arrived in Palestine a short time after its failure. In Palestine they wanted to set up a local version of the party, and they stressed the necessity of class warfare and of creating a society based on socialist principles. Po'alei Tzion saw itself as part of the worldwide Po'alei Tzion movement founded in 1906 at the Poltava Conference under the leadership of Ber Borochov. The "Ramle Program," the Po'alei Tzion party platform, formulated in 1906, stated that the Jewish Social-Democratic Labor Party in Palestine (Po'alei Tzion) "aims at the accumulation of the means of production and the construction of a society on socialist principles. The party regards class warfare, the forms of which depend on time and place, as the sole means by which this can be accomplished."[39] Ideological changes within the party began to take place with the rise of David Ben-Gurion, Israel Shochat, and Yitzhak Ben-Zvi to the party leadership. In addition to these two parties, there were also labor organizations with their parties, such as Ha-Horesh in 1907, the Histadrut Ha-Po'alim Ha-Hakla'im shel Ha-Galil (Federation of Agricultural Workers in Galilee) in 1911, and similar workers' federations in Judea and Samaria.

The workers' groups sought additional means of strengthening their position in the Yishuv and wanted greater representation in the Zionist Congresses in order to make the question of settlement and construction of the land of Israel the primary objective of the Zionist Federation. In 1907, the World Zionist Organization decided to set up a Palestine Office in order to coordinate the functioning of various Zionist institutions in Palestine and to offer advice concerning the acquisition of land. The Palestine Office in Jaffa helped a great deal with immigration, and its activities included the large-scale acquisition of land, the absorption of immigrants, the creation of neighborhoods, and the encouragement of new branches of the economy. In 1908 the World Zionist Organization founded Hevrat Hachsharat ha-Yishuv (Palestine Land Development Company), a company whose aim was to acquire land and prepare it for the Jewish National Fund and also for individual settlers who wanted to own land privately. The originator of the idea was Otto Warburg, who headed its board of directors. Arthur Ruppin was appointed head of the company and Jacob Thon was his deputy.[40]

The aim of the "conquest of guard" was achieved through the founding, in September 1907, of the Bar-Giora Organization, a guarding organization named after the leader of the revolt against the Romans in the Second Temple period. In 1909, the members of Bar-Giora founded *Hashomer*, whose program, endorsed by the general assembly in Passover 1909, was to promote Jewish watchmen in Palestine. The *Hashomer* company disbanded in 1920, but its members and deeds, especially in the case of those who fell, constituted one of the great myths of the period.[41]

In the period of the second aliyah, there appeared for the first time in Palestine women with a strong sense of the right to equality with men, and they wanted to become workers and tillers of the soil. The most outstanding of these were Ada Fishman, Mania Shochat, Sarah Malkin, and Rachel Yanait Ben-Zvi. But their struggle for gender equality only showed up the overall lack of equality in the workers' society: Instead of working in the fields, the women found themselves in the kitchen cooking for the workers. The pioneers could still not get rid of their traditional ideas about women despite their openness to other forms of change. It seems that both men and women remained captive to the prevailing concepts in the society in which they were reared.[42]

There were other groups belonging to the ideological elite apart from the socialist agricultural workers. For example, there were workers in the liberal professions, such as students, intellectuals, and teachers who settled in the towns and not in the villages; they represented the beginnings of a civil society in the Yishuv.[43] In the period of the second aliyah, the seeds were sown for the creation of fledgling institutions that to sprout at this time. Thus, the Palestine Office was the executive branch, the Teachers' Federation was the nucleus of the Ministry of Education, Beit Mishpat Ha-Shalom Ha-Ivri (the Hebrew court in Palestine) was the judiciary branch, and the Histadrut Ha-po'alim (Labor Federation) represented the desire for a representative assembly. This professional class of people also developed a new Palestinian Hebrew culture based on traditional Jewish culture. For instance, the Bezalel Academy of Art, Shulamit Ruppin's music school, the literary journal *Ha-Omer*, the Gymnasia Herzliya (Herzliya High School), and even the Maccabi gymnastics club were all founded during this period. Private enterprise also played an important part in developing the country in both the agricultural and the urban spheres. In the agricultural sphere, it was active in developing land, in preparing land for construction, and in founding new agricultural settlements. In the urban sphere, it was active in founding new neighborhoods. The climax of the activities of private enterprise in the urban sphere can be said to be the founding of the city of Tel Aviv.[44]

Among the waves of immigration to Palestine, the second aliyah is regarded as the most ideological of all, and it was celebrated in this way even before it ended. Its image was fixed as a unique phenomenon with its own human, social, and cultural character. According to a 1914 article in the newspaper *Ha-Ahdut* (organ of the Po'alei Tzion Party), this wave of immigration "was distinguished from those that preceded it not only in its large dimensions, but also, and chiefly, in its quality and social character." This aliyah, the article continued, was largely an immigration consisting of single men, and their objective was chiefly work on the land. Only "ideal young people came to the land who did not yet know the yoke of the life surrounding them, and they came with songs of rebirth on their lips." But those immigrants "burdened with cares and family concerns," who "had to bring food home, eschewed Palestine and made their way to America."[45] These factors distinguished aliyah to Palestine from immigration to other countries, and made it special and exceptional in Zionist historiography as well. In this way, the "laborers of the second aliyah" came to be seen as representative of the aliyah as a whole.

But was this really so? Was the image imprinted in the historical memory—of youthful pioneers draining marshes and setting up cooperative settlements, "conquering" the work of guarding—a true representation of all the Jews who arrived in the country during those years? Did Zionist historiography, which concentrated almost exclusively on the ideological aspect of the aliyah, not neglect other motives? This book sets out to show that the story of the period of the second aliyah is not complete without considering the activities of the majority group that reached Palestine at the beginning of the twentieth century. Its aim is not to relate the history of the labor movement and its leaders, nor tell of the attempts at settlement in Galilee and the struggle for the conquest of labor and guarding. The subject of this book is those ordinary immigrants who were not involved in political activities of the period and their collective story, which, though lacking heroism and pathos, brought little glory to the Zionist enterprise beginning to take shape in the country.

Methodology

Historical research on Jewish immigration to Palestine has usually been based on two assumptions. One is that aliyah is essentially different from all other forms of immigration; and the other is that aliyah is a central factor in the development of the national entity in Palestine from social, economic, and cultural points of view. Due to these assumptions, historical research has not examined immigration to Palestine according to the usual criteria in the investigation of immigration.

This practice leaves many questions unanswered. Thus, for example, the agricultural workers of the second aliyah have been made representative of the entire aliyah, as the primary sources consulted by the researchers were those of the ideological groups that immigrated to Palestine. These "conquering" groups had a highly developed national historical consciousness and embodied the Zionist idea as a whole. The written material they left behind was vast and varied: memoirs, letters, diaries, and newspapers with articles on a variety of subjects. These sources had the effect of making researchers describe the period from an angle that was valuable and important, but one-sided.

However, the sources that this study has relied on are essentially different from the abundant archival material left behind by the pioneers of the second aliyah. Because immigration to Palestine at the beginning of the twentieth century was an inseparable part of the Jewish migration from Eastern Europe to the West, the sources that can help one to investigate the population that immigrated to Palestine are the kind used for research dealing with immigration in general and Jewish immigration in particular. The main sources we have used come under three headings:

1. The Palestine Information Bureaus

The unprecedented scale of migration from Eastern Europe at the turn of the nineteenth and twentieth centuries led to the establishment of many information offices that helped migrants contend with the difficulties they encountered on their journey. From 1904 onward, a series of information offices arose along the routes of migration that provided Jewish emigrants with varied and valuable information. These constitute a source from which one may learn a great deal about the period of migration and about immigration to Palestine. Special information bureaus, in addition to the existing ones, were set up for Jewish emigrants who wanted to travel to Palestine, and these offices provided them with all the necessary information on the country. The first information bureau was established by the Odessa Committee in 1905 in Odessa, which was the main port of departure for Palestine at that period. In 1906 the Odessa information office set up a branch in Jaffa, headed by Menahem Sheinkin. Additional branches were set up in Istanbul, Beirut, Haifa, and in cities that were stops on the immigration route to Palestine. In 1908 a further information bureau was established in Palestine. It was part of the Palestine Office and was run by Arthur Ruppin and Jacob Thon.

In the publications of the information bureaus intended for immigrants traveling to America and Palestine, there is a gold mine of information for the researcher of the history of Jewish immigration in the period before World War I. The special feature of the Palestine information bureaus, in addition to the publicity and informational material, was that they preserved the letters sent to the bureaus. The letters relate the details of the "immigration drama" experienced by thousands of applicants, who wanted advice from the authorities on the fateful question that included all others. The many letters written in Yiddish and Hebrew, and the bureaus' replies to them, are a great treasure trove, preserved almost in its entirety in the Central Zionist Archives and in the Pinchas Lavon Institute for Labour Movement Research. From the letters, one can learn about immigrants' hesitations and difficulties in reaching a decision on whether to emigrate, not only in the case of Palestine, but in the broader historical context of the period of the great migration. These letters are a direct primary source representing hundreds of artisans, peddlers, and small tradesmen who in particular historical circumstances sought guidance and deliverance from their difficult situation in Eastern Europe.

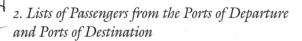

2. Lists of Passengers from the Ports of Departure and Ports of Destination

The main sources available to the researcher who wants to examine the composition of the population of immigrants arriving in Palestine at the beginning of the twentieth century are lists of immigrants who left from the two main ports of departure for Palestine, Trieste and Odessa, and similar lists of the Palestine Office in Jaffa. Jews from Galicia generally left from Trieste, and Jews from the Pale of Settlement left from Odessa. A very precise list of travelers to Palestine was kept by officials of the information bureau in Odessa, which was the chief port of departure for Palestine. The data published regularly by the information bureau concerned nearly two-thirds of the immigrants.

The statistical data were published about every two weeks in the World Zionist Organization's organ *Ha-Olam*, under the heading "Departures for Palestine via Odessa." These data were the basis of the annual summary of immigration to Palestine published at the end of the year in *Ha-Olam* and in other newspapers of the period that dealt with matters relating to immigration and were interested in immigrants to Palestine. The lists of passengers leaving from the port of Odessa include details about the emigrants' sex, age, country of origin, profession, capital, and reasons for leaving.

The list of immigrants from the port of Trieste is less precise, it is not continuous throughout the years, and it deals with only a few months during the years 1912–1914. The lists of immigrants sent from Vienna to the Palestine Office in Jaffa were sorted according to name, and only gave the names of immigrants to Palestine along with their age, occupation, capital, reason for traveling, and date of embarkation. The lists only report on the months October to December, and a few of them on the months January and February, and they give details for about 385 immigrants. Despite the small number available to us, it is possible to reach conclusions about the composition of immigrants who set sail at Trieste, but one has to be cautious in adopting categorical positions.

Another source from which one can learn about the composition of immigrants to Palestine are the lists compiled by Haim Ridnik, an official in the Palestine Office at the port of Jaffa who met immigrants at the port when they arrived. The statistical charts and lists are in the Palestine Office section of the Central Zionist Archives, and they are a remarkable source for learning the composition of immigrants and understanding the nature of immigrants' initial encounter with Palestine and its inhabitants.

3. Newspapers

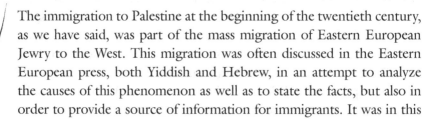

The immigration to Palestine at the beginning of the twentieth century, as we have said, was part of the mass migration of Eastern European Jewry to the West. This migration was often discussed in the Eastern European press, both Yiddish and Hebrew, in an attempt to analyze the causes of this phenomenon as well as to state the facts, but also in order to provide a source of information for immigrants. It was in this context that immigration to Palestine was reported on in various Eastern European newspapers: *Ha-Yom, Ha-Tzofe, Ha-Zman, Der Jüdische Emigrant, Neue Welt, Unser Leben,* and others. Many of the articles and much of the information treated immigration to Palestine as merely one kind of immigration out of many. The descriptions of the country and of the immigrants who reached it in these newspapers were often quite different from the descriptions in the Palestinian newspapers. The reason for this no doubt lay with the readers targeted by the newspapers, which also explains the Palestinian newspapers' avoidance of speaking of certain events in Palestine or their different approach to them. The difference between these two perspectives—the Eastern European and the Palestinian—not only enables researchers to view events in the country in a different, less ideological way but also to take note of the events and occurrences, especially those not to the credit of the Yishuv, that were not mentioned in the Palestinian press of the period.

＊

These primary sources—the information bureaus and especially the immigrants' letters, the lists of passengers to Palestine from the ports of Odessa and Trieste, and the Eastern European Jewish press—show the period of the second aliyah in a different light. This view is perhaps less heroic, but it is of great importance for an understanding of Eastern European Jewry and the Yishuv in the period before World War I.

In order to gain a better understanding of the motivations for immigration to Palestine and of the absorption of immigrants into the host society, and also to gain a better understanding of the motivations for immigration to Palestine and of the absorption of immigrants into the host society, I shall examine certain matters in a comparative perspective. Because the vast majority of Jewish migrants immigrated to the United States, I shall compare the Jews who went to Jaffa at the beginning of the twentieth century with those who went to Manhattan in the same period.

This book focuses on Jewish immigration to Palestine during the years 1904–1914 rather than in the previous period (1881–1903) for two reasons. First, the second aliyah is considered the most ideological of all the waves of immigration to Palestine before or after it. It is therefore interesting and important to focus on this particular aliyah and examine the role of the ideological factor involved in reaching the decision to immigrate to Palestine. If immigrants in this aliyah came to Palestine without any ideological motive, it may be assumed that in other and less inaugural periods the "push factor" in the countries of origin was stronger than the drawing power of Palestine. It was not Zionist ideology that drew these immigrants to Palestine but various prosaic motives, far less heroic than those described in Israeli historiography. Second, we possess very few primary sources concerning immigration to Palestine in the years 1881–1903. So far, no lists of passengers have been found who came to Palestine in those years, and we are consequently unable to examine the demographic composition of the immigrants, their motives for coming, or their places of settlement in Palestine. This period is a lacuna in Zionist historiography. The vast majority of scholars have dealt with farmers in the *moshavot* who were a small and unrepresentative minority during the period. Very little is known about the majority of immigrants who came to the country from the 1880s and 1890s to the beginning of the twentieth century, and until primary sources are found it will be difficult if not impossible to write about them and, certainly, to compare them with Jewish immigrants who went to other countries. This historiographical lacuna is similar in many ways to that concerning Jewish immigration to the United States before 1899, about which very little is known. Because it was only in 1899 that the American authorities began to ask immigrants about their ethnic origins, we do not know the exact number of Jewish immigrants that entered the United States, where they came from, what their occupations were, or answers to many other important questions. The relative abundance of primary sources we possess for the later period enables us to study Jewish immigration to Palestine at that time and compare it to immigration to the United States.

Despite the numerical difference between Palestine and the United States, there are certain things that characterize all the immigrants, such as the immigrant's experience from the moment he sets out from his Eastern European shtetl, his journey by train, his entry onto the steamship and the sea voyage, his encounter with the new country and fear of the unknown, his attempts at assimilation and absorption in the new country, and his confrontation with problems of existence such as livelihood, accommodation, and nourishment. All these things are common to every immigrant who leaves the familiar surroundings in which he was born and are not confined to any one group.

The book has six chapters. Chapter 1 investigates the causes of the great Jewish migration from Eastern Europe at the beginning of the twentieth century and, in this context, the reasons for immigration to Palestine. The aim of the chapter is to place the immigration to Palestine in its broader historical context and to show that its causes were not different from the causes of immigration to the United States and other countries during the years in question. The second chapter deals with the decision-making process with regard to immigration to Palestine and the implementation of that decision from the moment of leaving to the time of arrival in the port of Jaffa. This chapter attempts to determine the real place of Zionist ideology in the reasons for emigration before the decision was reached and the country of destination was chosen. Chapter 3 examines in a comparative perspective the demographic profile of immigrants to Palestine and that of immigrants to the United States; and chapter 4 deals with the journey to Palestine, the bureaucratic difficulties involved, the cost of the journey, the vicissitudes of the sea voyage, and immigrants' first encounter with the country. In the fifth chapter, I deal with the absorption of immigrants to Palestine at the beginning of the twentieth century. Finally, chapter 6 discusses the scale of emigration from Palestine, the profile of those that left, and their reasons for leaving.

One Three Revolutions and the Pogroms

In March 1913, at the height of the great Jewish mass migration, David, the oldest son of the Kohelet family, sent a letter to the directors of the Palestine Office in Jaffa. In the letter, he described without embellishment the miserable situation of his family in a shtetl in the region of Mogilev. He listed one by one the tribulations of this Jewish family's attempts to sustain itself in the economic and social conditions of the Russian Empire at the beginning of the twentieth century. In his letter, David Kohelet described the family's hesitations, difficulties, economic situation, and relations with the non-Jewish population of the shtetl. His presentation of the situation enables us to see the intentions of such a family in calculating a decision to emigrate even before it had made a decision to do so.

Kohelet's letter is an extraordinary document from the period of the great migration, and it embodies all the factors that gave rise to the Jewish migration from Eastern Europe. These factors, which will be discussed in detail in this chapter, combined relentlessly to upset the fragile economic situation of the Kohelet family and of many similar Jewish families in the Pale of Settlement, which drove the Kohelets and many like them to consider emigration.

The Kohelet family lived in Zakharino, a small village in the region of Mogilev.[1] There were ten people in the family: a father and mother, both 53 years old, and their eight children—six sons and two daughters. The letter described the situations of these eight children. The eldest son David, 27, ran a Talmud Torah (a religious school); two sons were shoemakers, who could not make a living from their trade and found work with a timber merchant close to their home, earning a wage of a rouble a day; two sons aged 15 and 17 lived at home with their sisters

33

aged 6 and 12; and an 8-year-old child was at school. The father of the family, whose name the eldest son did not give, was a shoemaker who, because of the many people practicing that trade and the great competition between them, earned very little and even that was obtained with great difficulty. The poverty and wretchedness of the family in Mstislawl, the town where they lived previously, had caused them to move to Zakharino. There the family rented a plot of land and grew a few vegetables, which it sold in the market on "one of the days of the week." In addition to their economic woes and the difficulties of providing for a family of ten people, the Kohelet family suffered from the behavior of its non-Jewish neighbors. "The family does not feel it has any ground to stand on, and life is against it," wrote David Kohelet. "You have to put up with the insults of the peasants in the village and flatter them when your blood is boiling at their cruelty."

This reality totally undermined the family's economic foundations and sense of security. The economic distress, paltry wages and constant search for work, being uprooted from place to place, and the father and sons' abandonment of the trade of shoemaking to go and work with a timber merchant—all this, plus difficult relations with the local people, made the family feel that its future was unclear and the basis of its existence was disappearing under its feet. They thus wrote the following letter to Arthur Ruppin, director of the Palestine Office in Jaffa:

> In light of all this, the family is thinking about leaving this country and heading for another country that will treat them in a more welcoming fashion. . . . We are not aiming for a life of luxury or asking for easy work; we just long for a quiet, satisfying life. We are not idealists, but we are willing to make sacrifices—provided that we are assured that our future will eventually be secure and stable, and that the ground under our feet will not collapse. If we see that there is no way for the entire family to leave the country all at once, then we have decided that the older sons—that is, the second and third sons—will emigrate first, and after a while the rest of the family will go. Sir! If possible, express your opinion on this matter. Please help us by sending us your instructions and your advice: Would we be able to move to Palestine and settle on the land or even in some city? Will we find what we are looking for in the Land of Israel? Or would we be better off heading for other countries, because the living conditions in Palestine are not suitable for us? We are afraid that we will fail and ruin our

already-precarious position. Please do not delay in replying. Respect-fully, in the name of the entire family, David Kohelet.[2]

David's letter reveals the family's hesitations concerning the destina-tion country, its fears of the future, its economic distress, and its longing for "a quiet satisfying life"—a place where it would feel secure and un-threatened. The troubles described in the letter show how the changes that took place in Eastern Europe in the second half of the nineteenth century undermined the basis of the Jewish family's existence in every sphere. Here we have an individual case that enables us to see how "macro" factors brought a single, but representative, Jewish family to consider immigration to Palestine or to other countries overseas.

Three revolutions took place in the Russian Empire from the mid-nineteenth century onward: a demographic revolution; an industrial revolution, followed by urbanization; and a revolution in public trans-port. In addition to these three revolutions, there were persecutions by the authorities and pogroms that hindered the activities of the Jews and worsened their socioeconomic situation; but, as we shall see in the following pages, these were only a catalyst and not a cause of emi-gration. The aim of this chapter is twofold: On the one hand, I will examine the macro factors that brought about the emigration of more than two and a half million Jews from Eastern Europe; and on the other hand, I offer an exploration of how the causes of emigration were reflected in letters to the Zionist information bureaus set up at the beginning of the twentieth century. The many letters sent to these Zionist information bureaus not only enable us to examine in a direct fashion "from below" how the demographic and economic changes af-fected ordinary Jews in Eastern Europe but also to see immigration to Palestine in a much broader perspective—as an inseparable part of the general Jewish migration. The letter of the Kohelet family and simi-lar letters of Jewish families who considered immigration to Palestine show, first of all, similarities in the causes of immigration to America and to Palestine at the beginning of the twentieth century. These mi-grations were not two parallel movements without any point of con-tact, but rather they comprised a single movement of immigration in which the points in common—even if the immigrants went to different countries—were greater than the points of difference.

The Demographic Revolution

One of the major changes that took place in czarist Russia between the beginning of the nineteenth century and the outbreak of World War I was its rapid demographic growth. The rate of natural increase in the Russian Empire as compared to other European countries was extraordinary and impressive in its scope. In the space of about only fifty years (1860–1913) the population of Russia doubled from 74 million in 1860 to 164 million in 1913. Between 1883 and 1887 and between 1909 and 1913 the population increased at a rate of 1.6 percent a year. This rate of increase was only matched in the United States, Canada, and Australia during the same time periods. But, whereas in these countries the growth was due to a continuous immigration up to World War I, in czarist Russia it was a natural increase of the population.[3]

The main reason for the growth in population in Russia was the sharp decrease in mortality as a result of the development of medicine and improvements in sanitation, even though the rate of births remained unchanged. An increasing number of children survived the first years of their lives, and as a result the difference in the total number of births compared to the total number of deaths increased significantly.

The rate of natural increase among the Jews of czarist Russia was far greater than that of the non-Jewish population. The economist Simon Kuznets has examined the growth of the Jewish population in relation to that of the non-Jewish population. His findings show that, averaged over the years, the Jewish population grew by 223 percent in the years 1825–1900, and the non-Jewish population by 150 percent.[4] In Minsk, for example, between the years 1847 and 1897 the Jewish population increased by roughly 300 percent, in Vitebsk the rate of growth was 248 percent, in Kiev 220 percent, in Vilna 199 percent, and in Grodno 185 percent.[5] In the south of the Pale of Settlement, in the regions of Kherson, Ekaterinoslav, and Taurida, the rate of increase was even more rapid. In 1844 the Jewish population there numbered about 95,000 souls, but by 1913 it reached 900,000. The Jewish population had grown by 844 percent. On the other hand, the non-Jewish population had only grown by 280 percent.[6] At the same time in these areas, as we shall see in the following pages, part of the growth was not due to natural increase but to a large-scale internal migration from the northwestern parts of the Pale to the south.[7] In Congress Poland and Galicia in the Austro-Hungarian Empire the demographic tendencies were not very different: In 1860 the Jewish population in Poland numbered about 600,000 souls and the non-Jewish population about 2,700,000. Fifty years later, the number of Jews reached two million—a growth of about 227 percent. As against this, the general population grew by about 170 percent, and in 1913 it stood at thirteen million souls.[8] In Galicia, the rate of growth was more moderate, but it was still high. Between the years 1869 and 1910, the Jewish population grew from 575,000 souls to 880,000.[9]

The difference in the rates of growth of the Jewish and non-Jewish populations appears to have been due to the special character of Jewish society: its concern for orphans and the poor, the existence of charitable institutions caring for the sick and needy, the stability of the family cell, a low rate of infant mortality, and preservation of the traditional way of life. All these factors constituted a kind of "life insurance" that reduced Jewish mortality in general and infant mortality in particular, bringing about a more than fivefold increase in the number of Jews in Russia over a period of a little over a hundred years.[10] There were a million Jews in the Russian Empire at the beginning of the eighteenth century; by the end of that century, their number had reached five million.

A by-product of this population growth was the large proportion of young people. From the findings of the Russian census of the year 1897, it appears that 29 percent of the Jewish population consisted of children up to the age of 9, 23 percent were from 10 to 19 years old, 28 percent were from 20 to 39, 14 percent were from 40 to 59, and only 6 percent were age 60 and above.[11] This situation was clearly reflected in letters sent to the Zionist information offices. Most of the senders were fathers, and they provided information on the size of their families. The Kohelet family, for example, whose story opened this chapter, is a good example of this demographic. Zalman Lifchitz of Kiev said in his letter to Ruppin that he was the father of five children: three sons aged 5, 13, and 20 and two daughters who were twins aged 22.[12] The Alterman family declared that it numbered "nine people, five of whom are familiar with work in the fields and are able to contribute, and another one or two who help in blacksmithing."[13]

This division of ages had far-reaching socioeconomic consequences. A third of the Jewish population consisted of small children who were unable to be self-supporting. This stratum of the population, together with those over 60, was supported and unproductive. The necessity of feeding so many mouths led to a very difficult economic situation and hard living conditions. The economic situation was only eased when children joined the workforce. In David Kohelet's letter to Ruppin, he said that "five years ago the family lived a life of poverty, barely earning enough for their dry bread because the children were still small," and "only recently, when the boys grew up and started helping out, one here and one there, did things improve a bit."[14] Alterman, in his letter to Ruppin, also spoke of the contribution of five of the nine family members to supporting the family. This demographic reality naturally worsened the economic distress and made many Jews consider immigration to a country overseas. Palestine was one of their options.

The Industrial Revolution and Urbanization

From the 1870s, the Russian Empire, a hundred years late, began a process of rapid industrialization.[15] Alexander II's ascent to the throne in 1855 brought a period of far-reaching changes in most areas of Russian life. The liberation of the serfs in 1861 removed a major stumbling block to industrial development in czarist Russia. At the same time, most scholars agree today that serfdom was not the main obstacle to the awakening of the Russian economy. There were many liberated serfs even before the official abolition of serfdom, and the majority of them were unable to contribute to the improvement of the czarist economy, even if they so desired. Vast distances between villages and cities, the scarcity of railways, and Russian peasants' attachment to their lands held back the entry of hundreds of thousands of people into the developing labor market.

Russia's defeat in the Crimean War (1854–1856) placed the Russian authorities in the position to make far-reaching changes in the country. The defeat by Britain and France, industrialized countries equipped with up-to-date warships, brought the Russian government to the conclusion that the Russian economy had to be developed without delay. This realization led to rapid industrial development throughout the Russian Empire. In the space of about sixty years, there was an industrialization process in Russia similar in character and consequence to what had taken place in Germany, France, and Britain fifty years before. Farming communities in Russia became urban settlements, new social classes emerged, and the family ceased to be the dominant unit of productivity. On the eve of World War I, Russia was an industrialized land with a powerful economy, able to compete successfully with Western and Central European countries.

The outstanding characteristic of this industrialization process was the exploitation of raw materials. New centers of industry arose in areas rich in coal and iron, especially the Ukraine, the Ural Mountains, and the Caucasus region. The iron industry developed a need for coal, as the iron had to be smelted and cast in unprecedented quantities. In the years 1860–1864 Russia produced about 400,000 tons of coal a year in all. Ten years later (in the period 1870–1874) coal production increased to more than a million tons a year, and shortly before World War I coal production reached a total of more than 33 billion tons a year—an increase of more than 300 percent.[16]

The most significant progress in the industrialization of Russia took place in the 1890s. The reason for this was the increasing involvement of the state in speeding up the process. This economic achievement may be ascribed to Sergei Witte, the Russian Minister of Industry from 1893 to 1903. In those eleven years, Russia became an industrial empire able to compete on an equal basis with the industrial countries of Western Europe. The Russian government invested a great deal of money in the railways, which began to connect small towns and remote villages to the developing industrial centers. This railway system crossed the length and breadth of Russia and made possible a labor force of hundreds of thousands of peasants who had previously found it difficult to integrate into the new economic order.

Investment in the railway infrastructure was the heart of the industrial revolution that took place on the European continent in general and in Russia in particular. In 1890 Russia took fifth place among industrial nations with regard to railways; but during the years 1890–1900, through an investment of 350 million roubles, Russia built the second-most-developed railway infrastructure in the world (after the United

States). The laying of the Trans-Siberian Railway was one of the most ambitious projects undertaken by the Russian government—equal in importance to the building of the Suez Canal in the mid-nineteenth century and the Panama Canal in 1900. From the beginning of the 1890s until the end of the nineteenth century, the size of the railway system grew from 30,000 kilometers to 53,000 kilometers.[17]

Another sector that developed rapidly from the second half of the nineteenth century onward was the textile industry. Until World War I the production of the Russian cotton industry was the fourth largest in the world. The replacement of the handloom by the steam-driven loom resulted in major changes in the scale of production. In the years 1887–1897, for example, the textile industry doubled its output from 460 million roubles to about 950 million roubles. Similar developments took place in the food and timber industries.[18] Although industrialization in Russia began about a hundred years later than in Western and Central Europe, in the last thirty years of the nineteenth century Russia succeeded in closing the gap. It entered the twentieth century as an industrial power in all respects.

The industrial revolution changed the lives of millions of Russian peasants. Hundreds of new factories drew myriads of peasants who found it difficult to make a living in the new economic situation. In thirty years, the urban population doubled from 6.5 million in 1867 to 12.5 million at the end of the nineteenth century. In the region of Taurida, for example, the population increased by 240 percent in only sixty years—from 600,000 in 1863 to 164 million in 1914. In Minsk it increased by 200 percent, in Bessarabia by 160 percent, in Kherson by 180 percent, in Moghilev by 167 percent, in Vitebsk by 150 percent, and in Vilna by 130 percent.[19] Before the 1917 Revolution, the population of the cities of the Russian Empire totaled about 25 million. The urban population had quadrupled in only fifty years. The population of Saint Petersburg grew from half a million in 1867 to 1.3 million in 1897 and 2.2 million in 1914. There was a similar growth in Moscow: from 350,000 in 1867 to 1.7 million in 1914.[20]

As a result of these changes, masses of peasants abandoned their original occupations. Because of increased efficiency in agriculture, which reduced the number of hands required for the production of food, hundreds of thousands of people had to go to the industrialized cities to seek a new source of employment. The internal migration from the impoverished villages to the industrial cities created a difficult situation in the towns. The great demand for employment combined with a limited supply of work in the factories brought about a lowering of wages and a rise in the cost of living, which in turn increased poverty and the gap between the classes. Moreover, the migration to the towns changed the traditional structure of the family. A family ceased to be a productive institution in itself, and its members became salaried workers who earned their living with difficulty in one of the many large-scale factories that had just sprung up.

These changes did not spare the Jewish population in the Pale of Settlement, and they were even more affected than others. The natural increase of the Jewish population resulted in an acceleration of Jewish migration from the villages and shtetls to the large towns. This migration weakened a sense of community in the Jewish population: A feeling of unity, which had previously centered on religion, was replaced by secularization and politicization. Over the course of the nineteenth century, the intimate communal feeling characteristic of small Jewish organizational frameworks in Europe began to disappear, and instead there arose new urban Jewish communities, larger but more alienated. By way of illustration, I will point out that at the beginning of the nineteenth century there were only three or four Jewish communities in the world that numbered a total of over 10,000 souls. But by the end of the century, not only was there growth in the number of Jewish communities within these cities; but now more than ten urban centers in the world had over 100,000 Jews.[21]

The progressive transformation of the Jewish people into city-dwellers changed its sociocultural character beyond recognition and resulted in a major change in its economic activities. When the Jews lived in villages and shtetls, far from economic and political centers, they earned their living mainly from renting land, from connections with the feudal authorities, and from buying and reselling agricultural produce. The move to large towns and industrial centers forced the Jews to abandon their traditional occupations and adapt to the new socioeconomic situation. Contrary to the stereotype of successful Jews advancing rapidly up the socioeconomic ladder, only a very small and unrepresentative minority succeeded during this period in adapting to the new reality by participating in capitalist activities and exploiting commercial possibilities. The vast majority of Jews were placed in a very difficult economic situation, struggling to survive and make a living from new occupations that involved hard and difficult manual labor.

The policies of the czarist government limited the settlement of Jews in villages. Together with the general economic processes taking place in Eastern Europe in this period, this edict forced Jews to move to the cities in order to earn their living. Eighty percent of the Jewish population at the end of the nineteenth century and beginning of the twentieth settled in the cities. These Jews sometimes relocated against their will. Zalman Lifchitz, discussed previously in connection with the difficulty of providing for ten family members, stated in his letter to the Palestine Office that "because of the bitter exile imposed on the Jews from the villages, including myself," he had to go "to Kiev to look for a morsel of bread, and the beadles of the synagogue met me. But because of the bitter exile, I have no authorization in Kiev either. And, here too, the possibility of making a living is very limited. I will have to leave Kiev."[22]

A petty tradesman named "Yitzhak," whose family name was not given, described a similar situation in his letter to Ruppin:

> As your honor knows, oppression and persecution of the Jews and harsh edicts occur every day until one no longer has the strength to bear them, and every day, the threat of expulsion hangs over me. I have therefore decided to ask your honor for advice, and if your honor agrees, I am ready to travel to Jaffa in the near future.[23]

In 1911, Z. Kurtzbach from Galicia described the economic situation of his family: "Dear Sir, because of the difficult economic situation in Galicia, I am forced to leave the country. I am the son of poor parents who earn their living by renting fields and who live in great misery. I am eighteen years old and I am familiar with farm work. It is my great hope to travel to Palestine and become a worker, and I am therefore asking you to inform me about the situation there—whether one can find work there, what the wage is, and what the journey costs."[24] And the Kohelet family discussed earlier, who found it difficult to earn a living in a large town because shoemaking "brings in barely enough for food, and even that with great difficulty," decided to move to the village of Zakharino, rent a plot of land there, and grow a few vegetables, which it sold in the market on one of the days of the week.[25]

As a result of the move from the villages and shtetls to the industrial towns, about 70 percent became small tradesmen or artisans.[26] The peddler who went from town to town offering his merchandise became a thing of the past. The resulting competition with the impoverished mass of peasants for places of work aggravated the situation of the Jews in Russia. Unlike their brethren in the West, they did not succeed in finding a place in the emerging economic situation. In the competition between Jewish and non-Jewish workers, who sometimes came to the town by the same train, the non-Jews were more easily absorbed into the large factories. The Jews were sent farther away, and they subsisted miserably in small, narrow, dark workshops.

The place and status of the Jew in the Russian economy was one of the subjects that preoccupied Jewish economists and researchers in the Russian Empire during this period. At the end of the nineteenth century and beginning of the twentieth, there began to be published— mainly in czarist Russia—a number of studies dealing with the economic problems of Russian Jewry. Three outstanding researchers who published in those years were Professor Andrei Palovich Subotin, Dr. Haim Dov Horowitz, and Jacob Lestschinsky. Each of these researchers in his own way noted the phenomenon of the deproletization of Jewish society.[27] The first to put forward this concept was the economist Dr. Horowitz. His studies were based on statistical material relating to the economic situation of Russian Jewry and on Subotin's researches on Jews in the Pale of Settlement published in two volumes in 1888–1890.[28] During 1901–1902 Horowitz published his comprehensive study, "She'elat ha-calcala u'mekoma be'tenuatenu ha'leumit" (The Question of the Economy and Its Role in Our National Movement), in the journal *Ha-shiloah*.[29] He declared that the aim of the study was twofold: first, to explain why "we are poor, and why our plight is so much worse than that of the other peoples that have natural, decent living conditions"; and second, to try to fight against poverty in order to improve "our shaky, poor economic status."[30]

Horowitz claimed that the poverty of Jewish society was first and foremost due to its employment structure. From his study, it appeared that 50 to 60 percent of Jews were artisans, 30 to 40 percent worked in commerce, and 10 to 20 percent were engaged in industry and agriculture. In his opinion, the fact that Jews did not engage in heavy industry caused an increase in the number of artisans among them, "of which there were so many that the work could no longer provide for them."[31] He said that in the city of Minsk there were 3,515 Jewish artisans with 1,812 assistants: There was one artisan to every twenty people. There were even more in the provincial capitals of the region in which there was one artisan to every seven inhabitants.[32] A similar process took place among Jewish industrial workers. Most of the large industrial concerns employed non-Jews, so that Jews were driven into light industry, which was close to being an artisanal type of employment: "We see that in the Vilna region as well the Jews are driven out of heavy industry and maintain their position only by the light industry."[33]

The economic options available to Russian Jews led to their overcrowding in a few, limited branches of employment. As a result, competition increased and earnings decreased to the point that the Jewish masses were impoverished. Adding to their difficulty, Jews did not succeed in gaining acceptance in more profitable branches of employment:

> The Jews are excluded from the professions on the higher economic levels; they do not hold respected positions in large-scale commerce and manufacturing, among factory-owners and commercial magnates. The Jews stop up every hole in the lower occupations until there is no more room, and despite this, the superfluous peddlers and artists have no possibility of moving to other branches of work, to professions that are not yet overcrowded like work in factories, and to places where such things are available.[34]

Dr. Horowitz saw the eviction of the Jews from these more profitable branches of employment as the birth of capitalist development, which he viewed as harmful not only to the Jewish population but also to Russian society. At the same time, the eviction of Jews from these other employment options had far graver consequences for Jews than displacement had for non-Jews. In non-Jewish society, the peasants displaced from their land abandoned farm work and moved to the towns, where most of them became industrial workers and a few became artisans. Thus, the peasants succeeded in being absorbed into the lower levels of advanced branches of employment. The eviction from the soil opened up new possibilities for them to earn a living and provided them with opportunities to progress economically, preventing their reduction to beggary. But Jews had no possibility of acceptance into the developing branches of the economy, particularly heavy industry. As a result, they were forced to earn a living with difficulty in their former occupations, with much more competition and great insecurity.[35]

Shlomo Kaplan's letter to the Palestine Office is one example of many that confirms the conclusions of Dr. Horowitz's study of the Jewish economy in the Pale of Settlement:

> I have been living for over ten years in a small Lithuanian town in the region of Minsk. Nearly all the inhabitants of the town are shopkeepers. I think this is the most loathsome and contemptible occupation. My forefathers were also shopkeepers, and for the last four years I have also been doing this work, although I feel it stupefies me and keeps me away from the world of the Holy One, Blessed Be He which is full of clear air and sunshine and all the other joys of nature in which our town is so lacking.[36]

Lestschinsky's 1906 study of Jewish workers in Russia also pointed out the lack of Jewish workers in mass-production industries: "The more the scale of production increases, the less the Jewish worker takes part in it and the closer we get to the most developed branches of production, the less the Jewish worker is involved in them."[37] The gates of the factories—both those owned by Christians and those owned by Jews—were generally closed to Jews. Non-Jewish industrialists preferred non-Jewish workers, as Jews were considered unskilled with no aptitude for manufacturing work. They were also viewed as socialists who instigated strikes to improve their working conditions. Factory owners preferred submissive non-Jewish workers, who were distanced from theories about class warfare. Jewish industrialists were also unwilling to employ their kinsmen, as for socioeconomic reasons it was more convenient for them to employ non-Jews. A Jewish industrialist did not feel any obligation toward their Polish or Ukrainian workers beyond an employer's obligation to a worker, while in the case of Jewish workers the relationship was complicated by their common origin.[38]

This situation had dire social and political consequences. Myriads of peasants taken off their lands, including Russians, Ukrainians, and

Poles, were subsequently absorbed into the great developing industries and became a strong proletarian class. But Jews found themselves in dark, miserable workshops in Minsk, Vilna, and other cities in the Pale of Settlement. The Jewish proletariat in Eastern Europe was, from the very start, a proletariat of artisans. There were no unionized skilled workers among them who played a central role in economic production, and thus the status of the Jewish worker in the labor force was frail and uncertain. The concentration of Jewish workers in small workshops and the constant threat of unemployment were factors that prevented them from fighting to improve their economic condition. The Jewish worker remained economically isolated, and the demands of the unionized proletariat in heavy industry were alien to him. Thus, economically cut off from the proletariat as a whole and engaged in light industries and workshops, the Jewish artisan and peddler in the markets was enfeebled and became nationally and politically worthless.[39]

The Jews' difficulty in finding a place in the new economic reality deepened their destitution and caused competition among Jewish shopkeepers and artisans for every piece of work. This competition resulted in a lowering of prices and forced many to sell their goods at a loss, a situation that soured the lives of Jewish artisans and tradesmen. Because Jewish artisans were not unionized, there was nobody to stand up for their rights, unlike the situation of workers in the great industrial concerns. Their living conditions were also hard to bear: Many families lived in cramped basements or dark rooms on the lower floors of tenements in the cities. An apartment unit often consisted of just a small, humid room, which usually served as a bedroom, a workroom, an eating place, a place of rest, and, for lack of an alternative, a playground for the children.[40] Many of the children had to help in providing for the family. There were long hours of work: in winter the working hours stretched from 8 A.M. to midnight, and in summer from 6 A.M. to 9 P.M., and sometimes more. In Vitebsk, for instance, Jewish artisans worked 13 to 18 hours a day, in Gomel 16 or 17 hours a day, and in Lodz, "the Manchester of Congress Poland," 13 to 15 hours a day.[41] The residential neighborhoods were dirty: Poverty, overcrowding, pollution, and foul odors prevailed.

In the studies of Subotin, one finds harsh descriptions of Jews' poverty and daily routines. At the end of the 1880s Subotin made a comprehensive survey of Jews in the Pale of Settlement. In almost all the towns he visited, he found a gloomy situation. Of Grodno, he wrote:

> We went to see the Jewish neighborhood. On the way we encountered a Jewish painter, and we asked him how to get to the riverbed. When he discovered the purpose of our trip, he offered to escort us. We went through filthy alleys, between crowded, burnt buildings. . . . We passed by a number of puddles and holes next to which half-naked children were playing. From there we reached an area of dense shacks, scattered along the river banks and separated by narrow, dirty passageways. . . . Very few of the shacks were upright and intact. The vast majority had become crooked and slanted over the years and were falling apart.[42]

After describing the area, Subotin turned to his visit to one of the shacks:

> Before us was a crumbling shack with a collapsing roof and slanting windows. The vast majority of the walls had holes with pieces of paper pasted over them. The shack itself was sunk into the earth and appeared to be on the verge of collapse. We entered the room, having to bend down to do so. We were very depressed at what we saw. . . . There was no furniture in the shack except for a broken table, two or three benches and rags scattered around the floor for sleeping. The sight of the room was difficult to take. Wooden boards from the ceiling were bent inward and looked as if they were about to fall down. . . . It is hard to imagine an intelligent creature daring to live in this decrepit ruin. Nevertheless, we saw twelve people in one room. The owner of the "property" is an old Jewish tailor, with his wife and ten children. The children had no underwear on; they were wearing some sort of torn garment.[43]

After this description of the Jewish neighborhood in Grodno, Subotin went on to Berdichev, where he reported that the economic situation of the Jews was worse than in any other town in the Pale of Settlement. The river in Berdichev, he wrote, formed "a large pool that serves as a major cause of the spread of epidemics. Sewage, garbage, and dead animals flow into it." It was also used for "laundry, bathing and watering animals."[44] Most of the homes in the town, he said, had no yards, "and all the refuse from the houses—rags, rubbish, fish-bones—is thrown from the houses into the street." The appearance of the Jewish neigh-

borhood was no different from that of the rest of the city: "The shacks
stood in a few rows, separated by narrow alleyways full of dirty water,
sewage and refuse." One might have thought that "in part of the town
there had recently been a bombardment by an enemy. Some buildings
were without roofs, with additions in ruins, cracked walls and peeling
plaster. Instead of yards and gardens, there were filthy puddles and piles
of garbage." Masses of poor Jews were crowded into this part of the
town, and, he said, "I don't remember ever seeing a more repulsive, dis-
gusting, suffering place" than Berdichev.[45]

As in Grodno, Subotin entered a typical Jewish home:

> In one of the shacks on the point of collapse we found a shoemaker
> with his household. He was renting a room to a poor Jewish woman
> for fifteen roubles a year. The conditions were really shocking. Even
> in the poor homes of Vilna and Grodno we did not see anything
> like this: dirty, unpainted walls, a sunken floor with wobbly boards.
> Sheer emptiness—bare walls, with no lamp, books or dishes in sight.
> Instead of furniture there was a miserable bench and table. Most
> of the homes had no beds, just rags on the floor. . . . Everything
> was stamped with depression and hopelessness. Yet, nevertheless,
> amidst that filth and the piles of rags, under these bleak ceilings,
> new life stirred. Masses of dark-skinned infants ran around between
> people's feet.[46]

In his article "Statistica shel Ayara Ahat" (Statistics of One Town),
published in the newspaper *Ha-Shiloah* in 1903, Jacob Lestschinsky
described his birthplace Horodyshche, saying it was typical of many
shtetls in the Kiev region. The picture he gave was very depressing,
similar to the one given by Subotin. Lestschinsky described a Jewish
home in Horodyshche as follows:

> There stood before us a low building, three and a half cubits long
> and two cubits wide. We went in. It was after the feast of Succot:
> a humid wind was already blowing outside and penetrating the house
> through the wide cracks. The house consisted of two rooms. In one
> room there was a small bed with just a few rags on it. We did not see a
> single pillow on the bed: it was covered only with the remains of an old
> blanket. Four boys and girls sat on the bed, warming their bodies by
> pressing against each other. They were all wearing torn, dirty shirts. . . .
> All the children's faces were very pale, without a drop of blood, and

one could see that they had not tasted bread that day. No breadcrumbs were visible either in the first room or in the second room, where there was a stove which showed it to be a kitchen. As is known, no one buys bread in bakeries in small towns as they do in cities, but every house-wife bakes bread herself for several days. Here there was no sign at all that bread had been baked in the past few days.[47]

The descriptions of Horowitz, Subotin, and Lestschinsky provide a depressing picture of the situation of Russian Jewry at the end of the nineteenth century and beginning of the twentieth, similar to descriptions in the letters to the Zionist information bureaus. It was not only pioneers steeped in Zionist ideology who wanted to go to Palestine but also Jewish artisans and tradesmen who sought an alternative to the difficult conditions of life in Eastern Europe. The absence of hope gave rise to a search for countries—including Palestine—where they could not only earn an honorable living but also, as the Kohelet fam-ily wrote to Ruppin, find a haven where they could enjoy "a quiet satisfying life."[48]

The Revolution in Mass Transportation

Railways were at the very heart of the industrial revolution in general and the industrial revolution in Russia in particular. The peak years of railway building were the period 1866–1900. In only thirty-five years, the size of the railway system grew tenfold, from 5,000 kilometers in 1866 to 53,000 in 1900.[49] But this period should not be seen as a single unit, for there were ups and downs during this time: The years 1866–1879, for instance, marked a turning point in laying railway lines and creating an infrastructure for the railways; and from 1891 until the beginning of the twentieth century, there was a renewed impetus for railway development, with more than 2,500 kilometers of railways built annually during that period.[50]

The railways changed Russian society and the economy beyond rec-ognition. Because of the large size of the empire, it is impossible to trace the development of every railway line that linked rural settle-ments on the periphery to the center. For the purposes of this study, we will focus on the railways in the Pale of Settlement where the vast majority of the Jewish population was concentrated. One of the first railway lines to be inaugurated was the Odessa-Yalta line, already in use in 1865; and five years later, in 1870, the important railway line from Yalta to Elisavetgrad was opened. In that same year, the railway line from Kiev to the port of Odessa was completed. By the beginning of the twentieth century, the length and breadth of almost all the southwestern part of the Russian Empire was covered with railways. From every major town in the Pale of Settlement and Poland, it was possible to reach any destination in the Russian Empire and beyond.[51] One could very easily reach the frontier towns and from there continue by train to ports of departure. The price of train tickets ranged from 1.5 roubles for towns and shtetls close to the frontier to 13 roubles for a journey from the Black Sea to the Baltic.[52] The upsurge in railway building in the southwestern part of the Russian Empire that took place in the 1880s corresponded to the period of Jewish and non-Jewish migration from Eastern Europe. From the moment that Jewish migrants could reach cities and from there continue to ports of departure, emigration became feasible. The journey was still difficult and dangerous, but as soon as a few set out on their way, they laid a path for those that came after, and the way thus was opened for major transit for emigrants at the beginning of the twentieth century. The new path of migration led westward to Manhattan, with secondary paths to Argentina, South Africa, Canada, and Palestine.

The steamships also made a real contribution to the migration westward. The possibility of crossing the ocean by steamship ushered in a new period in the history of maritime transport. The replacement of sailing ships by steamships facilitated ocean journeys as steamships were quicker, stronger, and larger. The first such ships were wooden sailing ships fitted with a steam engine. They were relatively small, the amount of coal they carried was limited, and they could handle no more than a few dozen passengers. The ships built later sailed by steampower only and were made of steel. Instead of taking forty days, these steamships crossed the ocean in only twelve days. For emigrants, the change to steamships meant a shorter travel time.

There were also major changes in the conditions of the voyage with the advent of steamships. Until the first half of the nineteenth century, emigrants on boats shared their living-quarters with animals and goods sent from Europe to America. In order to give an idea of the life of emigrants on ships, it should be pointed out that in the spring of 1849 one ship had in its hold 280 emigrants, who traveled together with 240 heads of cattle, 206 pigs, 19, sheep and 4 horses.[53] The steamships brought about a considerable improvement in travel conditions, although the voyage still involved many considerable difficulties, which I will discuss in chapter 2.

Shipbuilding, like the development of railways and the laying of railway lines, was an inseparable part of the industrialization process. The efficient exploitation of raw materials—iron and coal—was one of the main factors that made shipbuilding possible. In the second half of the nineteenth century, iron ships gradually replaced wooden ships. In 1876, for the first time, more steel ships than wooden ships were built in the dockyards of Europe and America.[54] The change from wooden ships to ships of iron and steel also had social consequences. Just as in the industrial revolution millions of peasants left their villages for the large industrial cities, so it was with the seamen. A whole class of deckhands, sailors, and seamen who were skilled in handling of the complex systems of sailing ships, such as ropes, poles, and sails, gradually disappeared. They were replaced by hundreds of stokers skilled in running steam engines—workers whose only task was to watch over the functioning of these engines.[55]

The steamships were built rapidly. In 1848, the average weight of a steamship was about 717 tons, its width was about ten meters, and its length 65 meters. At the beginning of the twentieth century, ships were built at a weight of 16,500 tons, a width of about 20 meters, and a length of 202 meters. And by 1911, the largest ship in the world, the *Imperator*, had a weight of 50,000 tons and a length of 268 meters, and it carried more than 5,000 passengers in a single voyage.[56]

Two factors gave an impetus to the process of building steamships. One influence was due to the Crimean War and American Civil War (1861–1865); the belligerent nations at war had an increased need for steamships of iron and steel. The other event that fostered the steamship industry was the opening of the Suez Canal in 1869. Sailing ships were unable to cross the canal on their own: Their limitations and unsuitability to the conditions made them irrelevant. A voyage to India and the Far East via the Suez Canal saved so much time and money that even the most conservative seamen, who doubted the usefulness of steel ships, understood that a new age was at hand.

The advantage of crossing oceans rapidly and safely was first of all economic: The trade routes expanded and grew larger. From the second half of the nineteenth century, the fleets of the European countries—not only steel warships but heavily laden cargo ships carrying hundreds of tons of industrial products—increased in size. Many shipping companies understood the economic potential of cross-Atlantic trade and began to adapt to the new conditions. There was no industrialized country in Europe that did not have an agent involved in this trade. Germany had two large shipping companies: Nord-Deutscher Lloyd, based in Bremen; and HAPAG (Hamburg Amerikanische Packetfahrt Actien Gesellschaft), based in Hamburg. Both of them had a shipping line to New York.[57] In Belgium, the large shipping company was the Red Star Line; in France, Messageries Maritimes; in Holland, the Royal Netherlands Steamship Company; and in Britain, the Cunard Steamship Company, owned by Samuel Cunard.[58]

The first ships of these shipping companies were cargo ships carrying goods and mail. In the second half of the nineteenth century, however, with the increase in immigration to the American continent, the shipping companies began to recognize the economic potential of transporting human cargo: vast numbers of immigrants who wanted to leave the European continent for the New World. Unlike the first steamships on whose decks there were only a few dozen passengers, the cargo ships were adapted to carry hundreds of immigrants. The originator of the idea was the German-Jewish shipping magnate and director of HAPAG, Albert Ballin. He eliminated private bedrooms on his ships, and then created spacious steerage accommodation between the upper and lower decks that could accommodate hundreds of immigrants. The large-scale exploitation of the structure of the ships for living-quarters enabled HAPAG to significantly reduce the costs of a voyage.[59] Ballin coined the motto *Mein Feld ist die Welt* (My Field Is the World) and initiated a competitive market for patronage from immigrants. This competition led to a further reduction in the cost of the voyage and the opening of direct new routes to ports of destination on the other side of the Atlantic. The number of immigrants grew from year to year. The official records of HAPAG reveal that in

1897 the company carried about 73,000 immigrants across the Atlantic, and in 1899 it carried more than 100,000 immigrants. Two years later more than 211,000 immigrants sailed on its ships, and in 1906 432,000 people used the services of the company.[60]

The steamships also ushered in a new era in the Mediterranean Basin that enabled immigrants and tourists to reach Palestine relatively easily. Until the 1840s, most of the ships that reached the port of Jaffa were sailing ships. Only then did steamships begin to visit the port, and the distance between Europe and Palestine was significantly shortened. In 1852 the French company Messageries Maritimes opened a regular line to the port of Jaffa. Shortly afterward, the Austrian Lloyd shipping company was founded and opened a line from the port of Trieste to Alexandria. This line was considered very fast, and it served passengers from Western and Central Europe. During the same period, the Russian shipping company began to operate regular lines for goods and passengers in the Black Sea and the Mediterranean.[61] On the eve of World War I, the steamships of six lines docked every week at the port of Jaffa: the French line Messageries Maritimes, which set out from Marseilles via the Egyptian ports for Jaffa, Haifa, and Beirut, a voyage of about ten days; the Austrian Lloyd line, which set out from Trieste; the Russian line, which set out from Odessa; the Egyptian line (in actuality British), which set out from Alexandria, via Port Said, for Jaffa, Haifa, and Beirut; and two Italian lines, Maritima Italiana and Servizi Maritimi, each of which ran a line twice weekly from Venice and Genoa via Alexandria to Jaffa, Haifa, and Beirut. The main port of departure for Palestine was of course Odessa, which at the beginning of the twentieth century became an important point of departure from the Pale of Settlement. On the other hand, the Jews of the Austro-Hungarian Empire, and of Galicia in particular, set out for Palestine from the port of Trieste.

The Pogroms

The Kishinev pogrom that broke out on April 8, 1903 constituted a great shock to Jewish society and triggered a turning point in Jewish emigration.[62] The pogroms of 1881–1882 were marked by destruction of property, but the Kishinev pogrom and the ones that followed were far more violent. In the years 1905–1906 there were 657 pogroms in which more than 3,000 Jews were murdered. The largest number of Jews murdered was in Bessarabia, 71 pogroms and 942 Jews murdered; and in Kherson, there were 82 pogroms/371 Jews murdered. In Kiev and Ekaterinoslav, there were 41 pogroms: In Kiev 167 Jews were murdered and in Ekaterinoslav 285.[63] The Jewish population was not used to persecution of this kind, and the acts of murder gave rise to feelings of shock and fear. On November 6, 1905, at the height of the slaughter in Kiev, Rabbi Moshe Rosenblatt, on behalf of the Jews of the city, sent a letter to Israel Zangwill, president of the ITO (Jewish Territorial Organization), begging him to make an effort to rescue them from their nightmarish situation.[64] Rosenblatt's letter, full of pain and despair, illustrates the fear and distress of the Jews during the pogroms:

> Our great president, head of the Jewish [Territorial] Organization, great author, crown of Israel, Mr. Israel Zangwill! Not in ink but in blood and tears are we composing these words to you! The hand trembles, the eyes tear, the mind is confused, and we cannot organize our thoughts and express them to you! A shout [is heard] outside in our city of Kiev. The soldiers, Cossacks, and police are slaughtering our brothers and sisters in the company of hooligans, and there is no one to protect them. The defense societies have become disheartened; they cannot stand up against the battle-hardened armies with their amazing tactics. Shouts outside, screams in the homes, in the basements, in the attics, in the caves. The screams of children and infants, the sound of women fainting, the groans of the dying, and the breaking of the bones of old people thrown from the upper floors deafen the air of Kiev! Infants and children are being torn up, ripped in half, and thrown to the dogs! They are slicing open the stomachs of pregnant women, cutting out organs from healthy people, and flaying them with iron combs. If the heavens don't explode at the sound of the cries, they must be made of iron and brass! If the earth doesn't shudder at the sound of the wails, then it is a bloody earth, a wasteland full of the fire of the inferno![65]

Rosenblatt's letter was written on the official stationery of Dr. Max Mandelstamm, an oculist, one of the first members of Hovevei Zion in Russia and a territorialist, so that Zangwill would see that the writer was "a man of Mandelstamm's circle—an honest man whose word can be relied on." About a month later, Rosenblatt sent Zangwill another letter in which he once again called for help:

> From the mountains of Kiev, from the vale of tears of the land of evil, we cry out to you for help! Please, prince of Israel, hurry up and save us from the teeth of the predatory beasts that are opening their jaws wide to swallow us alive! The pogrom ended back in October only officially; it is still going on, not noisily or tempestuously but slowly. Not a day goes by without hooligans or police attacking Jews who are passing by innocently on the street—killing them and robbing them of all they have, and even stripping off their clothes! Not a night goes by without murders, thefts, and robberies! The fear is escalating; none of the Jews living in the city can sleep at night due to fear! We sit here in groups at night, trembling at the sound of a driven leaf, and the sound of a mouse scratching at the wall freezes our blood![66]

The writer of the letter was not content with describing the fears of the inhabitants of the city, but he also depicted the consequences of the pogroms and their effect on daily life: "More and more people are being killed! The panic and flight have reached tremendous proportions here; emigration is increasing daily; almost half of the Jewish population has left Kiev! And the poor people who remain are starving to death! Blood is increasingly fertilizing this polluted soil, and brains are being mixed in with the earth! Not one of us has faith in life, for our lives hang in the balance! Every hooligan and every barefoot person beats Jews on the street and no one protests. The police and soldiers laugh at the sight and cheer. Almost all the civilian inhabitants of Kiev are members of the Black Hundreds, and they incite the people against the Jews! In brief, Mr. President, we are like a sheep among seventy wolves. We dwell among scorpions!"[67]

The inhabitants of the shtetl of Kalarash in the region of Kiev also described their harsh predicament in a letter to Zangwill:

> Exalted Sir who loves his people and helps it in its distress, Kalarash is a small shtetl. There are perhaps a thousand families there and there were about six hundred houses. Of these, three hundred were burnt down, and not a stone remains. All the shops in the town have been razed to the foundations. The plum trees, the nut trees, the apple trees were set on fire, all the furniture, cushions, featherbeds and dresses were taken, the silver, gold and jewelry looted. . . . Sixty

people so far have fallen victim to the hooligans and met all kinds of strange and cruel deaths, leaving a large number of widows and orphans after them.[68]

In the light of the harsh descriptions and cries of distress one finds in these letters, we may try to estimate the real importance of the pogroms among the causes of immigration to America in general and to Palestine in particular. There is no doubt whatsoever that the pogroms increased emigration. The proof of this is the simple fact that the number of emigrants increased significantly after every pogrom. In 1879 about 700 Jews immigrated to the United States; in 1888, 4,332 Jews emigrated from Eastern Europe; in 1881, there were about 5,700 Jewish emigrants; and in 1882, a year after the pogroms in the cities of the south of the Pale of Settlement, 13,200 Jews emigrated.[69] The same phenomenon of growth in the number of emigrants during and after the pogroms may be seen at the beginning of the twentieth century. In 1903, about 76,000 Jews immigrated to the United States; in 1904, there were about 106,000; in 1905, about 130,000; and in 1906, more than 153,000. At the height of the slaughter in the south and southwest of the Pale of Settlement, about 460,000 Jews altogether emigrated in a period of only four years. From these numbers, it is clear that the pogroms had an influence on the course of emigration and its scale.

However, the number of Jews who emigrated every year can be interpreted differently. From the numbers given previously, we see that the year 1881 was not a turning point or watershed in the history of Jewish immigration to the United States but, instead, the continuation of an existing tendency that began before the pogroms of 1881–1882. In 1880, for example, more than four times the number of emigrants reached the United States compared with the immigration rate in 1879. In 1881–1882 (the years of the pogroms), on the other hand, slightly more than twice as many emigrants reached the United States. The same applies to emigration at the beginning of the twentieth century. The peak of Jewish emigration was not during the years of the pogroms but in 1914, over the course of which there was an increase in the scale of Jewish immigration to the United States. In only eight months, 138,000 people immigrated to the United States, averaging more than 17,000 emigrants a month. It is reasonable to suppose that if World War I had not broken out, Jewish emigration would have reached a peak of 200,000 people a year. For this reason, one should see 1914, not 1906, as the year with the highest rate of emigration during the entire period of the great migration. In that year, there was no dramatic event—certainly not pogroms—in the lives of Jews of the Russian Empire, but emigration nevertheless reached unprecedented proportions. It should also be pointed out that there were also high rates of emigration from Galicia, although the Jewish population there had not experienced the horror of pogroms.

The question arises: Were the pogroms a direct or an indirect cause of the mass migration? The murders, robbery, and looting, combined with the tremendous damage suffered by Jewish businesses, worsened the existing destitution in the Pale of Settlement and increased the scale of emigration during the period of the pogroms. In other words, Jews who emigrated after the pogroms did include those whose families had been murdered and their property plundered (though one might think that these unfortunate people were not financially or emotionally capable of embarking on a long journey across the ocean). The example of what happened in the town of Brody in Galicia, where refugees fled from the pogroms at the beginning of the 1880s, only confirms this idea. In this instance, many of the refugees were brought back to the Pale of Settlement by the Alliance Israélite Universelle, which recognized that their chances of rehabilitation were much greater there than in America.[70] From the point of view of the activists of the Alliance, these refugees were destitute, and even if they were provided with tickets for the crossing to America it is very doubtful that they would have succeeded in rehabilitating themselves in the new country.

If this was the case, those that emigrated were those Jews who lived in shtetls close to the site of the pogroms. Increasing numbers of Jewish refugees began to flock to shtetls that had not been touched by the violence and then settled there. As a result, the shtetls became too small for the number of people, and the economic distress, already intense, worsened. The story of the shtetl Schpola in the Kiev region, which received many refugees from the pogrom in Kiev, is a good illustration of how the acts of violence led to emigration from a shtetl in which there had not been a pogrom.[71] In David Cohen's book published in 1965,

Schpola, masekhet hayei yehudim be-ayara (Schpola, Portrait of the Lives of Jews in a Shtetl), he said that the pogroms and expulsions caused real economic destitution in the shtetl:

> The Jewish occupations—petty trading, shops and small workshops—could not absorb the hundreds of Jews expelled from the villages, who earned their living in the villages from bartending and innkeeping. Life in the shtetl became a burden to its inhabitants, old and young alike: to the students in the house of learning and the *heder*, to the onlookers and those who had been hurt, to the learned, to those who engaged in trade, and to those who practiced crafts. . . . Many thought of leaving for America; a few for Palestine, but most of the Jews wanted a solution in the place where they were, and dreamed of settling outside the Pale of Settlement.[72]

The pogroms considerably increased the number of people who left the Russian Empire in view of the fact that the settlement of refugees in shtetls far from the centers of violence upset the fragile economic situation, which in any case had been difficult and intolerable. A family that had experienced a pogrom and whose property had been set on fire found it difficult to find the money to emigrate and go overseas. Leaving for a different town and settling there was easier and more convenient. In doing so, however, they became an economic burden on the towns they reached, and thus the pogroms led to a considerable increase in the scale of emigration. Consequently, those that emigrated as a result of the pogroms were mainly Jews who received the refugees rather than the refugees themselves.

Table 1.1 shows the size of Jewish emigration from the Pale of Settlement and Poland on the basis of the files of the information offices of the Jewish Colonization Association, and it enables one to see where there was most emigration in the Russian Empire.

From Table 1.1 we see that 32 percent of emigrants to the various destinations (mainly the United States and Argentina) left from the northwestern area of the Pale of Settlement (Minsk, Grodno, Mogilev, Vitebsk, Vilna, and Kovno). Twenty-eight percent left from the southwest of the Pale of Settlement (Kiev, Volhynia, Podolia, Poltava, and Chernigov), 16 percent from southern Russia (Bessarabia, Kherson, Taurida, and Ekaterinoslav), and 24 percent from the ten districts of Congress Poland. A comparison between the rates of immigration and

TABLE 1.1

Distribution of Jewish emigration in the Russian Empire, in percentages.

Region	Jewish Population in Russian Empire (%)	Jewish Emigration (%)
Northwest	29	32
Southwest	29	28
South	15	16
Poland	27	24
Total	100	100

SOURCE: Isaac Rubinow, "Economic Condition of the Jews in Russia," *Bulletin of the Bureau of Labor* 72 (September 1907): n.p.; reprint, 1970, 491. The data on Jewish emigration to different countries is based on about 150,000 applications to the information offices of the Jewish Colonization Association: Central Archives for the History of the Jewish People (CAHJP).

the concentrations of Jews in the regions of the Pale of Settlement shows that there were hardly any significant differences between the different regions.

At the same time, the rate of emigration from southern Russia is particularly interesting because this is the area where the pogroms occurred in 1903–1906, but the rate of emigration from the southern regions was nevertheless not much higher than the concentration of population there. Perhaps at first there was a low rate of emigration from the south and southwest of the Pale of Settlement, but the pogroms resulted in an increase in emigration so that the rate of emigration from this area became equal to the concentration of the Jewish population. However, studies dealing with the patterns of Jewish emigration to the United States from the Pale of Settlement support the idea that rates of emigration from areas affected by the pogroms not only were especially high but also were low in relation to other areas. Saul Stampfer reached a similar conclusion in his article "The Geographical Background to the Jewish Emigration From Eastern Europe to the United States Before the First World War." The data Stampfer used to ascertain the rates of emigration from the Russian Empire were not those of the Jewish Colonization Association (JCA) but of the *landsmanschaften*—organizations of people from the shtetls—which the emigrants established in New York in the period of the great migration. As the *landsmanschaften* were established on the basis of the shtetl or town of origin of the emigrants, one can attempt to examine and apportion them to different areas of the Russian Empire to evaluate the rates of emigration. According to Stampfer, 50 percent of the emigrants came from the northwest (according to the JCA, 32 percent); 20 percent came from the southwest (according to the JCA, 28 percent); and only 6 percent came from the south (according to the JCA, 16 percent).[73] A similar conclusion was reached by Joel Perlman, who based his study of the patterns of Jewish emigration from the Pale of Settlement on the lists of Jewish immigrants entering the United States via Ellis Island. It follows that the murder and robbery of the Jewish population had little influence on the dynamics and scope of Jewish immigration to the United States.[74]

The regional pattern of immigration to Palestine was different from that to the United States. From 1905 until the outbreak of World War I, the Zionist Information Office in Odessa published statistical data on immigrants to Palestine, including regional patterns of immigration. The publications of the office reveal that 38 percent of immigrants to Palestine came from the southern and southwestern parts of the Pale of Settlement, 25 percent came from the northwest of the Pale, and 17 percent were from Poland.

Figure 1.1 shows that the rates of immigration to Palestine were higher precisely in the southern regions of the Pale of Settlement affected by the pogroms. The data also show that acts of robbery and murder had more influence on the movement to Palestine than on that to the United States. When we examine the rates of immigration to Palestine from the point of view of the time when the pogroms took place (and not from that of the yearly average), we see that in 1905 and 1906 the rates of emigration from the southern regions were especially high and are estimated at 49 percent—52 percent in relation to the period as a whole. In the following years 1907, 1908, and 1909, after the waves of pogroms subsided, the rates of emigration from southern Russia decreased to 35 percent, 28 percent, and 32 percent, respectively, in relation to the period as a whole. The number of immigrants entering Palestine in 1906 relative to 1905 confirms this. In 1906, 3,450 immigrants entered Palestine, as compared to 1,230 in 1905. This was an increase of 180 percent in the number of immigrants to Palestine as against an increase of only 18 percent (from 130,000 to 158,000) to the United States in those years.

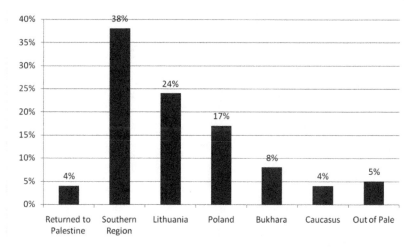

Figure 1.1 Distribution of emigrants from the port of Odessa according to countries of origin, 1905–1914.

SOURCE: "The Departure from Russia to Eretz Israel," *Ha-Olam* 17 (12 May 1910): 14–15; "The Departure from Russia to Eretz Israel," *Ha-Olam* 5 (13 February 1911): 18–19; "The Departure from Russia to Eretz Israel," *Ha-Olam* 16 (6 May 1913): 9–10; "The Departure from Russia to Eretz Israel," *Ha-Olam* 9 (10 March 1914): 15–16.

Immigration to Palestine must be seen in the context of this demographic, social, and economic reality. Immigrants to Palestine consisted not only of the ideologically motivated but also of ordinary Eastern European Jews who saw Palestine as a possible destination where they could have a better life than the one they knew in Eastern Europe. The letters to the information offices enable us to view the immigration to Palestine in its broader historical context and also to perceive other, more prosaic factors that are generally taken into account in immigration to the United States but less often in immigration to Palestine. The letters of the Kohelet, Lipchitz, Alterman, and Kaplan families (and many other letters) to the Palestine Office in Jaffa are evidence from the period of the great migration. These documents give us a better, firsthand understanding of the migration of more than two-and-a-half million Jews to countries overseas including Palestine.

Two Reaching a Decision

For researchers of emigration, one of the most difficult and complex matters is tracing the process of how individuals reached a decision to emigrate. Many historians of migration, both Jewish and non-Jewish, who have attempted to examine this aspect have remarked on its problematic nature. The first challenge they face is a lack of primary sources. This lack has forced scholars to rely on secondary sources—memoirs and oral accounts—that date from many years after migration and settlement in the new country. But these sources do not enable scholars to trace the dynamics of reaching a decision to emigrate. Nor do they allow historians to observe emigrants from the moment they set out until the time of their arrival at the new destination.

The historian Irving Howe, in his monumental work *The World of Our Fathers*, pointed out that it is doubtful if there is a reliable echo of the drama of uprooting even in memoirs: "The statements one finds in the memoir literature are persuasive through their repetition. We came because we were hungry; we came because we were persecuted; we came because life in Russia or Poland had grown insufferable. These are the answers one gets over and over again, and there is not the slightest reason to doubt them. But what they do not, perhaps cannot, explain is why some Jews acted on these urgent motives and others did not."[1] The historian Haim Avni wrote that "this subjective drama, multiplied hundreds of thousands of times, deserves a fascinating study in itself."[2] The initial process of hesitation and struggle in the family circle previous to emigration has not been researched and documented until now. Thus, the "emigration drama" of the ordinary migrant and his family is missing in the research literature, and, together

63

with hundreds of thousands of similar cases, it has been overlooked in quantitative statistics and research.

The historians who researched the non-Jewish immigration to America encountered a similar difficulty when they tried to understand how the decision to emigrate was reached and the obstacles migrants had to overcome in order to arrive peacefully and safely in the land of promise. As a result of this difficulty, they came to the conclusion that if one wanted to understand the motives for emigration, along with the environment in which the decision to remain in the country of origin or to leave for new countries was reached, one had to take into consideration the towns and villages the migrants came from. Philip Taylor, in *The Distant Magnet*, observed that "[i]t is never enough to think of migration continent by continent, or nation by nation. Emigrants were not Europeans or even Germans or Swedes: they were dwellers in a Norwegian valley, or in the Black Forest district of Württemberg: they were Slovaks from the northern hills of the kingdom of Hungary, Bulgarians from Macedonia, or Ashkenazite Jews from the Western provinces of Czarist Russia. No scholar, of course, will ever be able to comprehend all this local detail."[3]

In *Immigrants in the Lands of Promise*, Samuel Baily, the researcher of Italian emigration, stressed the importance of the "local level" in understanding the causes of emigration. Baily claimed that if one wants to know how the decision to emigrate was reached, the Italian village is the place where the "macro" factors that led to the migration westward are to be found. For this reason, among others, he chose the village of Agnone as the archetype of many in southern Italy from which Italians set out for the United States.[4]

Dudley Baines, in *Emigration from Europe, 1815–1939*, also maintained that the migrant's country of origin should not be seen as a single geographical unit but rather that one should focus on the provinces and villages from which the migrants set out.[5] Baines's book not only told the story of the migration from Eastern and Central Europe to America, but also raised a number of methodological problems and difficulties in connection with migration research, at the same time proposing solutions. Thus, for example, Baines recommended emphasizing certain matters that had been seen as secondary in research or had been regarded as self-evident. These matters included how the decision to emigrate was reached, how the country of destination was chosen, the stage of moving to the new country and the difficulties it involved, and many other such questions. In order to deal with the challenging questions that arose in his book, Baines suggested a number of sources and methods that could help migration research. For example, he suggested paying attention to the study of names, an area richer and more detailed than aggregative sources of knowledge.[6] Also, emigrants' letters are, in his opinion, an excellent source for understanding the dynamics of emigration and the motivation of the emigrant. Baines asserted that one of the main problems in emigration research is that "we cannot know what actually passed through the minds of potential emigrants."[7] However, the letters of ordinary emigrants written at the height of the emigration process permit us to see the predeparture hesitations and struggles of emigrants as they happened at the time.[8]

This chapter studies letters sent to the Zionist information bureaus in order to examine the following questions in a comparative perspective: How was the decision to immigrate to Palestine reached? What questions did those interested ask the information bureaus? What part did Zionist ideology play in the decision to emigrate? And, from letters written in reply to these requests, what can we learn of the Zionist immigration policies formulated in Palestine at the beginning of the twentieth century? However, before relating to these questions I wish to explain the background to the creation of the Zionist information bureaus, why the letters were sent to them, and the role these bureaus played in immigration to Palestine.

The Information Bureaus

Information bureaus were established in the countries of origin and the countries of destination of Jewish migration. They provided the emigrant with information before he set out on his long journey. In October 1904, there was a large conference in Frankfurt of major Jewish societies, such as Hilfsverein, the Jewish Colonization Association (JCA), and the Alliance Israélite Universelle, who wished to place Jewish migration and the problems that arose as a result on the public agenda. At this conference, it was decided to establish a central information bureau for the purpose of helping Jewish migrants. The information bureau, also known as the Central Bureau for Questions of Jewish Migration, was set up in Berlin, which was a central axis of migration at that period: "The greater part of the migrants, whether those who come off the boats at Hamburg or Bremen or those who sail from Rotterdam, Antwerp or Amsterdam, pass through Ashkenaz [Germany]."[9]

The central bureau in Berlin and the bureaus under it, which were scattered throughout the routes of migration, did not attempt to prevent migration or to limit it. The task of the bureau was to provide the migrant with the most relevant and exact information possible, starting with information about the cheapest and shortest way to the port and including details about buying tickets, cheap accommodation at the port previous to sailing, the logistics of absorption, and possibilities for employment in the country of destination. Moreover, the bureaus had to "ensure that the migrant had the necessary documents and had to be in contact with the ship-owners so that they knew that there is an eye watching over them and not maltreat the migrants, as often happens."[10]

The JCA was the first organization in the Russian Empire to help migrants and advise them free of charge. The JCA received its authorization from the Russian government in 1891. This authorization enabled it in 1894 to open an emigration department that was headed by the lawyer M. Bregman, the purpose of which was to solve problems that arose in matters relating to emigration. The department began to appoint representatives in several centers in the Pale of Settlement and to publish booklets on general information for emigrants. But Bregman's sudden death a short time after the founding of the emigration department, along with the small scale of emigration at the time, caused the department to shut down for a while.[11]

In 1904, following the Kishinev pogrom, there was a marked increase in the rate of emigration due to the great suffering of the Jewish population. The central committee of the JCA, in consultation with the administration in Paris and board of directors, decided to open an information bureau in Saint Petersburg. From 1904 onward, the JCA was the most important Jewish philanthropic institution dealing with emigration-related matters in the Russian Empire. The chairman of the central committee of the JCA in Saint Petersburg was Baron Ginsburg, who had overall responsibility for running the information bureau. The man who ran it on a practical level and saw to its day-to-day functioning was the lawyer Shmuel Janovsky. In order for the bureau to successfully achieve the goals it set for itself and create an effective information infrastructure for hundreds of thousands of Jewish emigrants, regional information bureaus were established throughout the Russian Empire. Within a few years, licensed information bureaus under the auspices of the JCA arose in all the cities and major centers of emigration. In 1906 there were 160 information bureaus in the Pale of Settlement, in 1907 there were 296, in 1910 there were 449, and by 1913 there were 507.[12] The information bureaus were a lifesaver for emigrants, sparing them unnecessary expenses and a great deal of distress. The newspaper *Hed Ha-Zman* wrote:

> In the dark world of the migrants, the bureaus that the central bureau of the JCA has set up in not inconsiderable numbers in the Pale of Settlement are like faintly shining stars. Every day, these bureaus receive many questions in writing, in very large numbers, on matters pertaining to emigration. Also hundreds and thousands of people go themselves to these committees to obtain information, and the latter help the emigrants, answering their questions and resolving their difficulties, telling them how to obtain passports to travel abroad and sometimes providing financial support for migrants who are not going to America.[13]

The central committee in Paris invested considerable sums of money so that the local bureaus could deal quickly and effectively with the problems of migrants, who often could not afford a delay. The Saint Petersburg information bureau's budget in its first years of operation stood at 14,000 roubles a year, and in 1913 the annual budget reached the sum of 20,000 roubles. Most of the bureau's expenditure was for salaries, publication of the journal *Der Jüdische Emigrant*, publication of pamphlets for the guidance of emigrants, books and posters, postage and telegraph costs, assistance to families, and so on.[14] Up to the outbreak of World War I, the JCA invested more than 130,000 roubles in the information bureau in Saint Petersburg. In addition to the regular budget of the central bureau in Saint Petersburg, money was also sent to the local information bureaus in the main centers of migration. During the years 1908–1914, the JCA financed the local bureaus to a total amount of 160,000 roubles. The information bureaus in the frontier stations, which were a bottleneck of Jewish emigration in which masses of emigrants were gathered, also had their budget.[15] The total sum that the JCA spent on the organization of emigration and alleviation of the distress of Jewish migrants was more than 300,000 roubles. The representatives in the local bureaus and the frontier towns had a kind of "small kitty" for the money that was sent to them, which gave them freedom to act and solve the problems of the emigrants quickly.

When the central bureau in Saint Petersburg began to operate and information began to arrive from the local bureaus, Baron Ginsburg and Janovsky set out the policies of the information office as follows:

> Not to rely on the recommendations of relatives to travel specifically to the places where they work, not to be drawn by the current to the large and beautiful cities over the ocean to which emigration naturally flows, not to be caught by the networks of agents who promise the earth, not to set out without first consulting an oculist, not to get on the train without showing the local representative all the necessary documents, not to take to America clothes and possessions that are not needed, not to turn to any benefactor or committee in the place you leave from or in the countries of transit unless they are authorized and duly appointed committees of the JCA in such and such a town of departure, such and such a town of transit, such and such a frontier town or such and such a place of entry.[16]

Janovsky had a Zionist outlook and saw Palestine as the true solution to the Jewish question. At the same time, he was careful in his work at the bureau "not to mix his personal Zionism with his work for the JCA."[17] For the purposes of the information bureau, he divided czarist Russia into three main parts: Congress Poland, White Russia, and Lithuania. The southern region included Volhynia, Podolia, and Bessarabia. There was a chief secretary in charge of each area who was an expert in matters of emigration and the specific arrangements required for it, and who was in constant touch with the emigration committees in the towns and cities of the Pale of Settlement. Previous to the outbreak of World War I, the JCA established about five hundred committees throughout the Pale of Settlement.[18] Many letters were sent directly to the central information bureau in Saint Petersburg, without passing through the committees. They were dealt with by Zalman Rubashov (later Shazar), who at that time was one of the officials of the bureau and an assistant of Janovsky. Rubashov described his work at the bureau:

> Every day, from eight in the morning until one in the afternoon, I was up to the neck in the troubles of the Jewish people. Reading and searching and answering and sorting, and sending my replies to the secretaries to be signed. . . . Jews who wanted to emigrate and did not know where to turn, emigrants who were cheated by exploiting agents and had no protection; the rabbi of a community who saw the poverty of the artisans in his shtetl who were penniless, had no customers and wanted to leave, but the rabbi did not know what to do about it; a shtetl intellectual whose heart grieved at the troubles of the Jewish people and wanted to play his part with the workers to improve the people's lot; a woman whose husband abandoned her and went abroad and forgot her and her children who were left to their plight with no one to help them. . . . Within a year I was expert in the whole range of these sufferings which bore within them the kernel of the approaching Holocaust.[19]

The hierarchical structure of the information bureau allowed dozens of local bureaus to operate effectively. Every problem that arose was submitted to the regional bureau, and if it could not be solved there it was passed on to Saint Petersburg. The larger regional bureaus were run by committees of three to ten people, in accordance with the numbers of those who wanted to emigrate from the area, and in the local bureaus in small towns and villages there was only one or two representatives at most.[20] Every few months there were regional meetings when local representatives would come together, discuss common problems, and consider possible solutions. At these meetings, the heads of the regional bureaus transmitted messages and requests to the local representatives from the central bureau in Saint Petersburg. These representatives were asked to keep precise records of those who applied to the local bureaus, publicize the aims of the JCA information bureau and disseminate its literature, warn immigrants about agents, and publicize the names of crooks and their illegal activities.[21] The aim of the local bureaus was to answer emigrants' questions, help them obtain passports, and sometimes offer financial support:

> The committees and representatives and correspondents who provide useful information to the emigrants already number a hundred and sixty in all the towns of the Pale. Every day, these bureaus receive questions in writing, in very large numbers, on matters pertaining to emigration. Also, hundreds and thousands of people go themselves to these committees to obtain information. The latter help the emigrants, answering their questions and resolving their difficulties, telling them how to obtain passports for travel abroad and sometimes also giving financial support to those who are not going to America.[22]

In the periods of massive emigration, there were two large general conferences: the first in Libau in September 1910, and the second in Vilna in May 1913. The conferences lasted for five days and included lectures. At Libau there was even a tour of the port, plus a visit to one of the ships of the Libau–New York line in order to find out firsthand about the difficult conditions of the voyage.[23] At these conferences, strategic decisions were made concerning emigration, including strategies for providing emigrants with medical assistance, offering financial assistance for purchasing tickets and obtaining passports, securing bodily protection for women emigrants, and making the work of the information bureau and its representatives more efficient.

One of the main aims of the information office was to wage a struggle against agents (who will be discussed in detail in chapter 4). Through the common effort of all the regional bureaus, it wished to rescue emigrants "from the wiles of the agents and their tricksters, and to remove these useless obstructions which have bitter consequences for the emigrants."[24] The information bureau waged an aggressive campaign against these swindlers and agents, and representatives of the JCA several times requested the help of the authorities. The bureau's primary objective was to help emigrants in every possible way: to protect them from agents and to provide help in solving their problems.

Besides the bureaucratic assistance, the JCA central bureau in Saint Petersburg sent out literature concerning emigration throughout the Pale of Settlement. In order to counter the influence of agents in the black market and their attempts to control information, the information bureau published a wide variety of pamphlets for the assistance and guidance of emigrants. It distributed these pamphlets—some of them free of charge and some offered at an especially low price—to the regional and local bureaus. By means of these pamphlets, the bureau wished to weaken the hold of the agents, whose only advantage was experience and knowledge in the sphere of emigration. "All information published about emigration, all practical advice, all help in obtaining a travel document was a blow to the agents. The emigrants came to realize that the bureau helped and served them for nothing."[25]

The bureau published material on various subjects in Yiddish and Russian. The booklet that had the widest circulation was *Algemeine Yedies Far die Vos Villen Forn in Fremde Lender* (General Information for Those Who Wish to Emigrate to Foreign Countries), which was distributed at the nominal price of 6 kopeks. The booklet contained a short explanation in simple language of what an emigrant had to know before setting out, practical advice on the process, and information about destination countries. After reading the booklet, an emigrant would be informed on how it was not advisable to set out without a certain sum of money; rates of exchange and frontier stations; the danger of agents; seasickness and how to deal with it; where to buy boat tickets; how to get a passport; and guidelines on weight for their baggage. There was also some advice on courtesy and details about various countries, including the United States, Canada, South Africa, South America, Australia, and Palestine. The JCA first published the booklet in 1906, and subsequently 10,000 copies were printed every year.[26] Emigrants could also get detailed, up-to-date information in special booklets devoted to specific countries: Argentina, Australia, Canada, South Africa, Chile, and of course the United States. Each booklet came out in several editions that were regularly revised. In these booklets the emigrant found a geographical account of the country of his choice with an accompanying map, information about the climate and wildlife, data on the local population, exchange rates and the value of the local currency, information about agricultural work and other occupations, details on the cost of living, and data on the cost of sailing to the chosen country. The most comprehensive booklet was the one dealing with the United States, which contained information about every single state in the country and the possibilities of employment there. The policy of the bureau was to avoid concentrations of emigrants in large cities and to encourage their settlement in towns of the interior. The booklet had a circulation of 6,000 copies a year, and it was brought up to date every year.

In 1907, the JCA began to publish a newspaper, *Der Jüdische Emigrant*, entirely devoted to matters of emigration. This journal appeared twice monthly, providing the latest information about countries to which emigrants wished to travel. Until his death in 1910, the editor of the paper was Baron Ginsburg, and from 1910 onward it was edited by the general secretary of the information bureau, Janovsky. In each issue, readers generally found one or two articles dealing with some aspect of emigration (with titles such as "Trade and Industry in Argentina," "Trachoma," "The Economic Crisis in the United States," "The Port of Bremen," and "Emigration from Bessarabia"). The paper also offered information from the regional and local bureaus, announcements from the central bureau in Saint Petersburg, readers' questions with answers, details on fraudulent agents, a list of prices for sailing, names of ships, and data on travel times for voyages (including mention of stops on the way). By the standards of the beginning of the century, the circulation of the paper was very large: in 1906, it was 5,000 copies; in 1907, 50,000 copies; and in 1908 (the peak year), 70,000 copies. In the following years, circulation ranged between 50,000 and 60,000 copies.[27] If one assumes that each paper was passed among a number of different readers, the circulation was even greater. Moreover, the bureau published dictionaries—such as Yiddish-English and Yiddish-Spanish—in order to smooth the path of the emigrant in the new country. Following the paper's great success, the Hebrew Immigrant Aid Society (HIAS) began to publish a bilingual edition of the paper in both Yiddish and English. The purpose of the English edition was twofold: first, to inform those interested in the United States on the difficulties of Jewish emigration and to permit an exchange of views on the subject; and second, to help Jewish emigrants while they were still in Eastern Europe, before their arrival in the United States.[28] As a result of this policy, a collaboration developed between HIAS and the JCA. The HIAS representative Alexander Harkavi began to publish booklets for the guidance of the emigrant of the kind that the JCA had done in the Pale of Settlement. He made a journey of two-

and-a-half months around the ports of Europe in order to gain a better understanding of the difficulties faced by Jewish emigrants on their way to the United States.[29]

In 1912, the JCA published a booklet entirely devoted to crooks. In this booklet, titled *Emigrantn un Aganten: Nit keyn oysgetrakhte mayses—nit keyn oysgetrakhte mayses* (Emigrants and Agents: Not Figments of the Imagination), the JCA information bureau informed emigrants of various cases of fraud.[30] The twenty-page booklet described fraudulent methods that the bureau had discovered when coming to the aid of the emigrants. There was a dual purpose in bringing out this booklet: First, it informed emigrants of the dangers that lay on their path and warned them of crooks out to cheat them; and second, it served to frighten emigrants so they would see that they had to rely on the aid of the information bureaus:

> The Jewish emigrant should know that he cannot undertake the great journey alone. After many years of emigration, the time has come to realize that one cannot migrate without assistance. We [the JCA information bureau] therefore provide information on how to obtain a passport, what routes to take, to which country one should go, conditions in the country of choice, and so on. For that reason, we are to be found in every major town in the Pale of Settlement so that the emigrant can receive the necessary information free of charge. The only way to prevent the Jewish emigrant from being immersed in problems is to accompany him from the moment he considers emigrating, and throughout his journey, until he steps on the soil of his new country.[31]

The Zionist Information Bureaus

The Zionist information bureaus that appeared at the beginning of the twentieth century, at the height of immigration to the United States, thus should be seen in light of this historical context. In January 1905, the information bureau of the Hovevei Zion in Odessa was established. Its aims were to provide immigrants wishing to go to Palestine with exact information about conditions in the Yishuv and to consolidate the information received "from reliable sources concerning the rights that have been granted and that are about to be granted to the Jews in

Palestine and Syria."[32] The information included data about the laws of the country, conditions for the purchase of land, and the possibilities of setting up businesses:

> The bureau will provide answers orally or in writing to all questions it receives, will inform applicants of decent, inexpensive hostels in Odessa and of banks where money may be exchanged or transferred cheaply. It will carry on a continuous negotiation with the shipping companies so that it can always provide exact information about the times ships leave for Palestine and Syria, and it will also try to obtain reductions in the price of tickets for applicants.[33]

The Odessa information bureau extended its sphere of activity and in 1906 opened information bureaus in Jaffa, Jerusalem, Haifa, Beirut, and Constantinople. The Palestinian information bureau in Jaffa was subordinate to the central bureau in Odessa, but it was financially supported by the central information bureau in Berlin:

> Palestine also has an important place among the countries of immigration, although in view of the terrible economic situation of the Palestinian Jews, the Berlin office of migration cannot explain this phenomenon. But it accepts it as a fact, and it therefore sees itself obliged to organize the migration in an orderly manner, to provide information about places of employment, and to set up reliable information bureaus . . . and it has therefore included among its expenses the general information bureau for Jewish migrants in Jaffa founded by the Palestinian Committee in Odessa.[34]

The Jaffa bureau was headed by Menahem Sheinkin, who directed it until the outbreak of World War I.[35] Its methods of disseminating information were similar to those of the JCA bureaus. In 1907, for example, Sheinkin published an information sheet specifying the activities of the information bureau that was distributed throughout Eastern Europe:

> The information bureau has the honor of requesting you to provide us with information in accordance with the present sheet of questions. The information bureau, for its part, is obliged to provide you with all the information in its possession concerning agricultural work, crafts, commerce and manufacturing in Palestine. The bureau is always ready to try to obtain all necessary information for the applicant and

to investigate all matters you require. The information bureau has representatives in all the towns in Palestine and Syria and in the Jewish settlements. The information bureau is open every day (excepting Sabbaths and holidays) from 10 to 12 o'clock in the morning and from 3 to 5 o'clock in the afternoon.[36]

The information sheet included accounts of the Jewish population in the towns and settlements of Palestine, exchange rates for Ottoman currency, information about "posts and telegraphs," and details of the transport facilities between the various settlements in the country. A year later, Sheinkin published an updated, detailed booklet about the journey to Palestine and the possibilities of absorption there. The information included descriptions of necessary preparations for the journey (obtaining passports and authorizations from the authorities), accounts of hostels in the port of Odessa, waiting periods before boarding the ship, the sea voyage and stops on the way, arrival in the port of Jaffa, the cost of living in Palestine, and languages that were spoken in the new country. There was also a special emphasis on possibilities of employment in Palestine in agriculture, local industries, and crafts. The booklet was updated every year and disseminated throughout the Russian Empire by the information bureau of the Hovevei Zion in Odessa.

In a lecture given in 1913, Sheinkin described the six main functions of the bureau:

(1) To give exact answers to all who turned to the bureau from far and near, whether orally or in writing; (2) To meet immigrants when they came off the ship and make sure they were not cheated; (3) To offer employment to workers and craftsmen; (4) To keep precise statistics on those entering the country; (5) To visit immigrants regularly in their hostels and deal with their problems; and (6) To serve as a postal service for immigrants who did not yet have a fixed address.[37]

The first years of the information bureaus in Odessa and Jaffa were marked by disorder and failure. "I am familiar with the situation in the Odessa bureau," wrote a man who called himself "Hadash," in an article in the *Ha-Po'el Ha-Tza'ir* journal:

I have carefully watched its development, and I want to say a few words about it. . . . Out of all the rooms in this place [referring to the building of the Odessa Committeee], in each of which sit one or two men,

workers of the Committee, there has been chosen for the bureau, where
you will sometimes find a whole *minyan* [quorum] of people at the
same time, the smallest and narrowest room, between the door and the
kitchens. . . . It must be said that Mr. A., to whom the management
of the bureau is confided, is totally unworthy of the highly responsible
position he has been given. . . . In the bureau of the Committee you will
always hear the travellers' questions: Should the Russian money be exchanged for another currency in Odessa? And the manager answers, it's
the same thing if you change the money here or somewhere else. Many
of the travellers don't change it at all, and they very soon see—especially
those that don't have a large sum—that it is not the same thing. At the
Turkish frontier they lose about five kopeks on every rouble.[38]

As a result of the inefficiency of the information bureaus, emigrants
incurred many unnecessary expenses on their way to Palestine. When
they reached the country, they complained bitterly to people in the
Yishuv about the inefficiency of the bureaus and about the needless
expenses they incurred because of wrong or irrelevant information provided by the bureaus. On several occasions it appeared that the head of
a family was made to buy tickets for his children when in fact they could
travel free of charge. When the mistake was discovered, it was too late:

The committee, after publishing the reductions it has made in the
sale of tickets for the voyage from Odessa to Jaffa, urges and obliges
the travelers in a bureaucratic way, arousing suspicion among many,
to buy half-tickets for small children aged three and four when in
fact this extra expense can be avoided. There have been cases when
it has forced the head of a family to buy tickets for his small children, threatening them that if they refused, they would not sell them
tickets at all, and they would later have to pay the shipping company
twenty-one roubles for a ticket. Later, when the officials of the ship
examined the tickets, they laughed at this ridiculous expense and left
the childrens' tickets with the fathers.[39]

Emigrants sometimes arrived in Odessa a few days before sailing and
found that the sailors and longshoremen were on strike and no ships
were leaving the port. The strike forced the emigrants to remain in the
city for a long time, a delay that made them even more vulnerable to
tricksters and involved them in needless expenses. When they reached
Jaffa, the emigrants reported their difficulties to officials in the Yishuv:

"The newspapers must warn the emigrants against staying in Odessa waiting for the end of the strike."[40]

The angry complaints of immigrants arriving in the country led to the setting up of a committee that first met in Beit Ha-Am in Jaffa in 1906. The initiators of the idea, who also became heads of the committee, were Akiva Aryeh Weiss, Y. D. Freyer, Raphael Sverdlov, and Mordechai Lederer. Their aim was "to investigate the sufferings of the immigrants on their journey to Palestine." In the month of Av in the year 1906, the meeting took place after "the travellers' stories of their troubles and adventures" had been heard "with serious interest, and after definitive proof had been given of the truth of these stories." The committee decided to write a letter protesting the shoddy work of the Odessa Committee, which they said almost "harmed the national enterprise." At the end of this letter of complaint, its writers asked that "for the sake of our sacred idea, we demand that our observations should be taken seriously and discussed at the next general meeting."[41] The head of the Odessa Committee, Menahem Ussishkin, replied that he took the complaints of immigrants described in the letter seriously. He said that in the minutes of the committee's meeting, it was written that:

> The information bureau must improve its methods of work in order that in future all the impediments that the Beit Ha-Am committee described in its communication should be removed or alleviated as far as possible. The meeting endorsed this response enthusiastically . . . and these seemingly minor impediments that have major consequences must be removed forthwith.[42]

Providing a similar function to the JCA bureau, the Odessa Committee's information bureau helped emigrants with the bureaucratic processes bound up with emigration. The bureau helped in obtaining travel documents necessary for emigration and subsidized the purchase of boat tickets (at the high rate of 40 percent). When the bureau provided the boat tickets, it also obtained the necessary travelers' tickets for getting off the ship at Jaffa: "And at Constantinople the bureau will help the travelers with obtaining the *Tazkara* [the Turkish document authorizing one to live in the country], with changing their money, with changing ships, with going from the shore to the city if necessary, and so on."[43]

In addition, the information bureau published booklets helping emigrants to overcome the obstacles they faced. These booklets specified the problems emigrants could expect, warned them of dangers, and attempted to guide them through the bureaucratic tangle of the emigration process. They also provided emigrants with all the necessary information on procedures to be followed before embarking on the journey, as well as warning them of the tricksters and crooks they could expect to find in Odessa. There were also tips on dealing with luggage, exchange rates, stops on the way, port information, and general information on Palestine.[44] The booklets were written and edited by the Jaffa information bureau under the management of Sheinkin, and their dissemination was the responsibility of the central information bureau in Odessa. A comparison between the booklets of guidance issued by the Palestinian information bureau and those issued by the JCA for Jewish emigrants to America reveals a great similarity between them. Sheinkin undoubtedly used the booklets of the JCA as the model for the booklets of the Odessa information office.

Another encounter of the JCA information bureau with Sheinkin's information bureau took place in 1911 with the arrival in Palestine of Zalman Rubashov, Janovsky's assistant in the information bureau in Saint Petersburg. After making a tour of the country that included Jerusalem, Haifa, and settlements in Judea and Galilee, Rubashov met Menaham Sheinkin in Jaffa. As a member of the JCA information bureau, Janovsky proposed to Sheinkin a collaboration between the bureaus that would lead to a considerable increase in the number of immigrants to Palestine. Sheinkin, however, as head of the Jaffa information bureau and the person most knowledgeable about immigration to Palestine, firmly rejected the proposal on the grounds that there should be no increase in the number of immigrants as long as the country was unable to absorb them.

Rubashov was not convinced by Sheinkin's argument, and he published an article titled "Nehutza Avoda" (Necessary Work) in the journal *Ha-Olam*, asserting that "Palestine must be included as a country of immigration in the list of countries that the people concerned with immigration deal with," and that the representatives of the bureaus should search for suitable immigrants to Palestine and tell them about life there.[45] Sheinkin reacted by publishing an article of his own in which he not only attacked the idea of a mass immigration to Palestine—and especially for workers with families who found it difficult to adapt and acclimatize themselves to the country—but also the transformation of the information bureau into a party concern. He said that as a realist and someone familiar with conditions in the country and options for settlement there, he thought that one should temper the desire for national rebirth with the realization that the country was "not yet ready for mass-immigration." Announcements of "vacant positions" were therefore not to be advertised in information bureaus other than those of the Hovevei Zion. His reasoning was that "there were so few such places, in fact too few to be advertised." Let us say, he wrote, that

> a tailor was needed in a certain settlement, a shoemaker in another settlement, three carpenters in one town and a bookbinder in another. A hundred and twenty-seven JCA information bureaus would soon be told about this, and as a result of our information at least ten times more people looking for work would come to the bureaus than were needed. Why should we not be content with offering these vacancies to the twenty carpenters, shoemakers, tailors and bookbinders that turn directly to us and wait for our answers?[46]

Strangely enough, Janovsky agreed with these arguments. He tried to explain to Rubashov that he should not mix one thing with another, should overcome his subjective Zionist desires, and not try to anticipate the end result. In order to console Rubashov, Janovsky told him that the work of the JCA information bureau was not fruitless and from a historical point of view constituted "a great laboratory for the governmental organization of a great *Aliyah* to Palestine in the future."[47] From this exchange between Sheinkin and Rubashov in the pages of *Ha-Olam* in 1911, one learns not only about Zionist policies concerning immigration to Palestine at the beginning of the twentieth century but also, above all, about the historical context in which the information bureaus operated. Sheinkin and Janovsky, as heads of information bureaus of the Zionists and the JCA, respectively, used similar methods to help Jewish emigrants—whether to Palestine or to the United States—deal with the problems they would confront on their long journey to the chosen country.

In 1908, the Palestine Office was established in Jaffa, headed by Arthur Ruppin and his assistant Jacob Thon. The Palestine Office was the executive branch of the Zionist organization in Palestine. Its main purpose was to promote, finance, and direct the settlement enterprise in Palestine, which included planning settlement, purchasing lands, allocating funds, founding of new agricultural and urban settlements, managing farms, assigning people to various settlements, providing guidance for existing settlements, helping workers, and providing information to those wishing to immigrate to Palestine and settle there. The activities of the Palestine Office overlapped with the work of Sheinkin's information bureau. The fact that two information bureaus operated in Jaffa—one under the auspices of the Odessa Committee and the other under the auspices of the Zionist organization—led to friction between Ruppin and Sheinkin. The more powerful and influential the Palestine Office became, the weaker Sheinkin became—and the more the bureau he managed lost its importance.[48]

Struggles and Difficulties in Reaching the Decision to Emigrate

Apart from publishing booklets of guidance that were disseminated in immigrants' countries of origin, the information bureaus answered written inquiries from emigrants requesting specific, exact information that they could not find in the publications. These letters, preserved in the files of the information bureaus, allow us to trace the path followed by an emigrant in reaching a decision during the transitional stage before he had decided to emigrate or where to go. Although each of the emigrants' letters to the information bureaus stands on its own and describes things from the point of view of the writer, one can nevertheless find a common factor among the thousands of requests. All the emigrants' letters—whether of those who wanted to go to America or of those who wished to go to Palestine—described a desire to receive information that would enable them to seriously consider whether it was worthwhile to uproot themselves and travel to the new country. A comparison between emigrants' letters sent to the information bureaus in the United States and those weighing immigration to Palestine show that there was no difference in the questions the emigrants asked the officials of the bureaus. Both asked for the most reliable and exact information possible about the chosen country and were interested in the economic opportunities it offered.

The profile of potential emigrants who considered emigration and applied to the Zionist information bureaus corresponded to the profile of the Jewish population in Eastern Europe. More than 50 percent of applicants to the Zionist information bureaus were tradesmen or artisans. About 23 percent identified as tradesmen, and 60 percent of these did not give an exact description of the kind of trade or business they practiced or intended to practice in Palestine. "I was in Palestine three years ago and worked for a year in the agricultural settlements," wrote M. Eisenstadt from the region of Plotzk in Poland, "but as a laborer I couldn't manage." Eisenstadt, a peddler in Poland, wanted to go to Palestine for a second time with his wife, but he no longer considered working in the agricultural settlements:

> I myself am thinking about the following things: for example, opening a small factory for buttons made of mother of pearl or linen thread, or maybe better—for candy or for umbrellas and parasols. If one cannot support oneself with these occupations there, then please tell me if there is any occupation that one can take up. Please just answer me as soon as possible.[49]

About 28 percent of the applicants to the information bureaus were artisans. "Yesterday a shoemaker from the Vilna region called Lieb Stefachnik, applied to me asking me to buy him a house with some land to grow some vegetables," B. A. Goldberg, representative of the Hevrat Hachsharat ha-Yishuv, wrote to the Palestine Office. "His sons are also artisans: one is a tinker, and the other is a bookbinder. He himself is fifty years old and has been an artisan from his youth. His wife is able to do gardening and to work in the fields with animals, and so is his twenty-one-year-old daughter."[50]

Of those who applied to the information bureaus, 20 percent were tailors, 11 percent were builders, 10 percent were shoemakers, and about 9 percent were carpenters. The other 50 percent of this group of tradesmen or artisans practiced various occupations: They were painters, glaziers, bone-setters, watchmakers, tinkers, locksmiths, bookbinders, and turners.

A relatively large proportion of applicants to the information bureaus, a percentage that did not correspond to their proportion in the Jewish population as a whole in Eastern Europe, belonged to the liberal professions. Twenty-two percent were pharmacists, who thought that their profession might be needed in Palestine because of the sicknesses there; and 16 percent were dentists, who wanted to know if one could open a clinic in Palestine. "I will ask the honored bureau to tell me clearly and as soon as possible where and in what way I can open in one of the towns or agricultural settlements of Palestine a *laboratorium* of my professionally certified craft," wrote Haim Levinsky to Ruppin:

> I should like after the holiday to change my place of residence together with the members of my family and settle in Palestine. I am outstanding in my profession, and I have made all kinds of artificial teeth; I heal and repair in an outstanding way. My certificate will confirm this, and I have great experience in much work of this kind. Apart from that, I ask you to provide me with information for my brother-in-law, who is an excellent barber and a fine artist, and his wife is able to make all kinds of plaits, wigs, locks of hair and tresses for plays in theaters.[51]

Of other applicants, 3 percent were students interested in attending the Technicon, the Bezalel School of Art, high school, or the Mikve Israel agricultural school. But some also asked for details about relevant studies in Europe in the hope that upon graduation they would find a livelihood in Palestine. This is how a student from Pshemishl, Galicia, described his problems concerning his studies and livelihood to Arthur Ruppin: "I am turning to you, honored sir, with a major request. This year I have finished gymnasium [high school] and received my matriculation certificate. I have always dreamed, and I still dream, of being a teacher in a gymnasium in our country. I am drawn to mathematics and physics and I want to do advanced studies in these subjects in the University of Vienna in order to teach them afterwards in the land of our hopes." The problem that arose was not a simple one. His parents did not agree to their son becoming a teacher:

> They strongly oppose this idea of mine and threaten that they will not give me the small financial support that they are able to give if I do not choose some occupation that provides for its practitioners in

comfort. In their opinion, one cannot hope that after finishing my studies in university I will find a decent position in Palestine. They claim that a great many students prepare themselves for these positions, of which there are not many as a result. They therefore advise me to choose medicine, which also gives one the possibility of living and working in Palestine. . . . Naturally, as a result of what they say, everyday life is becoming a heavy burden to me, doubts and misgivings are beginning to drive me to despair and the goal that I have set myself is fading away.[52]

About 15 percent of the applicants had no profession. This group was partly composed of young unmarried men and women who were interested in the possibilities of agricultural work in Palestine, but there were also people with families who had no profession yet hoped to find their salvation in the new country. Goldberg made enquiries on behalf of the young people who wanted to be laborers in Palestine: "I have to obtain exact information from you," he wrote. "Is there any certainty that they will find work there? Is it advisable now, at the time of the Yemenite immigration, to send a fair number of Ashkenazi workers?"[53]

In addition to showing the employment profile of applicants, these applications also demonstrate the role of Zionist ideology in the decision to immigrate to Palestine. From the 989 letters that have been examined, it seems that the Zionist idea was not a major motivation in the decision to emigrate, and only a few of the applications have a definite ideological coloring. Sixty-five percent of the applicants expressed a desire to go to Palestine, work in a trade or craft, and continue practicing their former occupations there; about 17 percent showed an interest in buying land; 10 percent specifically declared their support for the Zionist idea; and another 8 percent were interested in industry, studies, or other matters. At the same time it must be pointed out that in many letters there is not always a clear distinction between the choice of emigration for ideological reasons and the choice of it for economic reasons. However, it is absolutely clear from the content of the letters and from the formulation of the questions that Zionist ideology was not a central concern in reaching the decision to emigrate. This contention becomes all the more valid when one compares the letters sent to the information bureaus in Palestine with those sent to bureaus in the United States. The similarity in the formulation of the questions and in the desire to obtain exact and relevant information is striking. In the following, I offer some examples from these letters.

In 1907, Moyshe Zelnik of the shtetl of Dubassary in Bessarabia sent a letter to the head of the Industrial Removal Office (IRO) in New York asking for information on the drinking habits of Americans. Zelnik, who was an alcohol distiller, wanted to continue in his line of work in the United States. But before reaching a final decision, he sent the following letter in which there were a number of questions:

> Having nowhere else to turn for a satisfactory answer, I have the honor to write to you and I believe that you will not refuse me and will answer my questions below. By my profession I am a liquor distiller: that is, I have served in factories that make various sweet liqueurs and spirits, and now I have decided to leave for America as a result of the terribly critical situation in our area. But before I commit myself to the journey, I want to know whether there will be something to do in America connected to my profession, and therefore, I would need to know the following:
>
> 1. Do people in America drink a lot of liqueurs, or do they mainly drink unsweetened spirits like Gin or Whiskey and liquor distilled from wheat, corn, rye, and such?
>
> 2. Are there many distilleries in the United States of America and is it possible to quickly obtain a position in such a distillery?
>
> 3. If you happen to know, how much does the government get for each level of alcohol percentage per one hundred liters of liquor? If this is not practiced there, then I don't need the information.
>
> 4. Especially this one: How does one go about getting work and what does one need to do to obtain such a position? Is there a reputable bureau or society that can fill such positions or does one have to advertise oneself in a special journal devoted to my line of work?[54]

Moshe Borgin of the shtetl Kertingen in the region of Kovno also asked the head of the IRO for reliable information about the chances of absorption in the United States. Borgin was a pharmacist by profession, and he wanted to know about the following:

> I would like to know which region is more suitable for me and how prevalent my profession is there. I am a druggist. I have worked for

many years in drugstores (pharmacies). I know the business and the work very well. So, I'm requesting your help in answering these urgent questions for me:

1. What region or city is more suitable for me, considering my profession?

2. Can a person in this field find work in these kinds of businesses: drugstores, pharmacies, hospitals, drug warehouses, etc.?

3. What are the average earnings of someone working with these kinds of products?

4. What would a person from Russia be required to know to attain this goal?[55]

Ayzik Blum from the shtetl of Neswizsch in the region of Minsk asked if in America there was a place "for a young man of thirty with rabbinical ordination from rabbis in Russia, who knows how to preach, lead the prayer service, read Torah in shul, where he can obtain a position as a rabbi and be able to survive, because in Russia things are very bad since the war [Russo-Japanese War] has ruined the country."[56]

And from the town of Plonsk in Poland, a local representative sent a list of questions concerning potential immigrants who wished to know more about their chances in the United States:

1. A single man of eighteen. He is familiar with the textile trade and his capital consists of two hundred and fifty roubles (250 roubles). And he is fluent in Russian and Hebrew. Where in America should he go so that he can earn a living and learn the language?

2. A single man of twenty-three (that is, 23), a pattern designer, fluent in three languages: German, Russian, Hebrew, with capital amounting to one hundred and fifty roubles (150 roubles). Where in America should he go to be able to earn a living?

3. A single man of twenty, fluent in Russian and Hebrew, with capital amounting to six hundred roubles (600 roubles). Where in America should he go so that he can enroll in a technical school where his capital will last him until he will be able to earn a living in his field?

4. A single man of eighteen, an agricultural worker, fluent in Polish and Hebrew, and his capital amounts to 200 roubles. Where should he go to be able to earn his living in agriculture?[57]

The questions asked the directors of the Zionist information bureaus were not different from the questions put to directors of the information bureaus in Eastern Europe and the United States, and they demonstrate the importance of information in reaching the decision to emigrate. "In our town [Cherkassy] there is a strong desire to emigrate to Eretz Israel," Ben-Zion Lansky wrote to Arthur Ruppin, "but there is no one in our town who can provide the information that will give those that seek it the necessary knowledge. I ask his honor to please explain this matter and answer me as soon as possible because time is short and there is much to do." Lansky's letter also inquired on behalf of many people who had asked about the opportunities in Palestine. Each one according to his occupation and ability:

2. A strong and capable farmer, very familiar with work on the land. He has a total of a thousand silver roubles in cash (equivalent to 2,600 francs). In which colony could he be accepted as a worker and perhaps eventually as a houseowner? He is willing to travel first without his family: he will call for them later. Where should he turn to when he arrives in Palestine?

3. A Jew who could be a worker. He has a family, consisting of his eldest daughter, aged 18, a worker, a daughter aged 17, also a worker, a daughter aged 15, who does housework, and a boy of 12. He is a widower and has to travel with his whole family. Apart from his hands, he does not possess anything. Could he and his daughters find work as soon as he arrives? To what colony should they go? As they cannot afford any extra expenses, please assign them to a colony not far from Jaffa. When does the season for work begin?

4. Is there any room in Palestine for doctors, nurses, midwives, dentists, or watchmakers?[58]

N. Shmuglin of the shtetl of Konotop in the region of Chernigov wrote to Ruppin that "there has also been a movement towards emigration in our town, although it is one of the more prosperous in our region. And as the secretary of the association, whom everyone turns to (I have no exact information about what I should answer them), I stop the questioners and ask them not to emigrate to Palestine until I receive an answer on this matter from your honor, as I shortly will."[59]

These letters to Sheinkin and Ruppin contain many detailed questions that demonstrate the importance of receiving information that was very complete. Local factory owners, for instance, who earned their living from the wool trade, wanted to know more about "the industry of abayas [a simple, loose overgarment], of blankets, of down and other things specially needed by the masses of the population in the East." Because the information in their possession was only partial, they turned to Ruppin with a series of questions:

Concerning wool:

1. How many types of wool are there in Palestine, from sheep?
2. What is the price of each kind of wool: white, black, mottled?
3. How much weight does the wool lose in washing?
4. How many times are the sheep sheared: once or twice a year?
5. How and when can one obtain wool in Palestine and the surrounding area?
6. Should one buy a large quantity all at once or buy little by little?
7. Who are the purchasers of wool now and to what places is it sent?
8. Can one obtain wool-skin, and what is the difference in price?

Concerning camel-wool, wool of oxen and horse-wool, all of the above questions. Concerning artificial wool:

1. Can one obtain rags from the old woolen garments of the Arabs (abayas)?
2. Are there rags of a better kind? Could one arrange for the rags to be gathered together by collectors?

Concerning the woven label:

1. Find out if there are any workers with this skill in Palestine.
2. What machines would they use, and where?
3. What is the difference in price between a kilogram of wool and abaya? What are the conditions of buying and selling?[60]

Lipe Hertsbarg said that he was interested in immigrating to Palestine with his family and settling in Jaffa. He had heard that "Arabs with small boats ferry the passengers from steamships that arrive in the city of Jaffa," and he wanted to create a rival business in the city with cheaper and more attractive prices. At the same time, he was doubtful if he would succeed, because he was told "that the Arabs are bad people and they would not let a Jew run a small steamboat."[61]

Israel Nevelstein was also considering migration. To be sure of making the right decision, he sent Ruppin a few questions:

1. Can I establish a factory in our country for whatever oil is in great demand in Palestine or abroad? What kind of oil is this?

2. Can I obtain all the machinery and apparatus necessary for the factory there, and will 6,000 roubles be sufficient for establishing such a factory?

3. Can I hope to earn at least 100 roubles a month?

4. What is the name of the place where I can open such a factory?

5. Let me know the name of the flower or seed from which I can make oil. How much will it cost me by weight and volume before it is processed in the factory, and how much profit will I make on the oil produced from that quantity?

6. What would my monthly expenses be in such a factory?[62]

The letter of a certain "Rabinowitz" to Arthur Ruppin at the beginning of 1914 is yet another example of the similarity between the letters sent to the information bureaus in Palestine and those sent to the bureaus in the United States. Rabinowitz, an "unlicensed druggist," wanted to open a "pharmaceutical warehouse" in Jaffa or in one of the settlements in the Galilee or Judea. He was interested in knowing how much money he needed for this purpose and what difficulties he could expect:

Can anyone who wants to, even someone who is not a licensed pharmacist, open a pharmacy. . . . And if no one will prevent him, what does he have to do? Is it necessary to obtain a special permit from the government here in Russia? And if only a licensed pharmacist can open a pharmacy, can a simple man known as a druggist open a pharmaceutical warehouse in Jaffa or in one of the cities of Judea and Gilgal? How much money is needed to do so? Please tell me all this properly. Although I have a pharmaceutical warehouse here in the city of Jekaterinoslav in southern Russia, I am sick of my life in this land of new edicts, and with all my heart, being, and flesh I want to go to my ancestral land. But when such a thought occurs to me, a question immediately arises: What will you eat there, you and your household?

After all, you aren't trained as a farmer, and commerce and manufacturing have not yet developed in Palestine. So what will you do there? I don't want to go hungry anymore, not even in our ancestral land.[63]

Rabinowitz's letter perhaps demonstrates more than any of the others the complexity of the process of deciding to immigrate to Palestine. Although he regarded it as his "ancestral land," he was aware that one could settle there only if one's livelihood was assured and after the difficulties involved in moving to the new country had been reduced to the minimum. From the point of view of the druggist, if he was going to starve, it was better to do so in familiar surroundings than in a new country and in a strange society.

The process of reaching a decision, and the way the potential immigrants—to America or to Palestine—calculated and asked for information shows the rationality involved in reaching a decision. They were not motivated by the image of the United States as the *goldene medine* (Golden State), where the streets were paved with gold, or of Palestine as the national home of the Jewish people. Rather they were focused on considerations based on the given economic reality, on planning, on reasoning, and on a concern to reduce as much as possible the dangers involved in moving to the new country. The decision was only taken after they received the answers to their questions and knew how much it cost to open a business; learned the market conditions (at least to a minimal extent); understood the price of raw materials, the wages offered, and the cost of living; had thought of whom to send as their first connection with the chosen country; and calculated how long it would take to refund the cost of the enterprise.

Moreover, it appears from the letters sent to the information bureaus in Palestine that a large part of the applicants did not apply for ideological-Zionist reasons. Palestine, for them, was a possible (but not the only possible) place of immigration, and it was only natural that they would investigate the details of life there and the possibilities of subsisting. In addition, a comparison between migrants who considered immigration to America and sent their letters to information bureaus in the United States with migrants who considered immigration to Palestine and sent their letters to the information bureaus there shows a great similarity in the process of reaching the decision to emigrate, in the questions asked, and especially in the wish to receive reliable and exact information. In the case of Palestine, it appears that the role of Zionist ideology as a factor in reaching the decision to emigrate was extremely limited and was not a central motivation.

The Place of Women in Reaching the Decision to Emigrate

"Dear comrades! Two families that are about to be expelled from a small town have asked me whether they would be able to get by in Palestine." This is what a Zionist executive wrote on behalf of two poor families from a shtetl near Vilna to the directors of the Palestine Office in Jaffa:

> The members of these families are blacksmiths, and as they lived near a village they also worked the land. One of the families has a son who is also a blacksmith and three daughters who are seamstresses. The other has two sons who are blacksmiths and one daughter who makes corsets. Please tell me how these families can manage in Palestine. They are also asking whether work tools can be obtained there or whether they have to be brought from here. I await your prompt reply. With all respect and the blessings of Zion, B. Goldberg.[64]

Although this letter is not directly concerned with women and their place in the decision-making process, something is definitely to be learned from it about their economic importance in the family unit. From the representative's inquiry on behalf of the families, one gathers not only that the two families asked for information on the economic situation in the country to which they wished to emigrate and on their capacity to be absorbed there, but also that the very mention of the occupations of girls in the families shows that the women's contribution formed part of the economic calculations on whether to emigrate. The information office's reply indicates that the heads of the Palestine Office also saw the women in the family as a significant contribution to the workforce that could sustain the family economically until the blacksmiths could find their place in the local labor market:

> Master blacksmiths who are experts in shoeing horses may be able to find work and make a living from it. We therefore generally tell un-

married blacksmiths that they can come: they do not have the burden of a family, and they can move from place to place looking for work until they finally find it. But we cannot respond in the affirmative to people with a family who need immediate employment. Expert seamstresses can earn between 60 and 70 prutot a month (the prutah [pl., prutot] is a former monetary unit of Israel, equivalent to ⅟₁₀₀₀ pound). If they really know their work well, the three daughters can support the family while the father and son look for work. The corset-maker may also be able to find work. If they decide to come, they should bring the tools of their trade with them.[65]

From the questions put by the local representative on behalf of the two families, and especially from the information office's reply, one can see that the women had a central place in the considerations of whether to immigrate to Palestine. Their capacity to find work and perhaps even to support the family in the first months of their immigration shows their centrality in the process of coming to a decision.

The case of Yaakov Litvak, a teacher in a reformed heder in the city of Lodz in Poland, also shows us the interdependency of a family that found it difficult to subsist because of the low wages and high cost of living in Poland in the period before World War I. The general economic situation was so terrible that, as Litvak wrote, "there are no words to describe and explain the economic hardship of the Jews of Poland, oppressed and harassed by the Polish people." The members of the family decided to immigrate to Palestine in two stages. In the first stage, Litvak's wife and children would go to Palestine "because costs in Lodz are very high," and it was cheaper to send money from Poland to Palestine and maintain the family in Palestine than in Lodz. Then in the second stage Litvak would join his family:

> And when my wife and family are in our land, where things are not so expensive and needs are few, they will make do with little. In addition, my wife can earn some money by working because she is a seamstress. And then perhaps, with God's help, I will be able to save up a few hundred shekels and I, too, will be able to go to our land and purchase property there.[66]

The Palestine Office's reply was encouraging. If his wife was really a "skilled dressmaker, she could earn about seventy francs a month. If he could send her some money as well, she and the other members of the family could subsist here," wrote Ruppin to Litvak. Despite the fact that the head of the family intended to send money to family members living in Palestine, the role of the wife in the immigration process was very important. Unlike the husband, who continued his usual way of life in the land of his birth and his familiar environment, the wife had the responsibility of going forth along with the children and looking after them in a new country that did not resemble her hometown, Lodz, in any way whatsoever. Adaptation to the conditions of the new country and its climate, finding a place to live and a livelihood, and looking for a suitable framework for the children represented a real challenge for Mrs. Litvak. From the letter and the information office's reply, we cannot know if the family did in fact follow the office's recommendation and go to Palestine, but one can certainly appreciate the role of the mother of the family in the process.

One can thus learn about the centrality of the Jewish female emigrant in these letters, not only from the direct questions concerning the capacity of women to be absorbed into the labor market but also from the way the questions were put and the considerable use by the writers of the first-person plural ("we"). Although most of the letters were written by men—husbands or elder sons—the questions were quite often asked on behalf of both husband and wife. From some of the letters, it would seem that they sat together in their homes by the light of an oil-lamp and wrote the letter in consultation with each other. Expressions like "I ask you to inform us," "we do not ask," "we immediately decided that we wished to emigrate," "we wanted to buy some land and work," and many similar expressions appearing in these letters demonstrate a partnership in making decisions and a mutual dependency in the family circle before the decisions were reached.

There were, of course, cases in which the wife was not involved in the decision to emigrate at all. The case of the Kroll family is an example of a decision made unilaterally by the husband. In 1909, the Krolls moved to Palestine from Skaryszew, a small suburb of Radom, Poland. The head of the family, Mendel Kroll, was an expert at painting walls with oil paints. After arriving in Palestine, he earned a living whitewashing houses and decorating them with oil paints, using stencils prepared in advance. Many homes in the city of Tel Aviv, which was just starting to be built in 1909, were adorned by Kroll and his family with decorative bands painted along the walls, just a few centimeters below the ceiling. The Krolls' decision to move to Palestine at the beginning of the twentieth century was based on a combination of Zionism and a religious yearning for the land of Israel. They were a relatively affluent family that had made a living painting and whitewashing homes in Eastern Europe. Because their financial situation was not bad, there was no need for the mother, Tzirel Kroll, to work. Her role as a breadwinner was secondary, and hence her status and position vis-à-vis the issue of immigration to Palestine was marginal. She was not consulted as to whether to move; it was a done deal that she had to accept. "The desire to move to Palestine did not budge from Mendel's heart," their granddaughter Malka Kroll says in her memoirs, *Tsabaei ha-ir* (The City Painters):

> He shared his dream with his four sons and spun plans for emigration together with them. . . . Tzirel and the girls were not included in the Palestine plans. They didn't understand the language, since Mendel made a point of speaking with his sons in Hebrew. Sharp-eared Tzippora caught a few key words here and there and translated them for her sister Sarah. Tzirel tried to draw the big secret out of the boys—but they guarded it zealously for fear of the evil eye. Tzirel started suspecting that a big life-change awaited her—a change worse than the one she had known, having married and exchanged her pretty village for a small, crowded neighborhood.[67]

Another reflection of Tzirel's marginal status in making the decision to emigrate came up when the family arrived at the Jaffa port. The Krolls moved to Palestine in two stages. The two oldest boys, Abba and Chaim, went first, followed about a year later by the rest of the family. The reunification of the family after such a long time is described by Malka Kroll in her memoirs as an emotional event. The prolonged separation and the two boys' stay in the hot Palestinian climate had altered them unrecognizably. Abba had contracted malaria and lost a lot of weight. "What has this country done to you?" Mendel asked his oldest son when they were reunited. "You, who were called the manly one, you're skin and bones." "It's malaria," Abba replied.

"Everyone who guards orchards is stung by a mosquito and gets the disease," he explained to his worried parents.

> Why didn't you write to us that you were ill? Menachem Mendel demanded. So as not to scare you. We were afraid mother would change her mind and wouldn't want to come here. *Nu*, replied Mendel in a tone that sounded half-disparaging, half-angry, I decided to move to Palestine, and when I decide something, I do it. I don't need advice from women. A woman's place is in the kitchen.[68]

The image of Tzirel Kroll as reflected in her granddaughter's memoirs is that of a simple, illiterate woman who spent most of her time in the kitchen and on housework. Because she was not involved in the decision to immigrate to Palestine, she had a harder time integrating than the rest of her family did, and her difficulties lasted longer. Unlike the children, who fitted in with the children of other Jewish immigrants in Palestine, and her husband, who came into contact with the emerging Yishuv society through his work, Tzirel remained in the kitchen in a foreign country. One of many examples that illustrate her alienation and foreignness is the first time she went to see a movie at the Eden Cinema in Tel Aviv. Her husband "Mendel fell in love with the silent pictures instantly. He didn't hesitate to go to the same film two, three, or four times a week," but he never took his wife. Only due to pressure from the children did he decide to act "like a gentleman and take his spouse with him to the pictures." Tzirel wore "her silk Sabbath dress, her pearls, and her beautiful wig" and went out for the first time to spend some leisure time with her husband:

> When the lights went off in the theater she started screaming, "Mendel, are you here?" "Yes, I'm here," he replied softly. "Tzirel, calm down." Then the story started playing out on the screen. Shaken and agitated, Tzirel expressed her excitement vocally. "Oy vey iz mir, soon they'll kill him. Mendel, tell me he'll get away. Oy vey iz mir, the girl doesn't see the crook hiding in the closet. She has to be warned about him. Oy vey iz mir. . . ." The movie-goers stopped watching the movie. Their eyes were trained on the bewigged older woman who was screaming excitedly, "Oy vey iz mir!" Some of them even mimicked her and joined her in her excited cries, while the other viewers were convulsed with laughter in their seats. At that moment, Mendel

wished the earth would open up and swallow him. Menachem Mendel never again took Tzirel to the Eden cinema.[69]

The process of making a decision to emigrate for single women was different from that for mothers of families. Girls who wished to emigrate alone were dependent on the consent of their parents, who did not easily agree to their daughters going alone on a long and dangerous journey to some country overseas. The letter from Teyvl Kardash to the Palestine Office in April 1914 reflects the difficulties a young girl had to face if she wanted to emigrate alone:

Eighteen years have passed since I was born to my shopkeeper parents, who lived in a small, remote town in the province of Kiev. My father is a decent householder of good lineage, a good, honest man. He fears God, observes the Sabbath, and is meticulous about all the commandments. My mother, too, is a modest, decent woman, although she is more freethinking than my father. . . . For an entire year I have been fighting with my parents, who refuse to let me go for fear that I will have to work hard, since I don't have the means to support myself in a foreign land.[70]

The question she put to the head of the Palestine Office was whether it was possible to combine work with study in Palestine. Agricultural work was not attractive to the writer. However, "I very much want to gain an education, but I can't do it without money, and I have therefore decided to work in the daytime and study in the evening." In his reply, Ruppin supported the girl's decision:

Since you have no profession, you have no other choice but to be an agricultural worker. . . . But the season for this work is in the winter and you should postpone your voyage to that period. After the day's work you can study in the evening. Lessons are given nearly everywhere for free. Yet one cannot hope, of course, for much success at studies after the labors of the day. There is another way—to become a school or kindergarten teacher. Teaching requires training either privately or in a school. In Jaffa there is a seminary for school and kindergarten teachers and if you can obtain a certain monthly sum from your family for your upkeep, it is worth coming here and learning the Hebrew language so that you may finally receive a position in a school or kindergarten.[71]

Sheinkin, like Teyvl's parents, who were frightened of her traveling to Palestine, did not approve of single girls coming to the country, and several times he unequivocally rejected requests of this kind. In a letter in answer to Rivka Stein who wanted to come and settle, he wrote that "not only in Palestine, but everywhere, it is more difficult for a woman to manage than a man. Women are less well-prepared for the battle of life," he said, adding that "most of the women who have come until now miss Russia and want to go back there."[72]

We learn from many other letters sent to the information bureaus by potential male and female immigrants that the Jewish woman immigrant played an active role in the decision to emigrate. This is consistent with the conclusions of studies showing the importance of the Eastern European Jewish woman in the economy of the family group. It was her status as a provider next to her husband and her economic indispensability that gave her a central position in weighing up the complex considerations that were so crucial for her family.

Capitalists First: Zionist Immigration Policy at the Beginning of the Twentieth Century

The letters sent to the Zionist information bureaus enable us to gain a better understanding of the considerations involved in immigration to Palestine. The representatives' answers, on the other hand, reveal the Zionist policy with regard to immigration to Palestine and the kind of immigrants that the Zionist movement wanted. Until the outbreak of World War I, the Zionist movement did not have an official policy with regard to immigration, but an earnest debate took place within it on the question of "the good of the people" versus "the good of the land." Those that favored the good of the people desired a mass migration of the Jews to Palestine to rescue them physically and spiritually, while those who favored the good of the land claimed that the country was unable in a short time to absorb masses of Jews seeking to emigrate. They therefore claimed that people with capital or people able to work should be given preference to poor immigrants or those with limited capacities who had little to contribute to the Yishuv. In 1882, for instance, the secretary of the Hibbat Zion movement, Moshe

Lieb Lilienblum, said that "if we want to settle the land, we can only consider the rich, who can buy property at full price and prepare all the instruments at their own expense, but there is no room for the poor in Palestine."[73] However, Theodor Herzl, in his book *The Jewish State* (1896), took the opposite approach: "We must not visualize the exodus of the Jews as a sudden one. It will be gradual, proceeding over a period of decades. The poorest will go first and cultivate the soil. They will construct roads, bridges, railways and telegraph installations, regulate rivers, and provide themselves with homesteads."[74]

The answers of Sheinkin and Ruppin, the directors of the information bureaus, to those who approached them, show that both of them favored a selective immigration of capitalists first and preferred "the good of the land" to "the good of the people." In their opinion, Palestine was unable to absorb immigrants without capital, because they would be unable to subsist there. So if poor immigrants did come, they might endanger the whole settlement enterprise. Palestine, said Ruppin, was not a land of refuge, and it was incapable of absorbing unsuitable immigrants. The natural goal of immigration was therefore the United States and not Palestine.[75] Menahem Sheinkin said similar things when stating the policy of the information bureau on taking up his post:

> The information bureau for Palestinian affairs declares the follow-
> ing: the present situation in the country is that new migrants with no
> means have no chance of subsisting. The other type of people, who
> can come without asking if they have a place here, is those with capi-
> tal, with larger or smaller financial resources. For these, conditions in
> Palestine are very good, even if they are not specialists in any field.[76]

In a letter to Otto Warburg, a member of the executive committee, Sheinkin told him "that the Yishuv in Palestine is growing by thou-sands, and they want to come here and make a living from their work. The bureau must tell them once again that insofar as the Yishuv can absorb artisans, it has almost absorbed as many as it needs, for there are artisans for whom there is already no room in Palestine."[77] Even at the end of the period, Sheinkin continued to be of the opinion that only healthy immigrants with the financial means to set themselves up were needed in the country. If immigrants of the other kind arrived, the whole Zionist enterprise would be endangered. We all have one aspiration and objective, said Sheinkin,

> which is to strengthen and improve it through the entry into the country of an abundance of healthy and strong elements that have the means to strike roots, to live and to give life. We also know that, as against this, it would be a great danger to the Yishuv and all our work if, as a result of our advice and directives, undesirable elements—that is to say, ones that have no chance of managing here—would come to settle, because, in returning to the countries they came from, they have the power to destroy in one hour what we have built over a considerable length of time. We all know that it is much easier to destroy than to build or to reconstruct.[78]

Sheinkin claimed that "the undesirable elements" would not only be a burden on the Yishuv but also, in returning to their countries of origin because of their inability to support themselves, they would give Palestine a bad name. In this way, he said, they would prevent the arrival of immigrants with means and the capacity to pay their way who could contribute to the development of the Yishuv.

Sheinkin's attitude was also reflected in the answers he gave to people. To a Mr. S. Weisfeld, he wrote: "In answer to your letter, we write to you as follows: a young man with a wife and child who has little money cannot come to Palestine with a sum of 200 silver roubles: he cannot do anything here. The daily wage of a worker in an agricultural settlement (50 kopeks a day) will not be enough to provide for your family. Yours sincerely, with the blessing of Zion, M. Sheinkin."[79] However, in the case of "a young man with 3000 roubles who has five children and a wife, our advice is that at the present time he should come to Palestine alone and become acquainted with conditions here and see how it is best for him to settle. This man, with the sum of money that he has and with the knowledge that he has of agriculture and with the training that he has in this work, can settle in Palestine and practice agriculture."[80]

Arthur Ruppin's answers were similar to those of Sheinkin, and there was no difference between the immigration policies of the two bureaus. "Other kinds of work are also difficult to find here," wrote Ruppin to Abraham Persov of the Chernigov region, who wanted to find work as a teacher in Palestine. "The work is not permanent, and because you have a family it is hard to believe you could make an honorable living."[81] He told a certain Eisenstadt, who wanted to open a factory for making mother-of-pearl buttons or candy with an initial capital of 1,500 roubles: "It is generally difficult to start a factory or to do business here with a small sum of money and to expect to succeed." The button industry, he said, did not exist in Palestine, "and so I can't answer you on this." On the other hand, "factories for candy do exist here, but one cannot start a factory with a sum of 1500 roubles." The information bureau rejected Eisenstadt's application.[82] Many small-scale businessmen like Eisenstadt received negative answers because in the opinion of the bureau they lacked sufficient capital to succeed.

Table 2.1 shows that 61 percent of the applicants received negative answers from Sheinkin and Ruppin. About 18 percent of the replies had conditions attached, such as: come, investigate, and then decide; come only if you have enough money; or come only if you are prepared to manage with little. About 21 percent of the applicants received positive replies without conditions or restrictions. The criteria for recommendation were fixed according to the economic situation of the applicant, and there was a correlation between his capital and the answer he received. The smaller the capital at the disposal of the applicant, the greater the likelihood that he would be advised not to go to Palestine. People with capital, on the other hand, were generally advised to come and settle in Palestine. At the same time, those with

TABLE 2.1

Breakdown of answers according to information bureaus.

Recommendation	Sheinkin 260 answers		Ruppin 298 answers		Total Both together	
	Number	Percentage	Number	Percentage	Number	Percentage
Not recommended	154	59.0	186	62.4	340	60.8
Recommended	66	25.2	54	18.1	120	21.4
Come and investigate	11	4.5	39	13.0	50	9.1
Recommended on conditions	29	11.3	19	6.5	48	8.7

SOURCE: Database of the letters and answers to and from the Zionist information bureaus (author's personal collection).

capital were also rejected if it turned out that the economic initiatives they proposed were unsuited to the country. For example, Ruppin told Shalom from Galicia, who had a capital of 7,000 roubles and wanted to open a factory for copybooks: "There are no factories for copybooks in our country. The copybooks are brought here from Alsace in Germany. One printer in Jaffa tried to make copybooks here, but did not succeed. . . . Someone with a good knowledge of the business, and who can manufacture all kinds of good products, can hope to succeed, but because we do not yet have any experts in this field here, we do not wish to take responsibility."[83] And he told A. Rosenboim, who wanted to bring to Palestine buses "of the best French makes . . . very suitable for a regular service from Jaffa to Haifa and back . . . [which can easily cover] a distance of approximately 90 kilometers in 5 or 6 hours":[84]

> We have received your letter of the 23rd of March. We passed on your proposal to the Vinegrowers' Association in Rishon-le-Zion. . . . Mr. Gloskin, head of the Vine Growers' Association replied to us that your proposal cannot be adopted at the moment because the road between Rishon-le-Zion and Jaffa is not yet finished, but it will be kept in mind until a suitable time.[85]

The replies of the directors of the information bureaus clearly show that at the beginning of the twentieth century an immigration policy came into being that determined who was recommended to come to Palestine and on what conditions, and who was "refused aliyah" and was not wanted in the country. At the same time, it must be pointed out that this immigration policy was only advisory, and that Sheinkin and Ruppin did not have the capacity to impose it on those who came to the country.

The large number of rejected applications reveals a great difference between the directors of the information bureaus and the applicants with regard to their concept of the purpose of immigration to Palestine at that period. On the one hand, there were the directors of the information bureaus, who hoped that people with capital would come to the country and make a significant contribution to its development; on the other hand, there were the applicants, who saw Palestine as a place where they could continue to practice their traditional occupations and improve their economic situation without really changing their way of life. This difference in the concept of the purpose of immigration to the country led to the rejection of many applications.

The Zionist policy of "capitalists first" aroused the anger of labor circles. They did not accept the basic assumption that the wealthy should be encouraged to emigrate first in order to lay the basis for the Yishuv, while the middle and lower classes should follow later. The labor leaders insisted that those who thought that "the proper basis for immigration is the person with capital, as the worker, the artist and the member of the liberal professions can only provide for one person—himself—while the person with capital creates conditions that provide for many" were wrong:

> Everyone knows where America's enormous wealth came from. It was not the Huguenots, the exiles from France or Spain who brought their assets there, but the millions of wretched negroes who drenched its soil with their blood that laid the basis for the wealth of the "new world." It was not due to the English and German lords and deputies, but to the myriads of Chinese who built the railroads, and the millions of workers of all colors that even now are increasing their affluence.[86]

The labor leaders asserted that unlike the entry of capitalists, who came as individuals, the movement of workers was "at the same time a mass-immigration, and one, moreover, of masses who live from their own work," and in this way, immigration achieved its goal. It meant "an immediate extension and growth of the Yishuv that paved the way to the future."[87]

In labor circles there were also specific complaints against the policies of Sheinkin's information bureau. They said that people wanted proper information about their prospects as workers in Palestine, but from Jaffa and Odessa "they only received one answer—until capitalists come to the country, there will be no room for workers."[88] They claimed that the information they received from the bureaus, which was intended for those with capital, did not serve any purpose: "If a capitalist wants to immigrate, he does not need the bureau. He can travel round the country, investigate and ask questions, and has no need whatsoever to rely on the information we provide." But this was not the case with immigrants without means: "These, who for all their

goodwill and idealism, also have to know if they are destined to star-
vation here, are in need of information."[89] Because the information
bureau in its existing form was of no use to the workers, they held that
a special information bureau under their direction had to be created
for them in Palestine. Another example of the opposition to Sheinkin's
policies in labor circles can be found in D. Bader's reminiscences in *The
Book of the "Second Aliyah,"* edited by Bracha Habas: "I wrote a letter
to the information bureau in Jaffa run by Sheinkin and Dr. Hissin of
blessed memory, and the answer I received was roughly as follows:
if you have such and such an amount of francs, you can come, and if
not, stay where you are, for the work is hard and not always available.
Despite all this, and despite my advanced age (I was thirty years old), I
nevertheless decided to go to Palestine."[90]

Sheinkin's response to these people was to tell them not to make
the information bureau into a party affair, as "most of the workers do
not belong to 'Ha-Po'el Ha-Tza'ir' or to 'Po'alei Tzion'. . . . Nearly all
the members of 'Po'alei Tzion' and most of the members of 'Ha-Po'el
Ha-Tza'ir' have returned to where they came from or have remained in
Palestine without party affiliation, and most of those who have come
back do not belong to any federation."[91] However, in 1913, the Po'alei
Tzion Party set up its own information bureau, headed by Ephraim
Bloch-Blumenfeld, which served as an alternative to Sheinkin's information bureau especially where finding sources of livelihood for workers
was concerned. It likewise offered its services to inquirers abroad who
wanted to know about the situation in Palestine, and thus in practice
replaced Sheinkin's information bureau.

✳

From the letters to the Zionist information bureaus, we see that the
considerations involved in immigration to Palestine were complex
and bound up with the natural fears to be found in any immigration
movement. Indeed, there is a great similarity between the letters the
immigrants sent to America and the ones they sent to Palestine. Many
of those who turned to Sheinkin and Ruppin did not do so out of
ideological motives of settling the land or making the desert bloom.

Many of them only saw the country as a place where they could make a decent living. Some saw Palestine as a possible venue of immigration, and it was natural that they should inquire about the possibilities of subsistence and the details of life there. From the letters, it emerges that the Zionist idea did not always play a central role in the calculations of the writers, and even when it did, however strong the pull of ideology, it was the good of the family that finally decided where one was to go. The head of the family was first and foremost committed to providing for his family, and even if he was a great believer in Palestine as the answer to the distress of the Jewish people in exile, he would be very wary of going to a place where the means of subsistence and the chance of supporting a family were limited.

The letters of the Zionist information bureaus in answer to the applicants demonstrate the beginnings of the formation of a Zionist immigration policy with regard to Palestine. It was a policy of "capitalists first," which gave preference to middle- or upper-class Jews over poor migrants who had nothing. The Zionist immigration policy was faced with a dual problem. First, immigration was generally the consequence of a difficult economic situation and a desire to improve one's standard of living. As a result, those interested in coming were precisely those who were advised not to come. Those with capital were less inclined to immigrate because they had no reason to do so, and they did not expect an improvement in their standard of living but rather feared its deterioration. Secondly, Sheinkin and Ruppin did not have the capacity to impose their policy and decide who was going to enter the country. Their recommendations had a certain influence, but as we shall see in the following chapters, the vast majority of those who entered Palestine at the beginning of the twentieth century were migrants who did not meet their criteria.

Three Profile of the Immigrants

Letters sent to the information bureaus permit us to observe the process of how applicants reached a decision to emigrate and also to gain a better understanding of the factors that led to immigration to Palestine at the beginning of the twentieth century. While we can obtain much information from these letters, there is also much they don't tell us, such as which of the applicants actually went to Palestine, which chose to immigrate to some other country, and which decided to remain where they were. The letters tell us about the intentions of the applicants but not necessarily how they implemented those intentions.

This chapter develops a profile of immigrants to Palestine in the years 1905–1914 through an analysis of their sociodemographic composition. The immigrants can be classified according to their sex, age, occupation, capital, and reason for coming to the country. Unlike other chapters in this volume that deal with the inner world and the outlook of immigrants, discussion in the present chapter is based on quantitative data concerning the immigrants who registered at the information bureau in Odessa a short time before they embarked on ships sailing to Palestine.

Sources

There are three sources available to historians wishing to analyze the composition of immigrants who came to Palestine in the years 1905–1914. The first, main source is the newspaper *Ha-Olam*, the mouthpiece of the Zionist organization, which received statistical data from the information bureau in Odessa and began to publish it regularly in 1910.[1]

This data was also sent to the JCA (Jewish Colonization Association) information bureau in Saint Petersburg, which published it from time to time in its official journal *Der Jüdische Emigrant*.[2] The data published in *Ha-Olam* was provided by B. Spielberg, an official in the Odessa information bureau, which was run by the Odessa Committee. Spielberg, who was close to Ussishkin, recorded the particulars of the travelers who passed through his office on their way to Palestine. "Most honorable chairman," wrote Spielberg to Ussishkin, "as on every Sabbath eve, on this occasion also I am sending you a list of statistics concerning the travelers. The list is very encouraging; the work of the bureau in general properly [*sic*]. Everything is satisfactory."[3] Spielberg's lists were drawn up every two weeks—every time a ship left the port of Odessa for Palestine. He sent the lists to the editorial board of *Ha-Olam*, which published the data and made the following declaration:

> Readers will find here a list of statistics provided by the information bureau of the "Hovevei Zion" committee in Odessa on emigration from Russia to Palestine. . . . Almost all those leaving Russia for Palestine go via Odessa and come to this information bureau which offers them travel tickets at reduced prices. We are justified in thinking that the list provides us with information concerning all the Jews (apart from a small minority which we know nothing about) who left Russia for Palestine in the five years 1905–1909, and one may therefore learn from the list a great deal about the professions of the immigrants to Palestine.[4]

The great majority of immigrants to Palestine passed through the Odessa information bureau and registered there because it provided a considerable reduction in the price of a boat ticket: "The journey from Jaffa to Odessa costs about 20 silver roubles. If one obtains a ticket through the Odessa Committee, it costs about 40 percent less."[5] The lists printed in the newspaper *Ha-Olam* therefore provide a great deal of useful information. However, the data only related to emigrants leaving Odessa and not to those entering Palestine, nor did was it helpful for emigrants leaving from other ports, such as the port of Trieste (concerning which we have hardly any data). At the same time, Odessa was the main port for those leaving for Palestine from the Russian Empire. During the years 1905–1914, 23,000 of the 35,000 immigrants to Palestine sailed from the port of Odessa. The data in this chapter, based on those that sailed from the port of Odessa, therefore relate to two-thirds of the immigrants to Palestine in that period.

However, there is another source from which we can learn the profile of immigrants who entered Palestine through the port of Jaffa in the years 1912–1914— the records of Haim Ridnik, an official of the Palestine Office. The tables and lists Ridnik drew up are preserved in the Central Zionist Archives, and some of them were published in the journal *Ha-Po'el Ha-Tza'ir.*[6] In an article published in that journal titled "The Hebrew Immigration via Jaffa in the Year 1912," Ridnik spoke a little about himself and about the reasons he came to deal with matters of immigration when he reached the port of Jaffa:

> For three years now, I have been dealing with the Hebrew immigrants entering the country via Jaffa. In this period, I have seen many rises and falls in the numbers of those entering into the country, and the same applies to the numbers of those leaving it. In reading the many newspapers in this country and abroad on the development of our Yishuv, I became aware of how little idea our newspapers and communal workers have of the rise or decrease of the population in the country. . . . They have no true or even approximately true idea of the numbers of those entering and leaving, or of their age, occupation, capital, etc.. . . . Obtaining this information in the local conditions requires a great deal of time and work which are not within the capacity of the ordinary person. Rousing myself, I took it upon me to nevertheless achieve a small part of this objective.[7]

Ridnik, who was in Jaffa, met immigrants who came from Odessa, Trieste, and other places. He made lists of both those who entered and those who left. This is what Ridnik wrote about his methods of work:

> In publishing the following numbers, I feel it is my duty to preface them with certain observations: 1. One must realize that they come from a private source and do not have the exactitude of statistics such as those provided by customs officials in all countries. 2. I have registered the people coming from abroad on all the ships in various ways: through a careful questioning of the immigrants themselves, through an examination of the documents they presented, by investigating the ship owners and hotel proprietors. I have sometimes used several methods simultaneously, and used one method to achieve what

is lacking in another. . . . 4. In my questioning, I did not enter into many details, and I confined myself solely to questions concerning the family situation of the immigrant and his intention of going to or leaving the place he is asking about.[8]

A comparison between the lists of Ridnik, who was in Jaffa and received the immigrants when they arrived, and those of Spielberg, who sent his data from Odessa, reveals a certain difference in their approach. The number of passengers who left for Palestine according to Spielberg was greater than the number who entered it according to Ridnik. There could be various reasons for this difference: First, Ridnik worked alone, without assistants, and it is very possible that he was unable to document the data of some immigrants who entered the country. Another reason: From the time the passengers left Odessa, it was not clear who continued to Palestine and who left the ship at one of the stops on the way. Similarly, Ridnik only registered the passengers who alighted at Jaffa; he had no information about passengers who got off in Egypt and continued to Palestine by train or about those who got off in Beirut or in Haifa. It is also possible that immigrants were wary of identifying themselves to an unknown person immediately on entering the country and refused to give him information.

Despite the discrepancy between Ridnik's lists and Spielberg's tables, it should be pointed out that, as we shall see, there were quite a few points of similarity between them, especially in their analysis of the profile of the immigrants and their relative distribution. From both sources—the Odessa information bureau and Haim Ridnik's lists—one receives a very clear picture of the profile of the immigrants who came to Palestine between 1905 and 1914.

A third but problematic source for investigating the profile of immigrants to Palestine is the partial lists of passengers who sailed from the port of Trieste in the years 1912–1914. Because the lists of names were compiled for only a few months in each year, it is hard to draw conclusions from them about the profile of immigrants to Palestine from Galicia at the end of the period of the second aliyah. At the same time, these lists can be used to estimate the number of immigrants who arrived in the country during the period and to gain a certain idea of their reasons for coming.

How Many Came?

We do not have exact figures for the scale of immigration to Palestine in the period before World War I. Mark Wischnitzer gave two different assessments of the number of immigrants who came to the country in the years 1904–1914. One is a conservative estimate of about 18,000 to 19,000 souls; and the other, based on the data of Jacob Lestschinsky, estimates the number as 30,000 souls.[9] Aryeh Tartakower agreed with Lestschinsky's estimate: "Although we do not have exact figures for the scale of immigration to the country before the war," on the basis of separate numbers and pieces of information . . . "the conjecture closest to the truth is" that in the years 1904–1914 between 30,000 and 35,000 people arrived in Palestine.[10]

David Gurevich, Aaron Gertz, and Roberto Bachi, on the other hand, estimated the scale of immigration to the country in those years at between 35,000 and 40,000 souls.[11] According to the data of the Odessa information bureau and Ridnik's lists, it would seem that the assessments closest to the truth were those of Tartakower and Lestschinsky, who estimated the number of those entering the country during the whole period at between 30,000 and 35,000.

The little information we have on emigrants who left from the port of Trieste shows that in the years 1912–1914 between 80 and 100 people on average left for Palestine each month. That is to say, the number of emigrants from Galicia to Palestine did not exceed 10,000 to 12,000 a year. According to the estimate, a total of between 10,000 and 11,000 immigrants arrived in Palestine from Trieste during the whole period. Together with the 22,953 who arrived from Odessa, the total number of immigrants was about 31,000 to 33,000 souls.[12]

Figure 3.1 depicts the waves of immigration to the United States and Palestine and reveals a similarity between them. The years 1905–1906 were peak years in immigration to both countries; in 1907–1909, however, there was a decline in the rate of immigration to the United States but an increase in immigration to Palestine. The reason for this was the economic depression in the United States in those years, which caused a relative decline in the number of immigrants to that country but also increased the rate of immigration to other destinations such as Palestine and Argentina. When the United States recovered from the economic

TABLE 3.1

The number of emigrants who left for the United States and Palestine in the years 1905–1914.

Year	Number of Emigrants to Palestine	Number of Emigrants to the United States
1905	1,230	129,910
1906	3,450	153,748
1907	1,750	149,182
1908	2,097	103,387
1909	2,459	57,551
1910	1,979	84,260
1911	2,326	91,223
1912	2,430	80,595
1913	3,050	101,330
1914	2,182	138,051
1905–1914 (from Trieste)	10,000	—
Total	32,953	1,089,237

SOURCE: "The Departure from Russia to Eretz Israel," *Ha-Olam* 17 (12 May 1910): 14–15; "The Departure from Russia to Eretz Israel," *Ha-Olam* 5 (13 February 1911): 18–19; "The Departure from Russia to Eretz Israel," *Ha-Olam* 16 (6 May 1913): 9–10; "The Departure from Russia to Eretz Israel," *Ha-Olam* 9 (10 March 1914): 15–16; Liebman Hersch, "International Migration of the Jews in International Migrations," in *International Migrations*, ed. Walter Willcox and Imre Ferenczi (New York: National Bureau of Economic Research, 1931), 474.

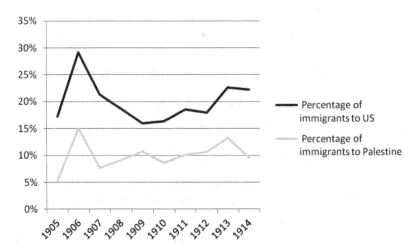

Figure 3.1 The waves of Jewish immigration to the United States and Palestine, 1905–1914.

SOURCE: "The Departure from Russia to Eretz Israel," *Ha-Olam* 17 (12 May 1910): 14–15; "The Departure from Russia to Eretz Israel," *Ha-Olam* 5 (13 February 1911): 18–19; "The Departure from Russia to Eretz Israel," *Ha-Olam* 16 (6 May 1913): 9–10; "The Departure from Russia to Eretz Israel," *Ha-Olam* 9 (10 March 1914): 15–16; Liebman Hersch, "International Migration of the Jews in International Migrations," in *International Migrations*, ed. Walter Willcox and Imre Ferenczi (New York: National Bureau of Economic Research, 1931), 474.

crisis in 1910, the number of immigrants there began to increase and the number of those to Palestine and Argentina declined. From 1911 to 1914 the rate of immigration to both the United States and Palestine increased considerably, a trend that continued until World War I.

Demographic Profile of the Immigrants, 1905–1914

Very few of the many studies on the second aliyah have included a sociodemographic analysis of immigrants.[13] One of the studies that dealt with the question of the social structure of immigrants was Yosef Gorny's "The Changes in the Social and Political Structure of the 'Second Aliyah.'" This study was based on the census of "Immigrants of the 'Second Aliyah'" taken by the Labor Archives in the mid-1930s and beginning of the 1940s. However, this census of 937 people, of whom 644 were men and 293 were women, does not inform us about the profile of the immigrants who came to the country at the beginning of the twentieth century, but only about that of the immigrants who were still there at the beginning of the 1940s.[14]

This chapter discusses the yearly tables published in the newspaper *Ha-Olam*, summarizing the scale and composition of immigration as given in the data provided by the port of Odessa. The tables have been converted into graphs (see figures 3.2–3.8) that represent the profile of the immigrants according to sex, age, country of origin, occupation, and reason for coming; there is also a classification for those who came to Palestine on the advice of relatives.

We see from the data provided by the information bureau (figure 3.2) that a comparison between the number of men and women that left the port of Odessa for Palestine in the years 1905–1914 that 60 percent were men and 40 percent were women. This distribution resembles that of Jewish immigrants to the United States in the same period: 55 percent of those entering the United States were men and 44 percent were women. If we take into account that not all the men came to Palestine alone and that some came with their wives, we see that it was an immigration of families and not of young unmarried men. Figure 3.3, showing the distribution of immigrants according to age, supports this conclusion.

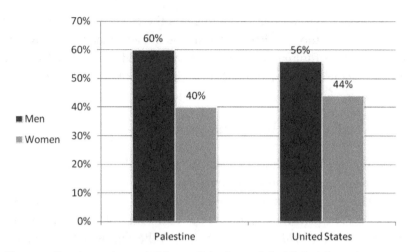

Figure 3.2 Immigrants' composition to Palestine and the United States by sex, 1905–1914.

SOURCE: "The Departure from Russia to Eretz Israel," *Ha-Olam* 17 (12 May 1910): 14–15; "The Departure from Russia to Eretz Israel," *Ha-Olam* 5 (13 February 1911): 18–19; "The Departure from Russia to Eretz Israel," *Ha-Olam* 16 (6 May 1913): 9–10; "The Departure from Russia to Eretz Israel," *Ha-Olam* 9 (10 March 1914): 15–16.

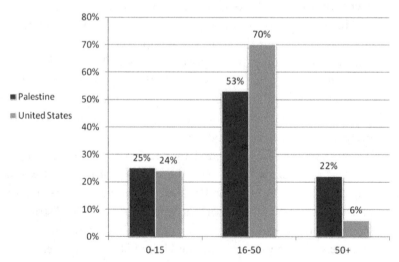

Figure 3.3 Immigrants' composition to Palestine and the United States by age, 1905–1914.

SOURCE: "The Departure from Russia to Eretz Israel," *Ha-Olam* 17 (12 May 1910): 14–15; "The Departure from Russia to Eretz Israel," *Ha-Olam* 5 (13 February 1911): 18–19; "The Departure from Russia to Eretz Israel," *Ha-Olam* 16 (6 May 1913): 9–10; "The Departure from Russia to Eretz Israel," *Ha-Olam* 9 (10 March 1914): 15–16.

A quarter of the immigrants who left Odessa for Palestine were children of up to 15 years old (a similar percentage of Jewish immigrant children reached the United States). One must assume that these children did not come alone but in the company of their parents, and therefore these figures, like those for the distribution of the immigrants according to sex, disprove the assertion that immigrants to Palestine were young unmarried men. A total of 53 percent of immigrants to Palestine were aged 16 to 50. Of this age group, one may say that 28 percent were aged 16 to 30, and 25 percent were aged 31 to 50. On the other hand, 70 percent of the Jewish immigrants to the United States were aged 16 to 44. There was a large and significant difference between Palestine and the United States in the 44–50 age group. Of these, 22 percent of immigrants to Palestine were 50 years old and over, while only 6 percent of those to the United States were more than 44 years old. An examination of the inner distribution of the people of this age group who reached Palestine reveals that nearly two-thirds (14%) of them belonged to the Old Yishuv; they were supported by charity and came to the country in order to study Torah and be buried there. Eight percent of the others were immigrants in the true sense who came to Palestine for a variety of reasons. We see from the letters sent to the Palestinian information bureaus that some of the immigrants aged 50 and over wanted to come to Palestine because they feared that their children would fall into bad ways in America; some wrongly thought that one could buy land cheaply in Palestine and make one's living from agriculture; and some simply came to escape the pogroms and bad economic situation.

The account given by Spielberg, an official of the information bureau in Odessa, of his meeting with a group of emigrants just before they sailed for Palestine confirms this. In his conversations with the emigrants, he came to the conclusion that "those that think that the travellers over the age of fifty are unable to work and go to Palestine only in order spend the rest of their lives in prayer" are mistaken and mislead others. In a letter to Ussishkin, Spielberg discussed the matter, and declared that "these people aged fifty and more can contribute" a great deal to the developing Yishuv in Palestine. In this letter in which he described the profile of the immigrants, he gave a few examples to support this assertion: "A man aged 56 and his wife aged 51 toured Palestine about four years ago, and now they have decided to settle there, and they are bringing with them a sum of 10,000 roubles." Another example: "A man and his wife, both aged 54, are going to Palestine with six dependents. Two of their children intend to enroll in a *gymnasia* [high school]. I understand that the family is very wealthy."[15] These examples and others demonstrate that a cross-section of the immigrants aged 50 and over consisted not only of old people who came to visit the holy places or to be buried in Palestine but also of families like the Kohelet family who thought that their chances of succeeding and rehabilitating themselves were greater in Palestine than anywhere else. That is to say, considerations special to Palestine, such as Jewish education and a religiously observant environment, were factors in preferring Palestine to other countries as a destination. It is also possible that America's bad reputation with regard to children's education, along with the fear that children would fall into bad ways there, contributed to the drawing power of Palestine.[16] There arose in Palestine a population of immigrants that, although according to ethnic characteristics and geographical location appeared to belong to the "Old Yishuv," in practice did not really correspond either to the categories "Old Yishuv" or "New Yishuv." Nothing is known of the profile of the 6 percent aged over 44 who went to the United States, and there is a lack of sources explaining why they went.

From the two preceding figures, we see that from the viewpoints of age and sex there is no evidence that immigrants to Palestine differed from those who went to the United States. The high percentage of elderly people aged 50 and over and children up to the age of 15 shows that most of those who came to Palestine were not young unmarried men, typically celebrated as pioneers in Zionist historiography, but immigrants with families who greatly resembled immigrants who went to the United States in the same period.

A comparison between those with professions and those without also shows a significant difference between figures for immigration to the two countries. In Palestine, 65 percent of immigrants had no profession, compared to 43 percent of immigrants to the United States. In contrast with other groups of immigrants who came to the United States at the beginning of the twentieth century, the highest percentage was for Jews without a profession. The reason for this was first and

TABLE 3.2

Those with professions and those without among Jewish immigrants to the United States and Palestine (from Odessa).

	United States	Percentage	Palestine	Percentage
With profession	841,000	56.7	8,123	35.3
Without profession	644,000	43.3	14,830	64.7
Total	1,485,000	100	22,953	100

SOURCE: "The Departure from Russia to Eretz Israel," *Ha-Olam* 17 (12 May 1910): 14–15; "The Departure from Russia to Eretz Israel," *Ha-Olam* 5 (13 February 1911): 18–19; "The Departure from Russia to Eretz Israel," *Ha-Olam* 16 (6 May 1913): 9–10; "The Departure from Russia to Eretz Israel," *Ha-Olam* 9 (10 March 1914): 15–16; Liebman Hersch, "International Migration of the Jews in International Migrations," in *International Migrations*, ed. Walter Willcox and Imre Ferenczi (New York: National Bureau of Economic Research, 1931), 474.

foremost the large proportion of women and children among the immigrants to Palestine. In addition, there were also many elderly people above the age of 50, which also helps explain the high percentage of immigrants without an occupation in Palestine as compared to the United States.

An analysis of the immigrants' composition according to occupation in figure 3.4 does not give us a clear picture of the employment profile of those who left from Odessa. Because the inner distribution of the categories is not sufficiently detailed, it is not clear which occupations are included in the category of "artisans"; what the difference is between "workers" and "agricultural laborers"; or whether "workers" is a term for those who had no profession. The same applies to those who engaged in trade and industry and those who followed the liberal professions. What kind of businessmen were included in the category "trade," and what kind were placed in the category "industry"? Who were those that followed the liberal professions, and did they include students?

At the same time, although these descriptions are general, it may be assumed on the basis of various sources describing the occupations of immigrants to Palestine and the United States that a large part of them were artisans and petty tradesmen. The composition of immigrants according to occupation shows that 19 percent of those who came to Palestine followed the liberal professions. In comparison with their overall percentage in the Jewish population of the Russian Empire (5% in all), and also to their percentage among immigrants to the

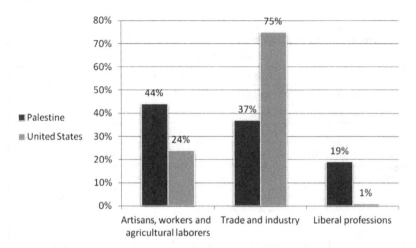

Figure 3.4 Immigrants' composition to Palestine and the United States by occupation, 1905–1914.

SOURCE: "The Departure from Russia to Eretz Israel," *Ha-Olam* 17 (12 May 1910): 14–15; "The Departure from Russia to Eretz Israel," *Ha-Olam* 5 (13 February 1911): 18–19; "The Departure from Russia to Eretz Israel," *Ha-Olam* 16 (6 May 1913): 9–10; "The Departure from Russia to Eretz Israel," *Ha-Olam* 9 (10 March 1914): 15–16.

United States (4.5%), it appears that a high percentage of educated people came to Palestine. At the same time, when the percentage of those that followed the liberal professions is seen in relation to all the immigrants that came to Palestine, the ratio is only 7 percent. Similarly, we see from figure 3.4 that the great majority of those employed did not consider themselves agricultural laborers in Palestine.

In the years 1905–1913, 36 percent of immigrants to Palestine wanted to settle in Jaffa and 38 percent wanted to live in Jerusalem and Hebron. Six percent of the remaining immigrants were divided among Safed, Tiberias, Haifa, and Beirut. In other words, 74 percent of immigrants wanted to live in the cities, and only 16 percent wished to live in the colonies. Those who wished to settle in the cities and not in the colonies did so for obvious reasons. First, the great majority of immigrants had lived in towns in Eastern Europe, and they continued to do so in Palestine. Second, immigrants had made their living from trade and various crafts and could not envisage themselves supporting a family merely from agriculture in conditions harsher than those they had known in their countries of origin. Third, the move to a new country

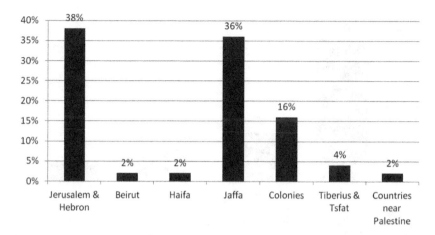

Figure 3.5 Immigrants' composition by their preference for place of settlement in Palestine, 1905–1913.

SOURCE: "The Departure from Russia to Eretz Israel," *Ha-Olam* 17 (12 May 1910): 14–15; "The Departure from Russia to Eretz Israel," *Ha-Olam* 5 (13 February 1911): 18–19; "The Departure from Russia to Eretz Israel," *Ha-Olam* 16 (6 May 1913): 9–10; "The Departure from Russia to Eretz Israel," *Ha-Olam* 9 (10 March 1914): 15–16.

meant completely changing their habitual way of life. They considered life in a village as too drastic a change, as they wished to continue the traditional way of life they had been used to overseas. These conclusions are confirmed by contemporaries' periodicals:

> Tel Aviv has an important role to play in developing the Yishuv.
> It draws new people, it makes the change of place, the move from
> Europe to Asia, easier for them. It binds them to the country, but
> there's a fly in the ointment. Many of the immigrants want to rest and
> choose to settle here rather to go out to a colony, build a two-story
> house and rent it, or plant an orchard or start a business.[17]

Figure 3.6 shows that about 60 percent of immigrants to Palestine in the years 1905–1910 told officials at the information bureau that they possessed less than a thousand roubles. In the context of the early twentieth century, this was a trifling sum that—as we shall see in the next chapter—was only just enough to cover the cost of immigration to the United States. One may cautiously presume that immigrants to Palestine as a whole were in a worse economic situation than those who went to the United States. The JCA information bureau pub-

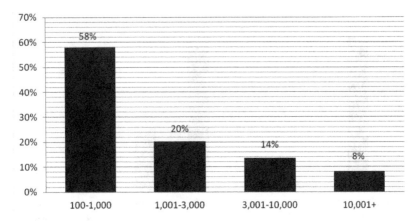

Figure 3.6 Capital (in roubles) of immigrants to Palestine who left from Odessa, 1905–1910.

SOURCE: "The Departure from Russia to Eretz Israel," *Ha-Olam* 17 (12 May 1910): 14–15; "The Departure from Russia to Eretz Israel," *Ha-Olam* 5 (13 February 1911): 18–19; "The Departure from Russia to Eretz Israel," *Ha-Olam* 16 (6 May 1913): 9–10; "The Departure from Russia to Eretz Israel," *Ha-Olam* 9 (10 March 1914): 15–16.

lished in the newspaper *Der Jüdische Emigrant* information about the economic situation of immigrants to Palestine that supports the findings in figure 3.6: "Immigration from our area has increased recently. The great majority of the immigrants goes to Argentina or Palestine. The hasty departure for Palestine, which has recently passed through a revolution [the rebellion of the Young Turks] is interesting. Many [of the immigrants] point out that Palestine is closer. Most of them are very poor, and they cannot travel far, and they have to choose a place that is closer."[18] And Sheinkin thought the same: "The current of immigration for the most part brings us poor people, for those who have some capital remain in Russia or go to America. Those who come to Palestine, on the other hand, are those who are down to their last cent, or old people who, if they do have any money, store it away in some bank or loan it to some shnorring [Yiddish for "cadging"] institution, and trade does not benefit in the least."[19]

Of immigrants who came to Palestine, 72 percent came in order to settle there (the large number of women and children supports this assertion); 8 percent came for a short time, to see the country, to visit relatives, to deal with business matters, and so on; and 13 percent came to spend their last days there (see figure 3.7). This latter group is particularly interesting, as we see from the immigrants' composition according to age that 22 percent of the immigrants were aged 50 and over, yet only 13 percent chose to die in the country and be buried there. This being the case, the other 9 percent of immigrants who belonged to this age group were not old folks who came to end their days in Palestine but rather active people who wanted to live there.

At the same time, it is not clear how to classify those who came to the country to study Torah and live from *haluka* (charitable funds from abroad), but not necessarily to die there. It is uncertain whether these immigrants should be included with the 9 percent who came to live and work in the country or with the 13 percent who came to end their lives there. It is reasonable to suppose that the category of those who had "come to die" refers to immigrants who came to the country for the religious purpose of studying Torah and not necessarily of dying in the biological sense, so the students of Torah would therefore be included in the 13 percent (see figure 3.3).

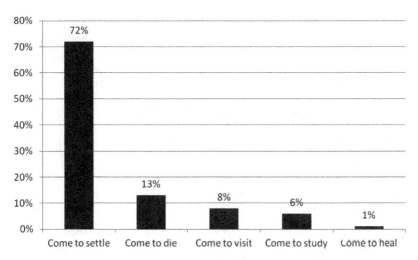

Figure 3.7 Composition of immigrants to Palestine who left from the port of Odessa, in accordance with their motives for traveling, 1905–1913.

SOURCE: "The Departure from Russia to Eretz Israel," *Ha-Olam* 17 (12 May 1910): 14–15; "The Departure from Russia to Eretz Israel," *Ha-Olam* 5 (13 February 1911): 18–19; "The Departure from Russia to Eretz Israel," *Ha-Olam* 16 (6 May 1913): 9–10; "The Departure from Russia to Eretz Israel," *Ha-Olam* 9 (10 March 1914): 15–16.

In 1905, 14 percent of immigrants to Palestine in figure 3.8 came on the advice of relatives. By 1913, their numbers had increased to 54 percent—a very significant number. This increase in the number of immigrants who came to settle on the advice of relatives was an outstanding example of "chain-immigration." In the earliest stage, the first members of the family arrived, toured the country, looked into the possibilities of employment, and even sent money; and in the second stage, other members of the family arrived. This is interesting, especially in view of the hypothetical question of what would have happened if the relatives had not recommended Palestine as a place to live. It is very likely that many of the immigrants would have accepted their advice and not come to Palestine. The immigration to the country as the result of these recommendations shows that the decision to immigrate was not necessarily motivated by ideological fervor, but rather it was the product of a mass of complex considerations based on the information of experienced relatives and family members who had already gone to Palestine.

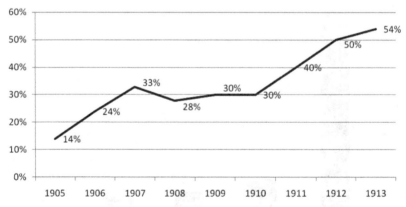

Figure 3.8 Composition of immigrants who sailed to Palestine on the advice of relatives, 1905–1913.

SOURCE: "The Departure from Russia to Eretz Israel," *Ha-Olam* 17 (12 May 1910): 14–15; "The Departure from Russia to Eretz Israel," *Ha-Olam* 5 (13 February 1911): 18–19; "The Departure from Russia to Eretz Israel," *Ha-Olam* 16 (6 May 1913): 9–10; "The Departure from Russia to Eretz Israel," *Ha-Olam* 9 (10 March 1914): 15–16.

"Wretched Immigrants"

Who were the immigrants who came to Palestine at the beginning of the twentieth century? Does the way they were described by contemporaries correspond to the statistical data furnished by the information bureau in Odessa? An examination of the way these people were depicted by onlookers can bring life to the dry facts and numbers. From the descriptions in contemporary newspapers at three points in time—1905–1906, 1908, and 1914—and from reports of the information bureau in Jaffa, we can see that immigrants of all types came to Palestine.

Articles in the newspapers of the period, Sheinkin's letters to the heads of the Zionist organization, and reports on immigration to Palestine all described immigrants who came to the country with concern and depicted them in dark colors. "The immigration does not stop; on the contrary, it is increasing," we read in the newspaper *Ha-Zman*. "Part of those who come remain in the country, part return to Russia, and the rest go on from here to America, Canada and Egypt. . . . It is necessary to say once again that poor people, fathers of families without any skills should not come here, as they will not find the means to live." On the other hand, rich people "have ample opportunities here for work either on their own or in connection with various groups, in trade, agriculture and industry."[20] Four months later, the newspaper described the immigrants as follows:

> Now the sailors' strike in Odessa has ended, the Russian ships have began to come in as before. New immigrants arrive, many from the Polish provinces. . . . There has been a great increase in poverty among the immigrants, there are eye-diseases among the children, and they have no one to support them or to help them, and generally the last two months of summer, "summer's end," are the most difficult for new people with families. This week we will open a cook-house for poor migrants. The cook-house is at present able to provide meals for fifty immigrants.[21]

The newspaper informs us not only that poor immigrants came to Palestine, but that among them there were immigrants with eye-disease who would have been most unlikely to have passed the thorough medical checks at Ellis Island. It seems that rather than being a "land of heart's desire," Palestine was a fallback option for Jews who wanted to emigrate from Eastern Europe but were unable to reach the United States. We read in the newspaper *Ha-Yom* a few months later:

> The immigration to Palestine, which had slowed down slightly between the festivals, has begun to revert to its former state—a state of confusion. They come without money, without skills, without preparation, without knowledge and—without any love of the country. And these wretches wander around in Jaffa like shadows, wander around and curse their lot, wander around and finally open one shop next to another: shops with some loaves of bread, some bottles of wine, some pounds of onions. And one wonders why this emigration does not strike roots.[22]

It would seem that in those years Palestine became a place of immigration rather than a site of aspiration. It was not only idealistic pioneers that came to the country but also the poor and wretched among the Jews of Eastern Europe who hoped there would be someone to receive them in Palestine:

> The immigration to Jaffa increases more and more. Each ship brings new migrants of various kinds, and they bring us the depressing news of a very strong movement of emigration from the towns of southern Russia, and they say that at Passover there began a mass-emigration to Palestine. In Jaffa we already see a mass of new arrivals wandering about and not being able to do anything with the small amount of money they have. We see masses of people wandering about in a state of destitution, who came here wrongly thinking that here there is great practical value to a working man or willing hands, as in the great countries of immigration such as the United States, Canada or South Africa.[23]

The newspaper *Ha-Yom* wrote, "On the whole, the current of immigration brings us only poor people, as those that have some capital stay at home [in Russia] or go to America." "Those that come to Palestine," *Ha-Yom* continues, "are those who are down to their last cent, or old people who, if they do have any money, store away it in some bank or loan it to some shnorring institution, and trade does not benefit in the least."[24]

A report of Sheinkin's bureau dated May 1906 describes the state of immigrants in the streets of Jaffa:

> Most of the immigrants come here without any means of support, without any skill, and without any talent for any kind of business . . . and we see here amongst us a large group of wretched immigrants who have no chance of settling in Jaffa and have no means to go to another country and seek a livelihood. . . . Eye-diseases are prevalent here among the poorer residents, as sanitary conditions in the towns in the Turkish domains are beneath criticism. So you can imagine the terrible situation of the great mass of poor immigrants here.[25]

Contrary to the hopes of the bureau, most of the immigrants who came to Palestine were miserable, suffering wretches who had fled from Europe and sought salvation in the country. However, they were not different from the type of immigrant who went to America. Although the newspaper *Ha-Po'el Ha-Tza'ir* saw them as anomalous elements in the human landscape who did not represent immigrants to Palestine as a whole at that time, the description of them in the newspaper account tallies with other descriptions of immigrants, such as the following:

> This disorderly current of immigrants, which bursts forth, has increased, and sweeps along with it all kinds of elements. Among them are extraordinary types we have not known here until now, for whom Palestine is not an ideal and an aspiration but simply a place of refuge and shelter in the most prosaic sense of the words. In the Jaffa area we find the type of Jewish "emigrant" that we used to meet crouching on his baggage at every intersection and at every station in the frontier towns on his way to the maritime cities; the troubled and miserable "emigrant" in whom the question "where to" has been stifled and remains without an answer, and who goes anywhere the wind takes him, anywhere his legs lead him. And with him comes the type of migrant whom thousands of reasons and blows in life's war have driven beyond the limits of his working life into lawlessness, the type that becomes the scum of society and is distinguished by his suspicious appearance, suspected by everybody.[26]

These testimonies and others support the conclusions of the statistical analyses in this volume. Many of the immigrants were not olim but simple Jews who sometimes came to the country by chance or treated it as a fallback option. The leaders of the Yishuv who, as we have pointed out, looked at the incomers with apprehension, were not hoping for immigrants of this kind. Menahem Sheinkin expressed this well in 1908 in a letter to his friend, Zionist executive Otto Warburg, wherein he spoke of his fears concerning the human material that was reaching the country:

> As long as you, the directors, don't attempt to attract capital by the million to Palestine, we are not worth a thing. Our position will not be strengthened by the poor people coming to Palestine on their own initiative. I say, quite the opposite, for our reputation is getting worse from day to day in the eyes of the officials and the general public because of this immigration. What they see is people who are down and out, downtrodden, patched up, with bundles of tattered clothes, the poorest of the poor, who cannot possibly be a blessing to the country, and it gives us a bad name. And if wealthy, respected people, well-groomed and well-regarded, don't come ashore, in the language of the port the term "Jew" will be synonymous with weak and poor, of little value, the dregs of society, and from there the idea will spread to the other sections of the people. This is the naked truth I have to convey to you as the representative of the information bureau, and every week I could say the same. Everything is static, nothing changes, and nothing is going to change until Palestine receives an injection of capital.[27]

*

This chapter describing the profile of immigrants to Palestine in the period of the second aliyah, in addition to the statistical evidence concerning the incomers and their characteristics, permits us to examine their motives for coming to the country. By means of the concept "second aliyah," historiography has already distinguished between the mass of immigrants who came to the country in the years 1905–1914 and the stratum of pioneers who brought with them a special national and social outlook.[28] Unlike the latter, who have been thoroughly researched, the former, although the majority, have been cast aside, and no one has attempted to examine their profile or characteristics. Thus, the focus of research on labor circles has blurred the image of the majority of immigrants, resulting in opaqueness and a lack of clarity concerning their characteristics and motives for immigration.

A comparison between those that came to Palestine and those who went to America shows a similarity between the two streams of immigration, but at the same time differentiates the immigration to Palestine and reveals its special character—and not only from the Zionist-ideological point of view. Forty percent of immigrants to the United States and Palestine were women, and about a quarter of immigrants were children. On the other hand, a higher percentage of people aged 50 and over went to Palestine: 22 percent of the immigrants to Palestine were over the age of 50, compared with only 6 percent of those to the United States. This difference is the main reason for the large proportion of immigrants without an occupation who came to Palestine, in comparison to those who went to America (64.7 percent in Palestine versus 43.3 percent in the United States). Among those who had professions, a definite majority of immigrants to both Palestine and the United States were artisans or small tradesmen who preferred to settle in towns and not in villages. An examination of the economic situation of immigrants to Palestine reveals that those that went to Palestine were from a lower stratum of Eastern European Jewry with a lower socioeconomic status than immigrants to the United States.

As against chapter 2, which discusses the decision to emigrate and the way it was reached in the family circle, along with the perspective of potential emigrants, this chapter deals with those who finally carried out their decision and came to Palestine. A combination of quantitative research examining immigrants as a whole and qualitative research focusing on the experience of the individual immigrant, as reflected in letters to Sheinkin's and Ruppin's information bureaus, provides a complex picture of the nature of the immigrants and of the factors that brought them to the country at the beginning of the twentieth century.

Four   The Journey to Palestine

The aim of this chapter is to examine the journey to Palestine in a comparative perspective, beginning with the bureaucracy involved in the emigration process, tracing the journey by train to the ports of departure Odessa and Trieste, and ending with the sea voyage and arrival in the Jaffa Port.

Once a decision to emigrate was made and Palestine was chosen as the destination, emigrants began preparing to move. Navigating the details of emigration was no small matter: Countless difficulties accompanied emigrants and their families from the moment they set out until they arrived in Palestine. These challenges included obtaining necessary documents to leave the country legally, selling their businesses and homes, buying railway tickets, traveling long distances by train from the shtetl to ports of Odessa or Trieste, and buying boat tickets to their destination. Finally, they faced their first encounter with Palestine and its population.

The Bureaucracy of Emigration

In order to leave czarist Russia legally, an emigrant needed three things: a passport, a boat ticket, and a state of good health to pass a medical checkup before boarding the ship.

1. The Passport, the Pilgrim's Certificate, and the Red Note

One of the outstanding features of this period of migration was a liberal immigration policy on the part of the countries of destination, which opened the gates to immigrants. Until World War I, there was no need for a passport or an entry permit in order to enter the destination countries overseas, including the United States. The borders of the American continent were open to an almost unlimited degree to the millions of migrants from Europe wishing to escape from the poverty and destitution of their daily lives. At the same time, in order to travel to the ports of departure and cross the borders of Russia legally and safely, an emigrant had to obtain a passport.

Obtaining a passport to leave the country was one of the most difficult and complex undertakings from the bureaucratic point of view. Russian law was not suited to a period of mass migration, and regulations differed from area to area. The problems that resulted were insurmountable, which paved the way for corruption and unforeseen expenses. In order to receive a passport, an emigrant had to obtain documents: an identity card; a document from the police certifying that there was no obstacle to his leaving the country; and those between the ages of 18 and 21 also had to obtain a document certifying that they had reported to a recruiting station.[1]

Obtaining the necessary documents was a problem in itself. Many emigrants were not registered in their place of residence and therefore did not have an identity card. Those who had cards found that they were often no longer valid or did not cover all the members of the family. In order to obtain a new card, emigrants had to go to the municipality where they were registered, however far it was from their place of residence. In October 1906 the law was changed, and people were allowed to have a permanent identity card (one without an expiration date) and a passport, which could be used for themselves and members of their family for travel anywhere in the Pale of Settlement and Poland. The one condition was that they had to produce all the necessary documents during transit. But this new law, which was made in Russia, was not disseminated properly in the Pale of Settlement, and so Jews had to obtain their cards according to the old arrangement.

One could only obtain a certificate of good character after obtaining an identity card and meeting the condition that there were no complaints against the emigrant and members of his family. When an emigrant was given a certificate of good character, he also got from the police the other documents necessary for obtaining a passport. All members of the family, of whatever age, had to be registered in the passport: one's wife, children, relatives, and even a maid if the family had one. If all the members of the family were registered in the emigrant's identity card, the process was very easy and there were no special difficulties. But if the emigrant's wife and children were not registered in the identity card, he had to obtain the children's birth certificates and to produce witnesses who knew his wife and children. Because in small shtetls it was usual to register a wife and children only in records of the Jewish community, many emigrants had difficulty in obtaining the necessary documents.[2]

Women who wished to join their husbands in the new country found it even more difficult to obtain a passport. According to Russian law, a woman could only obtain a passport with the permission of her husband, but many men with families emigrated alone in order to prepare the economic infrastructure for their families' arrival. They often failed to provide their wives with a separate passport or a paper signed by a notary affirming that they were married, and the wives consequently found themselves at an impasse.

This difficulty could be overcome in three ways. The first, least feasible way was for the husband living abroad to declare to a notary in the new country that he wanted his wife and children to join him. He had to get this declaration signed by the Russian consul in his area of residence and send it to his wife. When the wife presented the declaration signed by the notary and the consul, she received a passport without difficulty. The second way was for the wife to declare to the police that her husband had abandoned her and all trace of him had disappeared. After a short investigation to verify her claim, the police provided her with a document confirming her declaration and permitting the regional governor to issue her a passport.[3] The third, commonest way was to cross the frontier by stealth.

For a Jewish emigrant, the bureaucratic obstacles involved in obtaining a passport to leave Russia legally were almost insurmountable. Factors that complicated their goals included the custom of maintaining a separate registration of Jews by the Jewish community; and also internal migrations of Jews within the country, which resulted in geographical distance from the original area of their registration. These conditions contributed to difficulties in confronting the Russian bureaucracy in the early twentieth century and caused many emigrants to seek other, illegal ways of leaving the country. In the process, emigrants were exposed to crooks of various kinds who exploited their dependence and precarious situation.

Compared with obtaining a passport for the United States, the bureaucratic procedure for leaving Russia to go to Palestine was quite straightforward. In order to obtain a passport, an emigrant had to provide a certificate of good character from the police or from a representative of the Ministry of the Interior. He paid 15 roubles at a local branch of the Ministry of Finance, and in turn received a receipt. He presented this receipt of payment to the appropriate office and then obtained his certificate. The emigrant then took his certificate to the secretariat of the region where the passport was issued; acquiring the passport cost an additional 15 roubles.[4] Unlike those going to America, immigrants to Palestine had the option of presenting themselves as pilgrims. If they declared their intention of going to Palestine to pray, they could obtain a "pilgrim's certificate," which enabled them to acquire a passport for only 50 kopeks.[5] In order to obtain a pilgrim's certificate, these emigrants also needed a certificate of good character, a receipt from their branch of the Ministry of Finance, and a certificate from the rabbinate of the region confirming the intentions of the traveler. When he received his passport—whether for 50 kopeks or 15 roubles—the emigrant had to have it signed by the Turkish consulate and then buy stamps for a total sum of 2 roubles and 75 kopeks. Children under the age of 16 who had to obtain a passport needed an authorization from their parents or guardian agreeing to their journey. In view of the fact that the pilgrim's certificate was much cheaper, most of the immigrants to Palestine traveled on it, and thus for all intents and purposes pilgrimage was immigration.[6]

It was more difficult for youths of the age of military service to leave Russia, and most of them did it illegally. Their evasion of army service made it impossible for them to obtain the necessary documents, and many of them had to leave Russia by stealth or with forged documents. Those who engaged in political agitation against the czarist regime or were arrested in demonstrations against the government were also unable to obtain the certificate of good character needed to acquire the pilgrim's certificate, and they too had to leave the borders of Russia secretly.[7]

The acquisition of a passport permitted emigrants to leave Russia, but it did not enable them to enter the Ottoman Empire. At the stopover at Istanbul (see later for a description of the sailing route), the immigrants were expected to obtain a *tazkra* (red note). The *tazkra* was a document submitted to the Ottoman authorities by every Jew arriving in Palestine. It was really a commitment by the Jewish traveler to leave Palestine after three months. In order to obtain a *tazkra*, travelers had to produce a document from the Russian consul, which cost 80 kopeks, and then go to the Ottoman authorities with this document and their passports. The authorities charged 20 to 40 kopeks for each passport.[8] Travelers who did not succeed in obtaining a *tazkra* could receive one at Jaffa, but in that case they had to pay a fine. "Those who came without the *tazkra*," wrote Sheinkin, "paid the 2.40 fine. . . . For this fine, the port officials do not give a receipt, and one suspects that they take the money for themselves."[9] When travelers arrived in Jaffa, they deposited their "*laissez-passer* or passport with the official responsible for granting permits, and they received, in exchange of a grush (Ottoman monetary unit), a temporary document for visiting and residence stating that they were permitted to travel and stay in Palestine for three months. In order to distinguish this document from the others it had a different format and a different color."[10]

Jewish migrants who did not leave the country at the end of three months became, in effect, illegal inhabitants of the Ottoman Empire, but their rights derived from the capitulations (i.e., agreements between the Ottoman Empire and European powers) of the countries from which they came. Ali Ekrem Bey, governor of the city of Jerusalem, pointed out the paradox inherent in Jewish immigration to Palestine. The Jews, he said, fled from their countries of origin because of hatred and antisemitism, yet they were received gladly by the consuls of these countries and gained their protection:

> The policy followed by foreign states, and especially Russia and
> Austria, with regard to Jewish immigration, is to give protection in the
> Ottoman empire to the very Jews they expel from their countries, and
> whom in their countries they afflict with all kinds of punishment and
> oppression. . . . The Jews who even now are called in private conversa-
> tions at the consulates by the derogatory epithet "dirty Jew" because
> of the anger that exists in Christianity towards Judaism, are treated

with honor and respect the moment they write something to the effect that "I am a national of your splendid country" in the tiny official antechamber, even if it has nothing to do with nationality.[11]

Apart from needing to obtain the *tazkra*, there was no difficulty in entering the country, and immigrants met with almost no legal or governmental obstacles. At the end of an immigrant's three-month-long stay in the country and upon expiration of the validity of his *tazkra*, it was not a problem to extend his stay by various means with help from the consulate, which gave protection to its country's nationals.

2. The Boat Ticket

The price of a boat ticket to the United States from the main ports—Bremen, Hamburg, Rotterdam, and Antwerp—was about 75 roubles (equivalent to $37 in U.S. currency at the beginning of the twentieth century and about $755 today).[12] A child less than one year old paid 5 roubles, and up to age 12 a child could sail at half-price ($18 at that time, about $367 today). The sea voyage was cheaper from England: 65 roubles for a ticket from Liverpool to Philadelphia ($32/$663), but the journey to the port was more expensive. A ticket from Libau in Latvia to New York cost 70 roubles per person, and the terms for children were similar to those from the ports in Germany, Holland, and Belgium ($35 roubles/$714 dollars).[13]

Because the journey for a whole family was costly, the solution was for the head of the family to go to the country of destination as an advance party; after he had established himself economically, he would send boat tickets to his relatives waiting in the country of origin. The great danger with prepaid tickets of this kind was that cheats and swindlers could make a profitable racket from selling forged tickets of no value. The fraud would not be discovered until the family reached the port of departure and tried to board the ship, and by then it was too late.[14] Thus a family of immigrants could find themselves helpless and destitute in a new country without any means of support.

Another danger with these prepaid tickets was that they could be bought in installments from travel companies by the relative in the country of destination and sent to his relatives in the country of origin before the full sum was paid up. Because the company that provided the tickets had not received the full sum, it gave orders for the tickets not to be honored, and then the relatives would find themselves waiting in the port until the debt was paid.[15] These delays sometimes lasted for weeks, and meanwhile the relatives' money would run out while they waited for the matter to be settled.

Emigrants to whom prepaid tickets had not been sent bought their boat tickets in the offices of shipping companies located throughout the Pale of Settlement and ports of departure. The emigrants sometimes relied on agents to buy their tickets, and these agents sought to profit as much as possible from their intermediary role. Their mediation lent itself to corruption and made the tickets more expensive. The purchase was generally made in installments: An emigrant made an advance payment to the shipping company and registered his name and age, then paid the rest of the money as soon as he arrived at the port. In return, the company pledged to put him on the first ship sailing to the country he desired.[16]

Sailing to Palestine was considerably cheaper than sailing to the United States. The price of a boat ticket from the port of Odessa to Palestine was 20 roubles (the equivalent of $10 at the time, or $200 in today's value). After a 40 percent reduction if the emigrant agreed to sail via the Odessa information bureau, the price was only about 12 roubles ($6 then/$120 today).[17] Reaching the port of Odessa was also relatively easy compared with reaching ports in Western and Central Europe. An emigrant who sailed to Palestine did not have to cross the frontier of the Russian Empire to reach one of the ports in Europe. Railway lines came to Odessa from all parts of the Pale of Settlement, and the journey was relatively simple and did not require the emigrant to make his way in an unfamiliar country.

3. State of Health

In 1882, a law was passed in the United States prohibiting the entry of poor and sick immigrants and requiring shipping companies to send back undesirable immigrants to their port of departure. The shipping companies were required under this law to return immigrants at their own expense, and the resulting financial losses convinced the companies that it would be advisable to subject emigrants to medical examinations before they sailed to America. These examinations were made at the frontier stations and at the ports of departure before emigrants boarded the ships.[18] Emigrants suffering from venereal, skin, or eye diseases; tuberculosis; or other sicknesses were not allowed to leave the frontier station or board the ship. There were restrictions not only on those who were sick but also on deformed individuals—the hunchbacked, blind, deaf and dumb, the lame. Additional restrictions were applied to criminals, prostitutes, pimps, and their ilk.[19] In Palestine there were no similar restrictions, and no medical examinations were made either before the sea voyage or after it. The Ottoman authorities raised no difficulties, which is why, as discussed in the previous chapter, poor immigrants with eye diseases came to Palestine who would not have been allowed to cross the ocean even to reach the United States, let alone enter the country.

Agenten-Shwindler

Many people felt that the bureaucratic processes bound up with emigration were complicated and inconvenient, especially those connected with obtaining a passport. Regulations were contradictory and ill-understood. This, combined with the slowness and arbitrary nature of officials, high corruption, and the inability of the emigrant to make his way alone through the bureaucratic jungle gave rise to feelings of impotence and despair. As a result, emigrants began to look for shortcuts—generally illegal ones—to circumvent the bureaucratic entanglements. The search for shortcuts and help with problems that arose during the immigration process gave rise throughout the Pale of Settlement to a new profession—"migration agents." These agents claimed to be knowledgeable in the "secrets" of migration, and for a suitable payment promised emigrants that they would find solutions to their problems. Various kinds of crooks used the title "migration agent" to conceal their real identity and thus were able to exploit naïve emigrants, make false promises to them, take their money, and sometimes even endanger their lives. These fraudulent agents—*agenten-shwindler* or *geheime agenten*—were the main cause of emigrants' troubles. Their trickery was a by-product of the ramified, complex bureaucracy described previously. It is estimated that in Eastern and Central Europe there were thousands of agents recognized by the shipping companies, and many others were not recognized and worked independently:

> Agents of all kinds, official ones with firms, and secret ones, lesser ones and helpers of all kinds spring up like mushrooms and cover the face of the land. Every town, every shtetl has its agents. And it is not a single agent in every town but whole groups of agents competing with each other, quarreling, fighting and slandering one another.[20]

There was a direct link between the bureaucracy in place that presented difficulties in obtaining a passport and the *agenten-shwindler* that sprang up "like mushrooms" throughout the Pale of Settlement. Many emigrants who did not succeed in obtaining all the documents required turned to these agents and asked them to procure a passport in exchange for payment. By means of bribery, acquaintance with the local officials, and, above all, knowledge of the bureaucratic processes, the agents succeeded in satisfying the desires of emigrants and obtaining their passports. But not before they had generated needless expenses:

> The deceit and trickery of the agents is particularly great in the preparation of documents for going abroad. Ninety percent, if not more, of the emigrants do not know how to prepare these documents themselves and are frightened to do it. The people from small towns and shtetls, and often poor city-dwellers as well, imagine the process of preparing documents to be hard and difficult work and so turn to the "omnipotent" agent who offers his services.[21]

The most typical form of trickery was to obtain a common passport for several families who had no connection between them. According to Russian law, it was possible to register in a passport all the members of a family, close and distant, who wanted to emigrate. The agents exploited this legal sanction to create a common passport for several families and, without asking them, made them into one large family:

> They take it upon themselves to prepare a travel document, but instead of preparing a special travel document for every single emigrant or every family as is proper and according to the money they received, they "make" out of isolated individuals, complete strangers, a single large "family" and prepare for all of them a single travel document, and in this way earn scores of roubles on the side.[22]

At first glance, this arrangement seemed reasonable to an emigrant, who thought that he could probably manage with it. But the reality proved to be far more complex. After obtaining this common passport and setting out on his journey, an emigrant found that he "could not move or lift a hand or foot without his forefathers, his brothers and sisters, his wife and the new children that had been born to him thanks to the 'wonder-working' agent."[23] The movements of emigrants and their families were restricted under this scheme. As a result, quarrels broke out between the emigrating families who shared the common passport. There were cases where one of the families wanted to stop an extra day at a station on the way, and the others wanted to press on toward the port. Their total interdependence did not allow them to go forward without the agreement of the entire "united family." The real trouble, however, was what transpired at the medical examination before they boarded the ship:

> Here [at the port] they think that they have already passed through the seven sections of hell and that they can travel onwards without interference. But no—it suddenly appears that some member of this big family cannot travel because of an eye-disease or some other illness, and all twelve or fifty emigrants have to stay here or return home because according to the law a family is not allowed to travel if one of its members is not permitted to travel on account of a sickness, and his name is registered in the travel document. . . . All their entreaties and all their insistence that they are travelling alone without a family or relatives are to no avail. . . . There are many victims like these, who all of a sudden are made desperate because of the insatiable greed of the agents and their despicable hope of enriching themselves at the expense of the emigrants.[24]

The financial loss to emigrants in these cases was enormous. After they had sold their possessions, bought a boat ticket, and embarked on their long journey to the port, they found that it was all in vain. Their connection with the agent had dissolved, and they felt themselves to be quite helpless.

Another form of trickery practiced by the agents was to promise emigrants repeatedly that a passport could be obtained not only in their place of residence but also in the port of Libau before boarding the ship. The agents therefore urged travelers to buy their tickets through them and to set out on their journey before they had dealt with all the bureaucratic procedures.

In fact, in October 1906 the law for obtaining passports in czarist Russia was changed. Unlike in previous years, when it was only possible to obtain passports in the town in which emigrants were registered, from 1906 onward emigrants could obtain a passport anywhere in the Pale of Settlement. But, as we have mentioned, there were necessary documents, like the one recording an emigrant's marriage and children, that could only be obtained in the emigrant's place of residence, and they could not obtain a passport without these documents:

> Until now, emigrants have known that one could not leave without
> a passport because one had to obtain them in the region in which
> one lived. Now, as we know, passports for traveling abroad can be
> obtained by emigrants here [Libau]. On the face of it, everything is
> fine, but even this concession has proved to be an obstacle for the
> emigrants. The agents tell the emigrants: go, and you'll get everything
> there, and when they come here, they find that they do not have
> the document of the chairman of the administration and other such
> documents, without which a passport for traveling abroad cannot be
> obtained here.[25]

The agents exploited the helplessness of emigrants in order to extort more and more money from them on the pretext that funds were needed to obtain passports and other documents. "The agents and owners of the shipping companies exploit this for their benefit and profit and flay the emigrants."[26] This bureaucratic imbroglio held up emigrants and caused them financial expenses, wasting funds that were needed for the period of acclimatization in the new country. Most of emigrants' money was spent on food and lodging in the port town. In order to save on expenses, emigrants generally stayed in cheap hotels in the most wretched conditions: "There are hundreds of emigrants who have to stay here for months on end waiting for their travel documents, and they are incarcerated in cramped, dingy hotels like fish in a barrel. There are three and four in a bed, men and women in the same room; there is no sense of modesty or conception of hygiene."[27]

Another form of trickery was the fraudulent sale of boat tickets. Apart from "prepaid" tickets sent to emigrants and their families, emigrants could also obtain tickets on their own—either directly from the shipping companies that had branches in all the large towns of the Pale of Settlement or from certified agents. Many crooks posed as agents, took money from the emigrants, and promised that they would receive their tickets as soon as they arrived in the port. After emigrants had begun their journey, traveled hundreds of miles to the frontier stations, crossed the frontier, and successfully passed medical examinations at the frontier stations, they went to the shipping company to retrieve their tickets. They then found out that the agent had not sent the sum they had paid, and they had to wait until this money was received. Many weeks passed before emigrants made contact with the agents—if they ever did—and asked them to deal with the matter of payment. Meanwhile, their money ran out, and emigrants had to go begging or find support from Jewish philanthropic organizations.

The newspapers of the period reported a great deal on incidents of this kind, and they repeatedly warned emigrants against crooks posing as certified agents. One of the most cunning of these agents worked in the Kiev area, and he managed to ensnare quite a number of families before he was caught. In January 1909 this "agent," Moshe Mafter, undertook to send a group of six emigrants to Argentina. He received 400 roubles from the group for his efforts, and in return he gave them a letter to the Carlsberg shipping company confirming that he had received money for the boat tickets. When these six emigrants reached Hamburg they presented the letter to the representative of the company, but to their astonishment they found that money from the agent had not arrived and therefore they could not receive the boat tickets.[28]

In November 1908, a mother paid an agent 225 roubles to send herself and her two children, aged 4 and 9, to Winnipeg, Canada. The agent promised her that she would receive the boat tickets in Vilna and that from there she would proceed to the port of Libau. But when she reached Vilna, she found that the agent had only sent 195 roubles, and until the missing 30 roubles were paid up she could not receive her boat tickets. The desperate woman sent a letter to her husband in Canada describing the situation that had arisen, asking him to send the rest of the money so that his family could soon join him. Eight weeks passed between sending the letter and receiving a reply. The result was that the husband did not have the money she needed, and so his wife and two children were stalled without further assistance. She finally received financial assistance from the information bureau of the JCA.[29]

Emigrants who went to Palestine were cheated in the same way as those who reached America—by dishonest agents who exploited their naiveté and lack of knowledge of the arrangements involved in the emigration process. The main ports of departure for immigrants to Palestine were Odessa and Trieste. These ports were a bottleneck, crowded with emigrants waiting for a ship to take them to their countries of destination. The concentration of emigrants in these ports attracted crooks, pickpockets, and thieves of various kinds who wanted to pocket some money illegally. The booklet on immigration to Palestine that Sheinkin wrote for the information bureau warned emigrants of thieves and crooks in Odessa looking for "an opportunity to make them some generous proposal that would finally steal their money."[30]

Emigrants also lost money through the owners of hotels and their intermediaries, who used the visiting cards of the Odessa Committee in order to lure the many emigrants who arrived in the city a few days before sailing. For many emigrants it was their first time in a large city, and they soon found themselves in expensive hotels that quickly exhausted the little money they possessed. Or else they stayed in lodging-houses that served as a cover for brothels, which led to complications with the police:

> The committee distributes cards of recommendation to various hotelier-intermediaries in Odessa, and the travelers from the provinces fall into the trap. There was one case where one of these intermediaries brought the travelers to a hotel of you know the kind . . . which also led to unpleasant incidents with the police. And even after it looked into the matter, the committee did not see fit to take back his cards.[31]

The intermediaries and owners of hotels exploited the "authorization" of the Odessa Committee in order to obtain passports and entry permits and make various bureaucratic arrangements. These uncalled-for arrangements unnecessarily extended a traveler's stay in the city, exacting high prices for documents and hotel accommodations:

> The issuing of passports by the consulates in Odessa, when done through these hotelier-intermediaries, results in a lot of extra expenses. There was a case where the emigrants came to Odessa on a

Monday, a day before their ship sailed, and the owner of one hotel nevertheless kept dealing with the passports until they had to remain in Odessa—in the same hotel, naturally—for a whole week, although this whole business, if it had been done honestly, would have taken only twenty minutes.[32]

Constantinople was likewise a port city that attracted a great many fraudulent agents. Because it was an important stopping-place on the way to Palestine, the immigrants would stock up on food and drink before continuing on their way. They would also make preliminary arrangements for obtaining the *tazkra* (red note) that would enable them to enter the country without interference. The confusion at the port—the first encounter of many of the immigrants with the Orient—made things easy for crooks to exploit the newcomers. These crooks posed as Yiddish-speaking religious Jews or as Zionist activists and took advantage of the short time the immigrants had for obtaining the *tazkra*, their dependent situation, and their ignorance of the local language. Thus the new arrivals often willingly accepted the Jewish agents' proposals, made in their own language, and offers of assistance. By the time an immigrant discovered that the Jewish agent was no more than a crook, his money had been stolen and the agent had disappeared without a trace:

In Constantinople there is a man who appears on every ship, a real "Shulchan Aruch" type complete with sidelocks and yarmulke, and claims to be the son of a Galician rabbi. He offers the passengers to Jaffa his help in obtaining the *tazkra*—the ratification of one's passport by the Turkish authorities. There is a also a young man wearing a top hat who offers these same services, but as a representative of the Zionist Organization . . . I am warning against this pitfall. The passengers should know that they are dealing with a band of crooks whose only aim is to take their cash, and many emigrants have walked into the trap together with their money.[33]

Sometimes the deception was discovered in Jaffa, but by then it was too late. Not only had the emigrants given money to crooks, but they had to pay a fine of 2.40 roubles:

In many cases, when they ask an immigrant why he did not get the ratification of his document, he cries out that he gave the money for the permit to some man whom the Odessa Committee told him to turn to. Many people complain that in Constantinople a man approaches them in the name of the committee and then exploits them terribly. . . . This dreadful situation can only be avoided if landing-tickets are provided so that the immigrant does not have to stand there, crushed in a crowd of people, and when he wants to pay them what he has to, they stare into his open wallet and crowd around him until he is confused.[34]

Immigrants suffered a great deal. Every case of trickery and robbery was a tragedy for their families. They had sold their possessions, had been defrauded by an illegal agent, and as a result were destitute and helpless. It could happen that families were down to their last crust of bread and had to knock on doors in the frontier or port towns to ask for help. One of the newspapers of the period compared the victims of emigration to the victims of the pogroms and saw the agents as one of the greatest dangers to the Jews of the Pale of Settlement:

God's curse is upon the Jews of Russia. If the slain of the persecutions and pogroms are few, the slain of emigration are added onto them. This is our special malediction. . . . The Jew escaping from terror falls into the trap the agents have set for human souls. These leeches clinging to our flesh, which suck the strength of the emigrant, his blood and his money, also multiply the slain.[35]

And in another newspaper of the period, the agents are again described as "leeches" and "bestial":

As then, so now, they fall into the hands of the agents who suck their blood like leeches and abandon them to their fate. . . . Many of them are caught, beaten, wounded and even killed at the frontier by the guards. As then, so now, the doctors who examine them mistreat them, take their last pennies from them and send them home because their eyes were a little bleary from lack of sleep or the trials of the journey. . . . As then, so now, these beasts-among-men go about in all the coastal towns and treat the emigrants' tickets as if they were their own; and as then, so now, masses of people are turned back from America because they could not answer the official's questions, and so on.[36]

In this respect, the journey to Palestine was not different from the journey to the United States. In both cases, people fell victim to acts of deception. The only difference was in the methods used and in the ways of taking the immigrants' money. In the case of Palestine, the crooks exploited the Zionist ideology for their own illicit purposes. By posing as Zionist representatives they laid a trap for immigrants and exploited their naiveté.

The Cost of the Journeys to Palestine and the United States

The cost of immigration to the United States for an individual migrant was about 179 roubles up to the year 1908, and about 232 roubles from 1908 onward. From that year, immigrants to the United States had to prove to officials at Ellis Island that they had a hundred roubles ($50 in U.S. currency at the time) in their possession, and not fifty roubles ($25) as previously. Because Jews generally emigrated in families, the journey was very expensive. Quite often there were dual expenses. It often happened that a wife did not succeed in obtaining a passport on her own, and being unsuccessful, she paid smugglers to take her across the frontier (generally at a slightly lower cost than that of obtaining a passport). Children up to the age of 12 sailed at half-price. If a family convinced immigration officials in the United States that it was joining the head of the family, it was spared payment of the sum of money required to enter the country. Thus, up to 1908, the cost of immigration to the United States of a family of ten people (two parents and eight children, four over the age of 12 and four under) was 600 roubles for the boat tickets, 15 roubles for obtaining a passport or crossing the frontier illegally, 256 roubles for the train journey within the Russian Empire or beyond (the price varied in accordance with the length of the journey), and 10 roubles for board and lodging. The total cost of the journey for each member of the family can be estimated at about 881 roubles ($441 in equivalent U.S. currency at the beginning of the twentieth century). This was a huge sum of money for an average Jewish family, whose yearly income was only about 500 to 600 roubles ($250 to $300). It was extremely difficult to obtain this sum, and the family sometimes had to wait for years until the head of the family succeeded in finding the money and bringing over the others.[37]

In order to understand the true cost of emigration and the risk taken by Jewish (and non-Jewish) migrants, it is worth translating the value of the dollar at the beginning of the twentieth century into its present value. A boat ticket for the Hamburg-Amerika Linie Company on the direct Hamburg–New York line cost $37 in 1908, which is equivalent to $755 dollars.[38] The cost of emigration for the individual migrant was $89–$116 dollars—in today's terms $1,816–$2,367 dollars—and for a whole family, $440, equivalent to $8,979 today. These figures support the assertion that the poorest elements in Jewish society were not able to go to America. Those who did were people whose lives were undoubtedly hard and sometimes unbearable, but whose income enabled them at least to obtain the sum needed for the head of the family to travel.

On the other hand, as we saw in the last chapter, the poor were able to reach Palestine. The cost of emigrating for a family of ten was 74 roubles for a boat ticket, half a kopek for a pilgrim's certificate, 90 roubles for the train journey, and 10 roubles for board and lodging. The total cost of the journey for the whole family is estimated at 174 roubles ($87 U.S. at the beginning of the century/$1,775 today). Compared with traveling to the United States, the journey to Palestine was not only much cheaper but relatively free of risk. The migrant did not cross any international frontiers, he sailed from a port in the Pale of Settlement, he did not have to pay money to the Ottoman authorities, and he did not go through a medical examination. The migrants knew that if they failed in Palestine and did not manage to settle down there, they could easily find the money to return to the Pale of Settlement. In a 1906 report describing the wretched situation of immigrants in Jaffa, one writer said that many migrants came to Palestine because "Palestine is the country closest to Russia and the journey from there to here is inexpensive."[39] In an article on Jewish immigration to Palestine in 1906 in the newspaper *Ha-Yom*, which was published in Vilna, Zeev Smilansky wrote:

> The small cost of the journey is a notable factor which makes it easy for the emigrants to leave Palestine. While the journey to America, South Africa and Australia costs a large sum which for average emigrants would be a large part of their capital, the journey to Palestine costs very little. . . . The journey costs so little that someone who has 15 or 20 roubles in his pocket can easily return to Russia.[40]

The Sea Voyage

Jewish emigration was chiefly from two countries: czarist Russia; and Galicia, located in the Austro-Hungarian Empire. Jews who lived in the northwestern part of the Pale of Settlement generally crossed the Polish-German frontier, and from there they traveled by train to the ports of Hamburg and Bremen. On the other hand, those who lived in the south and southwest of the Pale of Settlement crossed the Russo-Galician frontier and generally proceeded to ports in Belgium and Holland. The most popular sailing routes were those from Hamburg and Bremen, but there were obviously cases that did not correspond to the usual pattern and took a different route from the one generally taken by Jewish migration.

The ships on which immigrants sailed to their chosen destinations were the most up-to-date of their time. A ship's flag represented the power and prestige of the state it represented. The capacity of the ships to cross seas and oceans was an expression of imperialist ambitions and their ability to reach distant parts of the globe. Ballin's slogan *Mein Feld ist die Welt* (My Field Is the World) was an expression of the globalization of the beginning of the twentieth century and the power of the shipping company that sent its ships to distant places overseas. If one examines the advertisements of the time, one will see that, apart from bringing immigrants to their chosen countries, voyages were also a leisure activity for wealthy Europeans. Cruises leaving from the ports of Europe offered civilized Europeans a fascinating encounter with an element of "the wild" in Africa, Asia, and the Middle East. The HAPAG company, for example, had more than sixty shipping lines that sailed to almost every continent. Its ships sailed to North America (New York, Boston, Philadelphia, New Orleans, Galveston, Montreal, and Halifax), to Central and South America (Mexico, Cuba, Veracruz, Colombia, and Buenos Aires), to Asia (Shanghai, Manila, Singapore, Bangkok), and to many ports in the African continent.[41]

The steamships were sailing vessels of huge dimensions. Steerage passengers who were not experts in physics had difficulty in understanding how these steel monsters could sail the oceans without sinking. Each company had its own flagships. For instance, HAPAG had three main ships that crossed the Atlantic Ocean, the *Amerika, Deutschland,* and

President Lincoln; Ballin in 1913 launched the flagship *Imperator*, the largest and fastest ship in the world; and the East Asia Company in Libau had Russian, Lithuanian, Estonian, and Korean ships.[42] The Norddeutscher Lloyd had a fleet of eighty-four ships, the largest of which were *Kaiser Wilhelm der Grosse*, *Kaiser Wilhelm II*, *Kronprinz Wilhelm*, and *Kronprinzessin Cecilie*.[43] The ships were not all of the same size: Some were large and spacious, others were small and crowded. *Amerika*, for example, had a length of about 210 meters, a breadth of 22 meters, an underwater depth of about 16 meters, and a weight of about 22,600 tons;[44] *Wilhelm der Grosse* was about 198 meters long, 20 meters in width, 13 meters underwater, and weighed 14,359 tons.[45]

The steamships sailed at a speed of 23 nautical miles an hour, and they significantly shortened the time of a voyage. At the beginning of the twentieth century the sailing time from the European ports to New York was about 12 days on average; the time of sailing from Bremen to Galveston in Texas was about three weeks; the time of sailing to Argentina was also three weeks; and to South Africa and Australia it took more than a month. Those who wished to go to South Africa stopped in England on the way. Their stop in English ports and waiting time there gave rise—as in Hamburg, Bremen, and Libau—to problems and needless expenses, and many people had to remain in England. Anglo-Jewry came to their aid. On the one hand, this was a form of philanthropy; but on the other hand, the help was given out of a fear that these poor migrants from Eastern Europe would settle in England. In the 1890s the "Poor Jews' Temporary Shelter" was consequently set up in London. There the migrants received lodging, a hot meal, and above all help in reaching the ports of Liverpool, Hull, and Grimsby, where they could board ships sailing to South Africa.[46]

Two factors influenced the day-to-day lives of migrants on board ship: (1) the ethnic composition of migrants and the cultural differences between them; and (2) the conditions of life on the ship and the quality of the service they received. Each ship was a modern Tower of Babel, where hundreds of travelers from different nations were jumbled together. One must suppose that contacts were made in the course of the journey and that travelers got to know one another. Edward Steiner, in his book *On the Trail of the Immigrants* that was published in 1906, described the variegated, happy encounter of the passengers in steerage on their way to the United States in 1906:

> Greeks, Serbians, Bulgarians, Magyars, Italians and Slovaks laugh at one another's antics and while listening to the strange sounds, are beginning to enter into larger fellowship than they ever enjoyed; for so close as this many of them never came without the hand upon the hilt or the finger upon the trigger.[47]

The only ethnic group that did not take part in the singing and dancing in steerage was that of the Jews. Throughout the whole of the voyage, Jewish immigrants kept away from non-Jews and functioned as a separate group that had no contact with the others. "No morning," wrote Steiner, "no matter how tumultuous the waves, but the Russian Jews will put on their phylacteries, and kissing the sacred fringes which they wear upon their breasts, will turn towards the East and the rising Sun, to where their holy temple stood."[48] In the light of this description, it is easy to imagine what the travelers in steerage thought when they saw the Jews wrapped in their prayer shawls, bedecked with phylacteries, and praying eastward to the rhythm of the swayings of the ship.

The alienation of the Jews, their self-isolation, and above all their position as an exceptional ethnic group brought them close to one another and led to mutual support and aid in steerage. The story of the immigrant Sarah Leah Levine is an example of comradeship among the Jewish immigrants. In April 1909, Sarah Leah Levine sailed from the port of Antwerp with her three children; they were on the way to her husband in America. A short time after Sarah set out, she fell ill and died. As is usual on board ship, the captain wanted to throw her body into the sea, but a burial of this kind was completely contrary to Jewish tradition. The other Jewish immigrants would on no account agree to a "burial at sea" but insisted instead that she had to be buried in a Jewish grave when they reached the United States. After consultations with the captain, it was decided that the immigrants would pay for construction of an iron coffin at a cost of $250 to prevent the spread of diseases liable to result from the rotting of the corpse. As the immigrants did not have this sum at their disposal, an English-speaking Jewish immigrant came to their aid, and by speaking to the captain succeeded in bringing down the price to a hundred dollars. Ultimately Sarah Leah Levine's corpse was not thrown into the sea, but was given to her husband in America.[49]

Life as a minority in the belly of the ship was nothing new for Jewish migrants. The twelve days on the ocean were a concentrated version of life in their country of origin. The sea voyage was really a continuation of their way of life in the shtetls of Eastern Europe and their complex relationship with the general population. Their basic suspiciousness, like their religious practices and laws of kashrut, distinguished them from the other travelers and made it difficult for them to take part in the daily routine in steerage.

In order to allay the fears of Jewish (and also non-Jewish) migrants, the shipping companies published booklets to provide them with information on what to expect on the sea voyage. The Nord-deutscher Lloyd company, for instance, brought out a booklet in Yiddish for emigrants titled *Durkh Bremen Keyn Amerika mit dem Dampf Shifen fun Nord-deutscher Lloyd* (From Bremen to America with the Steamships of the Nord-deutscher Lloyd). The booklet gave a detailed description of the shipping company, its fleet of ships, the agents of the company in Europe and the United States, an explanation of how to reach Bremen from the frontier, information about the port city, the stay there before sailing, conditions of the sea voyage, and an explanation of the laws of entry into the country of choice. The Nord-deutscher Lloyd company naturally described the voyage as a positive experience that would be comfortable and without problems. Life onboard ship was described in this ideal manner in order not to exacerbate the fears of potential emigrants.

The information bureau of the JCA (Jewish Colonization Association in Saint Petersburg, on the other hand, described a completely different state of affairs. Representatives of the bureau were sent as hidden reporters on trans-Atlantic voyages so they could describe their experiences in the newspapers. In 1909 there appeared in one of the issues of *Der Jüdische Emigrant* an article by S. Bloch, a representative of the JCA who was sent by the bureau on a voyage from Bremen to Argentina and back in order to report on the conditions of the voyage. In the article, Bloch drew the attention of readers to the distribution of fresh water on the voyage and the struggle to obtain it, writing,

"Quarrels often break out over the use of fresh water."[50] The passengers in steerage did not receive enough water, and Bloch advised them to insist on getting the amount of water that was due to them. Descriptions of this nature obviously did not appear in the booklet intended for Jewish emigrants put out by Nord-deutscher Lloyd. But what is interesting in Bloch's narrative is not the struggle over the distribution of water but the way in which he explained to Jewish emigrants what fresh water was: "Sea water is salty and unsuitable for drinking, and the ship must therefore obtain supplies of drinking water while still on dry land. This is called fresh water."[51] The very fact of this explanation shows the lack of general knowledge on the part of Jewish migrants. Many of them had never seen seawater and did not know what it was. Crossing the ocean was an emotional experience for them, and in memoirs the journey is often described as a trauma.

Because a large percentage of the passengers were Jews, and in order to fully realize the economic potential of Jewish emigration, shipping companies gradually began to maintain kosher kitchens on the ships and provide kosher food for the passengers. There was sometimes a Jewish worker in the kitchen authorized by a rabbi, and he was the one who dealt with Jewish emigrants during the voyage. On some of the ships that left from the port of Libau there was a full-time monitor of *kashrut* (kosher eating).[52] In 1904, HAPAG began to serve kosher meals.[53] It was followed by Nord-deutscher Lloyd, which kept a kosher kitchen and provided Jewish migrants with kosher food during the voyage. The kitchen in some of the company's ships was under the supervision of the Bremen rabbinate, and it served four meals a day that contained vegetables, milk, grits, rice, soup, meat, and fruit.[54] On the other hand, the ships of the Belgian Red Star Line did not have a kosher kitchen, because "the policy of the company was to give equal treatment to migrants of all nationalities." Those who refused to eat the food provided were given bread, potatoes, and salt herring.[55]

There was a great difference between the literature of guidance put out by the shipping companies and the actual conditions of the sea voyage, so emigrants did not receive all the information needed for sailing. The American immigration authorities were well aware of the conditions of the sea voyage, and from the second half of the nineteenth century the U.S. Congress began to pass a series of laws to oblige shipping companies to provide passengers with more humane conditions onboard ship. The aim of the laws was to protect immigrants from the arbitrariness of the shipping companies during the long voyage from Europe to America. The laws restricted the number of immigrants allowed to board the ship, and the shipping companies were also obliged to provide passengers with decent food and reasonable living conditions.

The increase in the stream of immigration to the United States beginning in the second half of the nineteenth century, and the transition from sailing ships to steamships, led to additional legislation to supervise shipping companies and enforce the law. As the heads of shipping companies wanted to profit as much as possible from each voyage, they did not adhere to the laws and thus harmed the rights of passengers. The U.S. government therefore sent agents posing as immigrants to travel from Europe to America and examine the conditions of the voyage. One of these clandestine agents was Anna Herkner, who sailed from Bremen to the United States and reported on conditions onboard ship. Herkner's report and reports of the JCA information bureau enable us to perceive the difficulties of the voyage and the attempts of immigrants—both Jewish and non-Jewish—to confront them.[56]

According to Bloch's account, when immigrants came on deck, they were separated into three groups: women, women with children, and men. The ship's crew also separated—through temporary partitions—the Jews from other groups of immigrants because the needs and requirements of the Jewish immigrants were different from those of the non-Jewish immigrants. The sailing conditions were not easy for anyone on board. The beds on the ship were made of iron and were only 1.80 meters long (by comparison, the average height of an emigrant was 1.60 meters [or 5′2″]), and on each one was a straw mattress. The ship was crowded, insufficiently ventilated, suffocating, and ill-smelling.[57] There was no room on the ship for hand luggage, and passengers therefore placed their possessions on the beds. There was great overcrowding, and the swayings of the ship caused the luggage to fall down and scatter in all directions. The ship had wooden floors, which were only occasionally cleaned from the dirt and infection they had accumulated from previous sailings.

Passengers in third class had only two washrooms at their disposal. The area of the washroom was 7' × 9', and passengers could use ten taps with cold seawater for washing. As only ten passengers at a time could wash themselves, and two washrooms were not enough for 1,500 passengers, the separation of men and women was not observed, and the attempt to wash during the sea voyage was on a basis of "first come, first served." Conditions in the lavatories were much worse: Anna Herkner reported that there were only six lavatories for women and five for men. About 1,500 men and women had to use eleven lavatories that were cleaned only once a day in the evening. Needless to say, the lavatories were dirty for most of the day. The smell seeped into the immigrants' living-quarters and made it difficult to be there.[58]

In order to escape the crowdedness and stench in the belly of the ship, many passengers passed their time on deck, where one could breathe clean air, take exercise, and enjoy the infinite horizons of the ocean. But in storms and bad weather the passengers were forbidden to remain on deck.[59] The lives of passengers huddled in steerage were hell during the lurching of the ship during storms. The seasickness to which most of the passengers were prone caused nausea and vomiting, and it is not difficult to imagine the scene in the belly of the vessel when a storm tossed the ship up and down.

Meals were not a pleasant experience either. In the ship's dining room, seven tables with a bench on either side were at the disposal of passengers. As the tables could not accommodate all of them at once, they had to eat in turns. Food was placed in large pots in the center of the tables without any serving utensils, and the migrants had to fend for themselves as soon as they heard the bell, which was rung at the start of the meal. When they heard it, there was a great commotion and they all fell on their food. Anna Herkner wrote in her report:

> If the steerage passengers act like cattle at meals, it is undoubtedly be-
> cause they are treated as such. The stewards complain that they crowd
> like swine, but unless each passenger seizes his pail when the bell rings
> announcing the meal and hurries for his share, he is very likely to be
> left without food. . . . When I went for my breakfast, it was no longer
> being served. The steward asked why I hadn't come sooner, saying
> "The bell rang at 5 minutes to 7, and now it is 20 after." I suggested
> that twenty-five minutes wasn't a long time for serving 160 people,

and also explained the real reason for my tardiness. He then said that under the circumstances I could still have some bread. However, he warned me not to use that excuse again.[60]

The gulf between first-class and steerage passengers as described in Herkner's report accentuates the difference between emigrants who were seeking a new way of life and those for whom the voyage was more like a pleasure cruise.

The experience of sailing to Palestine was not different from that of sailing to America. Although the distance from the port of Odessa to Jaffa was shorter than that from Hamburg or Bremen to New York, immigrants to Palestine also sailed in steamships in similar conditions. And because of the many stops on the way, the voyage had a similar duration: eleven to twelve days.

The main shipping companies the immigrants could use were the Austrian Lloyd company, which ran the Trieste-Alexandria-Jaffa line, and the Russian shipping company, which ran the Odessa-Beirut-Jaffa line. The ship that sailed from Trieste left every Sunday at 1:00 P.M., and on Monday at 4:00 P.M. it made the first stop at Gravosa. From there it sailed on Tuesday to Brindisi, arriving at 11:00 A.M. on the same day. From there it sailed to Alexandria, arriving on Friday at 3:30 P.M. In Alexandria the immigrants had to wait for three days to change ships. On Monday at 5:00 P.M. they left on the new ship for Port Said, reaching it at 7:00 A.M. on Tuesday. At 7:00 P.M. on the same day the ship left Port Said for Jaffa, arriving at 7:00 A.M. on Thursday. The voyage, including the long stopover in Alexandria and the change of ships, lasted eleven days.[61]

The immigrants who sailed from Odessa took a different route. The ship left every Wednesday at 4:00 P.M. for Constantinople, arriving on Friday at 7:00 A.M. There was a stopover in Constantinople until Saturday at 4:00 P.M., and during that time the immigrants tried to obtain the *tazkra*, for without it they would have to pay a fine at the port of Jaffa. From Constantinople the ship sailed to Izmir, arriving on Monday at 5:00 P.M., and from there sailed on to Beirut, arriving on Saturday at 3:00 P.M. There was a stopover at Beirut until 10:00 A.M.on Sunday, when the ship sailed to Haifa, arriving at 3:00 P.M. the same day. In Haifa the passengers waited until the ship was loaded, and then sailed on to Jaffa, which they reached at 5:00 A.M.on Monday, the following day. From Jaffa the ship continued on its way to Port Said and Alexandria.[62] The duration of the voyage to Jaffa was twelve days, including stopovers, without a change of ship. The voyage from Odessa was easier and more comfortable for the emigrants, or at least their families, who must have come with belongings but did not have to take them from ship to ship but instead unloaded them directly at the port of Jaffa.

The companies that took travelers to Palestine had an economic interest in attracting a large number of migrants moving to the east, including Jews traveling to Palestine. In 1910 the Russian shipping company consequently began to realize the economic potential of Jews immigrating to Palestine and started to make its ships kosher. For this purpose, the company set aside three rooms, "a room for cooking, a room for preparing food and a dining and prayer room. The supervisor of *kashrut* and the kitchen was rabbi Abraham Chernivsky who was certified to teach by our greatest sages."[63] A year later, the Austrian Lloyd shipping company also began to serve kosher food to Jewish passengers on its ships to Jaffa and back:

> It is written in one of the advertisements that "the ships of the Austrian Lloyd sailing from Trieste to Jaffa and back" are preparing preserved foods in Frankfurt-on-Main under the supervision of the rabbi *gaon*, our teacher (may he have a long life, amen), and will provide a new copper kettle on every ship for the sole purpose of heating these preserved foods which will gladden the hearts of these people.[64]

The trials and tribulations of the travelers did not end when they boarded the ship. The conditions of the sea voyage were difficult and sometimes quite inhuman. Most of the passengers were unused to sea travel and in a short time suffered from seasickness: "I never liked the sea," wrote one of them, "and the sea took its revenge on me, as if to show me that we do not control it, but it rules over us. I was laid out for two days and couldn't move. The waves hurled the ship hither and thither with cruel lashings. . . . Groans were heard on every side from the passengers who were not used to this and who all fell prey to seasickness."[65] According to the notes of B. Spielberg, an emigration official at the Odessa information office, most of the emigrants traveled in the third class without food, and water was only available from a single tap on the deck of the ship. The provisions the emigrants brought with them were insufficient; the food spoiled in the course of the sea voyage and so the travelers suffered terrible hunger.

A few of the passengers slept on the deck of the ship during the voyage and suffered from the cold and bad weather. "That night, the cold woke me up several times," wrote one of the passengers. "It was dreadful to be awake at night with everyone around me sleeping and the engine roaring. . . . My eyes were full of sleep and I was shaking with the cold. I wanted to go, but because of the strong swaying of the ship I fell on the railing. The dark horizon rose up and the sea looked like a bowl of water in a trembling hand."[66] Conditions were hard, and the vomiting in the dirty, crowded cabins was very difficult for the passengers, who had to endure this situation for nearly two weeks. This is how Haya Rotberg described the sea voyage in her memoirs:

> I got on the ship. I "got organized" together with all the Jews who entered the steerage. One person lay next to another in congestion and filth. In the morning I went up from the steerage. The passengers crowded around a tap to get some hot water. I saw a ladder next to the side of the ship and I climbed it. Before me was the deck, empty and washed clean. In its center were white rescue craft, and all around, the endless expanses of the sea merged with the blue of the sky.[67]

David Smilansky, one of the founders of Tel Aviv, had a similar experience. He arrived in Palestine in March 1906, and entered the country as a partner in the Atid (Future) Company, which set up factories for the production of oils for soap, and was later a partner in Leon Stein's factory in Jaffa. After Tel Aviv was founded, he became one of the communal workers of the city. This is what he wrote:

> The ship swayed; the passengers felt quite good. Only a few of them suffered from sea-sickness. When we left Odessa, the weather was chilly and it was snowing. We wore winter clothes and we didn't take them off until we got to Constantinople. They didn't use to light stoves in the third class of the ships. The passengers down below very quickly caught cold and fell sick en route. They were always exposed to cold and humidity and wallowed in dirt and uncleanliness. The people who ran the ship paid no attention to such small matters and

regarded third-class passengers as almost beneath consideration. . . .
Next to the coal-burning steam boilers there were some places for
third-class passengers. Only the lucky ones could get these places, and
even then after a scramble. Of course, one couldn't speak of comfort
in these corners. At one moment you were enveloped in heat from the
boilers and the next moment you were assailed by drafts from all sides
and you were caught between frost and heat.[68]

The greatest dangers lay in wait for the travelers at the intermediate stops. As soon as they stepped ashore, the stunned migrants were
set upon by porters, hotel representatives, crooks, middlemen, and
other dubious characters. The bewildered immigrants, who did not
always have their wits about them, often made the wrong decisions
under these pressures and fell victim to acts of deception. One of the
commonest methods of exploiting the travelers was employed when
they were taken in a rowboat from the ship to the port of Constantinople. The owner of the rowboat generally fixed a certain price for
the journey to the harbor, but after the passengers had left the ship,
"the owner of the boat took them out to sea, insistently demanded a
sum he had decided on, and would not budge from the place until his
demand was met. And all this was done in broad daylight in the open
sea. The captain of the ship and his officers did not care about the
fate of the passengers."[69] The unfortunate passengers had no one to
complain to or relate what had happened, and moreover they had no
knowledge of the local language and so were at a complete loss:

> There were cases where the owners of the rowboats came to an agree-
> ment on the ship to take the travelers from the ship to the be-Hadera
> coast for the price of ten kopeks per person, and once at sea they took
> by force forty francs for a single family. And without knowing the lan-
> guage of the country and being ignorant of French, they could obvi-
> ously not complain about this to anyone.[70]

The solution recommended to the travelers was to remain on the deck
of the ship and to stock up on food and drink from hawkers selling
their provisions, and as far as possible to avoid going on shore.

The stopover at Alexandria was the most problematic of all, because
of the long wait (three days) before travelers could board the ship to
take them to Jaffa. There was no information bureau in the city, and

the travelers often felt bewildered and helpless in the face of the noise and confusion that surrounded them:

> When someone gets off the ship, the Arabs and hotel-owners surround him [sic], and they all cry, here at [my place] is the cheapest accommodation, and when [the traveler] goes there, they demand a completely different price. Sometimes they delay his departure so that he will stop an extra day and the hotel-owner will earn a little more.[71]

The Jewish community in Alexandria, which saw what was happening, wrote to Ruppin, asking him to do something about it. "From the day I came here," wrote Abraham Yitzhak Neustein, a Hebrew teacher in Alexandria, "I have heard that nearly all visitors, and especially the Jews, complain of the disorder. They are surprised that there is no information bureau here."[72] Ruppin turned to the Jewish hotel proprietors in Egypt, asking them to "find a trustworthy man whom the Jews coming and going via Egypt can turn to in matters of emigration and immigration, traveling and accommodation," but he was not able to set up an official, organized bureau like that in Palestine.[73] The Odessa information bureau, on the other hand, did set up bureaus, but only on routes taken by the emigrants from Odessa. As these routes did not pass through Alexandria, the city remained without a bureau.

The lack of an information bureau in Alexandria was exploited by the hotel proprietors, who sent out representatives to meet the travelers and take them to the hotel (their own, of course), where they remained until their boat left for Port Said and Jaffa. "A man such as you asked for is really needed here, for many of our brethren who pass through here . . . suffer from the go-betweens," a hotel proprietor in Alexandria wrote to Ruppin. As a result, the owner of the Hotel Carmel was given the responsibility of "dealing with everything to do with the migrants coming by ship or railway."[74] It was decided that the representative of a hotel would have an outward sign that identified him, similar to the representatives of the reputable travel agencies waiting at the port for their arrivals:

> This man must have an outward sign, just as the translator of "Cook" or the Hamburg-America Line or other tourist companies have an outward sign. That is to say, he must wear a cap or an overcoat by which everyone will recognize him as "the translator of the Jews." On

the peak of his cap or on the lapel of his official uniform there should be a small decoration . . . for example, a star of David . . . or a cluster of grapes, etc., so that nobody can be taken by another translator. In order that he should also recognize the travelers, it would be a good thing if every traveler would buy the identical sign—a brooch showing the cluster of grapes or the star of David—from the information bureaus in the coastal towns, and when the ship reaches the shore this brooch will be on the right side of his chest on the lapel of his overcoat, and each person will recognize the other immediately.[75]

The First Encounter with Palestine and Culture Shock

For many immigrants, the experience of immigration was the first time they had left the Pale of Settlement. One should remember that for most of them it was also the first time they had left the town or shtetl in which they had lived. The first encounter with the new country was a shock for many of them, leaving them excited, confused, and sometimes at a loss. This feeling was particularly strong in immigrants' first encounter with the United States. When they arrived in New York, it was the first time they had seen a noisy, overwhelming city, with skyscrapers and underground trains traveling at a tremendous speed. The immigrant who had come from a small, remote shtetl in the Pale of Settlement, or even from one of the large towns there, could only be amazed and excited at what he saw.[76]

The immigrants' first encounter with Palestine and the stops on the way was different. They did not see enormous buildings, nor did they have a trip on an underground railway. But their first encounter with the East nonetheless gave them a shock and made a great impression on them, which was reflected in their letters and memoirs. The ships' sailing routes took them to two large cities of the period—Istanbul and Alexandria. The encounter with the smells of the East, the people, and the unfamiliar lifestyles evoked wonder and amazement. One passenger, Yitzhak Ben-Zvi, was enchanted by the new impressions: "The travelers were able to leave the ship for a few hours and to take a close look at the cities of Anatolia and Syria, and observe the customs of these countries and their inhabitants. . . . The strange sounds and the colorful and picturesque costumes and especially the bargaining in the markets." Ben-Zvi realized that he was now in a "new world," different from the one he had known.[77] The Jewish press in the Russian Empire also provided descriptions of Palestine and the Orient. These reports are interesting because they describe the feelings of contemporaries and are not retrospective like later memoirs. This, for example, is how Havvah Shapira described her encounter with the city of Alexandria in the newspaper *Hed Ha-Zman* in 1911:

> We went ashore, and this was a different country, a different atmosphere, and people who were so different and strange. And among the types gathered on the shore, each one pushing and shoving the other, there were all sorts: Arabians, Egyptians, Negroes, Jews, all speaking some peculiar language that did not seem to be rich in vocabulary because the people supplied what was missing with shouts, grimaces and strange sounds. And all these people were rushing, running about and pushing each other, and all was shouts and noise. The European stood there and was surprised . . . at the strange place he had come to, a place where they were unfamiliar with his ways and customs and manners, and where he too was pushed around, and where they paid no attention to him and his astonished reactions. And everything one sees is so interesting, so new, a completely different world.[78]

This colorful description demonstrates the cultural gap that existed between the Eastern and Western consciousness. The account reflects the great difference between the writer's world and the "new" world. The tumult, the shouts, and the pushing and shoving were not interpreted by her as the usual Oriental way of doing things but as a primitivism that served as a cover for a poor and undeveloped language.

The arrival at the port of Jaffa also made a strong impression on the travelers. Before they reached the town and its streets, they had to undergo yet another kind of voyage. Jaffa did not have a port in which ships could dock quietly and safely. Most of the ships dropped anchor about a kilometer from shore. The passengers were then taken onto rowboats, which navigated between the rocks and brought them to the customs house in Jaffa. Sometimes, in bad weather, the passengers had to wait a long time on the ship until calm returned and the rowboats were able to draw up to the ship and collect the passengers. At other times, when it became clear that it was not going to be possible to reach the shore, the ships sailed back to Beirut or Port Said, returning to Jaffa some days later: "It is not unusual for ships which come to Jaffa in wintertime to run into a storm so that they are unable to unload the passengers onto the boats. At such times, the ships move around for some days off the coast of Jaffa or sail to Port Said together with the passengers and then turn back to Jaffa again."[79] Even once the travelers were on the rowboats, their troubles were not over. The journey required great skill and the capacity to maneuver between the rocks that lay between the port and the open sea. Sometimes the boats capsized, together with the passengers and their cargoes: "The sea gets stormier day by day. Yesterday, some boats capsized and the goods they were carrying fell into the water."[80] Sometimes the passengers got soaked to the bone:

> I suffered very much from the sea. The sea was very high and we couldn't leave the ship. The ship waited from 12.00 to 6.00, and at six began to sail to Beirut. But suddenly there was a signal from the shore that the ship should wait a little longer, and now a boat approached and we were very happy and went down into it. When the boat came to the rocks it almost overturned, but in the end we were saved and arrived wet on shore.[81]

The "welcome" the passengers received from the boat owners and stevedores who had to take them to shore was different from the relatively orderly reception of passengers in European ports. The sight of the stevedores and sailors suddenly taking passengers and their belongings down into the rowboats, without asking their permission, gave the immigrants a feeling of confusion:

> When the ship dropped anchor, the sailors appeared without waiting for the bridge to be let down. They leapt quick as monkeys onto the ropes of the ship. They came onto it from all sides, and without asking the passengers seized their belongings and threw them down to the boats tossing on the waves. With their wide trousers, their wild cries, and their terrifying expressions, they were like pirates. The Jewish passengers were stunned and did not know what to do. One of the passengers took hold of his umbrella in order to prevent the Arab from taking his things, but the broad-shouldered Arab stevedore put his hand on his shoulders to quiet him and said to him in Yiddish, "Yafo neyt ganev," which means, "There are no thieves in Jaffa."[82]

In his book *Shanah rishonah* (First Year), Shlomo Tzemach wrote:

> Already before the ship anchored . . . we saw boats and small fishing
> vessels shooting toward us like arrows from all sides. . . . They suddenly
> surrounded us, shrieked, wrestled with us for our bags and suitcases,
> and we went onto the boats overshadowed by their burning eyes and
> the exposure of their white teeth, and they hastened like thieves. . . .
> We were taken in the arms of the sailors who carried us here and there
> and threw us from hand to hand like balls until we were inside the boat
> . . . and a broad-chested, big-faced, big-nosed, and big-mouthed Arab
> rubbed his face against us, enjoying it immensely. . . . The same broad-
> chested Arab took up position in the center like a cantor with his choir
> and began singing, and the eight sailors responded. . . . The staccato
> rhythm of their intonation and the rhythm of the beating of a drum
> blended with the swaying of the bodies and the movement of their
> arms and of the oars. I sat there bewildered and depressed. I had not
> expected this kind of welcome.[83]

The travelers' initial shock—a result of this unexpected experience of
being surrounded and brought down into the boats amid shouting
and turmoil—led to a state of confusion and sometimes caused them
to make wrong decisions under pressure. Sheinkin, the director of the
information office in Jaffa, wanted to warn travelers of what to expect.
He sent a letter to the information office in Odessa in which he asked
the office to explain to travelers what awaited them at the port:

> You must also tell the passengers not to be impatient, not to be in a
> hurry to get off the ship, and not to be overawed by the shouts and
> cries of the Arab sailors. . . . Teach the travelers to Palestine the im-
> portance of the words "Shwaia, shwaia" [slowly, slowly] and tell them
> that if they say this to the Arabs suddenly appearing on the ship, they
> will calm down a bit and not shout "Yalla! Yalla!" [hurry, hurry]—a
> cry that has something contemptuous about it.[84]

Sheinkin also asked the information office to impress upon travelers
going to Palestine the importance of their external appearance:

> Likewise, ask them to pay attention to order and cleanliness, so that
> the local people will not behave contemptuously toward them . . . and
> tell them that when they get off the ship they should tidy themselves
> up a bit and clean up their clothes and put some order into their bag-

gage so that there will not be rags and packages everywhere and all kinds of tiny parcels. Such precautions bring respect to the visitors and also sometimes reduce expenses.[85]

But more than advice was involved. The Jaffa office asked for a man of their choice to be appointed who would meet passengers on the shore, take care of their luggage, and alleviate as much as possible their initial shock upon arrival. In July 1907, an agreement was made between Resnick, a local hotel keeper, and the committee of the town of Jaffa, whose representatives were the rabbi of Jaffa; Abraham Yitzhak Hacohen Kook; and Dr. Haim Hissin, Sheinkin's deputy at the information office. "We have appointed D. Resnick to take [the travelers] off the boats and bring them ashore at Jaffa, and to bring them with all their belongings, whatever their weight and number, to a place where they will receive further instructions."[86] By means of this agreement, Resnick became the official representative of the Hovevei Zion in Jaffa, was responsible for travelers' safety, and took care that they would not fall into the hands of crooks. The payment Resnick asked for bringing travelers ashore with their baggage was 3 francs per man or woman and 1.5 francs for travelers sailing on a half-price ticket. No payment was made for children who were allowed to travel on the boat for free.[87]

Unfortunately, Resnick himself proved to be a crook who exploited the agreement in order to raise excessive sums of money from immigrants. "Two weeks ago, we heard that the executive committee of the Hovevei Zion negotiated with Mr. Resnick and appointed him to bring down [from the ships] all the Jews coming to Palestine for a three months' stay, at a rate of three francs per person," wrote Hillel Arnov, a hotel keeper in Jaffa and one of Resnick's competitors. "Finally, the thing stopped, and the owners of the boats were also forced to reduce the price to three francs, and I was later surprised to learn that David Resnick, the 'community representative,' took five francs per person."[88] Perhaps the competition between the two hotel proprietors and the struggle for a livelihood led to hostility between them and mutual recriminations. But Sheinkin, in a letter to the Odessa information office, also gave his opinion of Resnick:

> Concerning Resnick, after all the complaints, we did not find him guilty of any great offenses, but he is no saint. He is a hotel-keeper and a man

of the seafront typical of such people of his age, not a Zionist and not an idealist and definitely not one of us. He has undoubtedly tried to make a rouble on the side, and who knows what has gone on between him and the harbor officials or between him and the shipping agent?[89]

✳

The move from the country of origin to the land of choice involved many difficulties that immigrants had to confront. These difficulties, whether bureaucratic or physical, are called "intervening obstacles" in the literature of migration.

The trials experienced by travelers to Palestine—from the time of their departure from the towns of the Pale of Settlement and their arrival in the port, during their sea voyage, and up to their first encounter with the East—were not different from those of their brethren who sailed to America. Both groups attracted dubious characters who tried to defraud them of the little money they possessed. Sometimes the acts of swindling and deception that immigrants to Palestine encountered were more cunning than those directed at immigrants to America. The trickery was often masked with a veneer of Zionist ideology and rhetoric about return to the land of Israel. The naïve immigrants never imagined that these fake "Zionists" were exploiting them and taking their money by fraudulent means.

The sea voyage also involved a great deal of suffering, especially for poor migrants without a kopek who traveled by third or fourth class. Hunger, dirt, and cold were inseparable from the sea voyage. The encounter with the East and entry into the port of Jaffa, with porters and sailors yelling and falling on incoming passengers, were also part of the sea voyage from Odessa and Trieste to Palestine. There is no doubt that these conditions tarnished somewhat the romantic aura of the return to the ancestral land after the long exile of almost two thousand years.

Five Adaptation and Acclimatization
in the New Land

This chapter examines the adaptation and acclimatization of immigrants to their new country after they left their ships and passed through customs at the port. The town of Jaffa plays a central role in our account for two reasons. First, Jaffa was an important metropolis for most of the new Yishuv in Palestine. The town was where the peripheral population from the Jewish settlements and the immigrants from Eastern Europe gathered. Tel Aviv, which was founded in 1909, did not yet play a central role in the life of the Yishuv, and before World War I it was no more than a suburb of Jaffa. Second, Jaffa was a major port that absorbed thousands of immigrants. Thus the immigrants' patterns of adaptation and acclimatization in the town can be compared to those in other ports of immigration during the same period.

With this in mind, we shall take a close look at the economic situation of the immigrants. How did they make a living? What were the possibilities of employment? How much did they earn? What were their working conditions, and how many hours a day did they work? What was the price of basic commodities at that period in relation to their wages? What proportion of their wages was set aside for rent? What were the housing conditions in the town? In other words, we shall try to reconstruct the cost of living in Palestine at the beginning of the twentieth century in order to understand the daily difficulties that immigrants encountered.

In order to gain as complete a picture as possible of economic realities, we shall make a comparison between Jaffa and New York—the main city of immigration at that time—and see where it was easier and cheaper for the immigrant to manage as he started out. Estimating the cost of living is not a simple matter, especially in the case of a ten-year period in places geographically distant from each other, when even during that period there were many changes in conditions. Consequently, we shall focus our assessment solely on the years 1907–1910, a time for which we have full information both for Jaffa and New York.

An understanding of the objective difficulties that immigrants experienced will also make possible a better understanding of the ways they adapted to life in the town. How did they grapple with the new reality? How did they deal with the problems they found on their path? When they came to the country, did they have an already-formed "settlement" mentality? And did ideology play a central role in their actions in the new country, or were their actions determined by the harsh reality in which they found themselves? As a consequence, were ideological considerations postponed for a period of economic prosperity and integration into the new country?

The immigration to Palestine not only attracted young pioneers who wanted to work on the land but also poor, ordinary immigrants for whom the country was only a fallback option. These people, who came chiefly because of the push factors that drove them out of their home country rather than the pull factors that drew them to Palestine, tended to settle in Jaffa and hardly left it. As a bustling port, Jaffa was a center of attraction for all sorts of dubious types wanting to provide services to meet the needs of the varied mass of immigrants residing in the town. Just as crooks "accompanied" the immigrants on their way to the new country, so crooks also awaited at the port in hopes of exploiting them.

The First Night in Jaffa

When immigrants reached Jaffa, they looked for somewhere to stay so that they could rest after the long sea voyage, visit the town and the surrounding area, and begin to search for employment and a place to live. The number of hotels greatly increased when the immigrants began to come, and by 1907 there were ten such hotels. "The Ashkenazi immigration to Jaffa created this phenomenon [of the increase in the hotel business]," wrote Zeev Smilansky in 1907. The increase in the number of immigrants arriving in the town—and thus in the need for places to stay—made the hotel business one of the most profitable and successful in Jaffa in the period before World War I. Smilansky observed that before the waves of immigration reached Jaffa, the available hotel rooms "were in small attics and tiny little apartments." When the immigrants arrived, hoteliers realized the economic potential of their business. Thus they expanded and increased the number of rooms, so that "now they are all situated on higher floors and in more spacious apartments."[1]

These hoteliers took advantage of the shock of the immigrants' initial encounter with the port of Jaffa. They "ambushed" the travelers, bringing them to their hotel and making every effort to ensure that they would stay for as long as possible. "Another sore point is the question of lodging places," wrote Haim Ridnik, an immigration official of the Palestine Office at the port of Jaffa, in a report:

> The hoteliers and the people from the boats already on the ship fall
> upon the immigrant with great shouts and cries and, frightened for his
> luggage, he hands himself over to some hotelier. And if one of them
> is obstinate and goes down to the shore, his fate is even worse, for
> they open his belongings in the middle of the street among a crowd
> of people, and he and his family get pushed around . . . and he stands
> there confused, depressed, and full of bitterness.[2]

The struggle over the immigrants led to an abundance of acts of deception and exploitation, which began the moment an immigrant left the ship. "The Jewish middleman has also developed at the expense of this immigration," we read in *Ha-Po'el Ha-Tza'ir*. "An ugly type is coming into being who smells out every hole and crack and seeks out any Jew with a farthing in his pocket."[3] The hotelier Resnick, for example, exploited the concession he received to help the travelers coming down from the ship in order to take them to his cramped and dirty hotel. The services he provided there were second-class and cost three francs a night. For this reason, Sheinkin wanted to separate the concession granted to Resnick from the question of hotel accommodation and to protect the immigrants from being taken to his hotel against their will. In a letter to the information bureau in Odessa, Sheinkin wrote:

> Travelers think that because Resnick is entrusted with taking them
> off the ship, they will also obtain the best and most reliable lodgings.

Thus, many of them come to his cramped hotel, which, like other second-class hotels, is not very distinguished for its cleanliness. Sometimes, rich people arrive there who are willing and able to pay an extra franc a day (four francs instead of three), providing they get a clean and spacious room. And I say once again, Resnick's hotel is no worse than others of the second class, but not everyone has to stay there, and in other words, you [the Odessa information bureau] do not have to recommend it. When they come ashore, they should be able to select the hotel they want.[4]

As in Odessa, the immigrants were sometimes taken to brothels masquerading as hotels. They also sometimes found themselves in hotels that were beyond their means and spent all their money in a few days. In order to lengthen their stay in the hotel, the proprietors were in the habit of "losing" passports and *tazkras*, a loss that forced the immigrants to wait for a few days in the hotel until their affairs were set in order:

They get taken to hotels they cannot afford or to hotels that deliberately exploit the immigrant, or to houses in a street unsuitable for families because there are grown-up girls there suspected of prostitution. And then the hoteliers find ways to take their *tazkras*, and they mislay them, and the documents are lost, and they delay their guests unnecessarily for some days (if they have missed the train or the coach) and use up their money. When the immigrant does finally catch his train, the hotelier buys his ticket for him, giving it to him at the very moment when the train leaves the station, and then he quickly passes the ticket and the note to the hand stretched out of the window but does not have the time to give him the bill and the change.[5]

Menahem Sheinkin and Haim Ridnik, who as part of their job accompanied immigrants from the moment they left the ship to the time they left customs, had very strong views on the hoteliers. "Most of the hoteliers are rabid anti-Zionists who condemn all Zionist institutions and representatives and speak evil of the country, and the immigrant's soul is filled with bitterness and despair," wrote Ridnik.[6] And Sheinkin wrote, "It is no secret that many mean-spirited and corrupt hoteliers are contemptuous of Zionists and make propaganda against what they do, and use every opportunity to poison the minds of visitors with fabricated nonsense."[7]

The solution proposed by Ridnik was to create an immigrants' house: "[T]o rent some building near the port where the immigrant could rest from the strain of the journey and leave his things, without being under pressure to look for lodgings."[8] But Ridnik's idea was not carried out because of budgetary difficulties, and the hoteliers continued to exploit the immigrants.

Immigrants did not expect a reception of this kind when they came to Palestine. The situation was similar to that in other countries of immigration, but the people who chose to go to Palestine perhaps thought that there they would be spared the "speculators, usurers, and moneylenders of every kind" who set about exploiting them the moment they got off the ship.[9] It was perhaps precisely because of their high expectations of the country, which were different from those of travelers to America, that these immigrants fell prey to the crooks more easily. Moreover, it should be remembered that Jaffa was first and foremost a port town that subsisted on immigrants and visitors. The hoteliers were primarily businesspeople and not representatives of the Zionist movement in the country. They understood the financial potential of the new wave of immigration that began to arrive in the country in 1904, and they exploited it to the full. As often happens, immediate financial gain overruled ideological considerations.

Prostitution and the White-Slave Trade

There was also prostitution and white slavery in Palestine at the beginning of the twentieth century. Prostitution is closely connected with the immigration process; it develops in countries with immigrant populations. There are several reasons for the link between prostitution and the presence of an immigrant population. First of all, the immigration process often weakens the solidity of a close family framework, which faces difficulty in continuing as before in the new country. Secondly, the number of men immigrating alone is always higher than the number of women. Many of the men come to a new country in order to make money and then return to their old one or, as in the case of the Jews, in order to send money home and then bring their families to the new country. The ratio of men to women is thus upset, with generally a higher proportion of men than women and thus heavy psychological pressures on male immigrants. Finally, crowded living conditions of immigrants hindered sexual relations between husbands and wives, which led to a search for other sexual outlets.

Palestine was no exception to this phenomenon. As a site of immigration it attracted crooks, pimps, and traders in white slavery who found Jaffa to be fertile soil for their dubious activities. Prostitution, of course, was not a new phenomenon. It existed in Palestine earlier, but immigration brought a new kind of prostitute, those of Ashkenazi origin:

> Prostitution, as we know, is not an alien growth in the East in general and in the Arab world in particular. Ten measures of prostitution were given to the world, and the East took nine! And it is no secret that there is not a single brothel in Syria and Palestine where you will not find a significant number of Jewesses. But our Ashkenazi sisters were not to be found in this muck; they were not to be found there at all, or only once in a blue moon.[10]

Jaffa was the main gate of entry into Palestine. As in all ports—which are visited every month by many ships carrying thousands of sailors far from their homes—there were brothels in Jaffa. Prostitution in the port city flourished in the period of immigration to Palestine, but many writers and editors of newspapers at the time tended not to mention the phenomenon and perhaps even tried to cover it up. Zeev Smilansky, for example, wrote a long article titled "The Jewish Community in Jaffa," which was published in the newspaper *Ha-Omer* in 1907, and did not mention the phenomenon at all. The matter was dropped from the article either due to censorship of an editor or self-censorship of the writer. Whatever the case, in the manuscript of the article in Smilansky's private archive, he spoke clearly about the phenomenon:

> We have to point out, that together with the new waves of Jewish immigration that are washing over Jaffa, a fair amount of dirt and filth has also been swept in. A few have opened taverns in which people sin and get drunk, and we should hide our faces in shame that the new Jews engage in such occupations. And not only that, but licentiousness is spreading among the new Jews. Among the hoteliers there are some who are pimps who provide prostitution for their guests. They often

get their "live merchandise" from the new immigrants, and how dreadful it is that a Jew who has fled from a country of persecution should sell his daughters into shame! Because of these pimps and whores we are disgraced in the eyes of the other inhabitants of the town.[11]

Thus the prostitution trade began to flourish in Jaffa with the arrival of the immigrants. Pimps, who understood the economic potential of this activity, began to set up brothels that served both Jewish and non-Jewish populations as well as crews of the ships that came into the port. The Jewish community found it hard to accept this new "trade."

Arguments put forth against the spread of brothels were based not only on a moral condemnation of the phenomenon but also on a fear of "what people will say"—in other words, of a lowering of the status of Jews in the eyes of Arabs, who unlike Europeans were not tolerant of houses of prostitution:

One of the most depressing sights in this country are the houses of prostitution continually being opened by people whom others to our misfortune call Jews because they have not yet left the Jewish community. This does terrible harm to our country. While in Europe certain things are considered important and the public shows acceptance in matters of vice and prostitution, the Arab with his strange tradition concerning modesty is like an innocent babe in comparison with European attitudes.[12]

Thus, the real fear of these commentators was that Arabs would be unable to distinguish between Jewish prostitutes and ordinary Jewish women, consequently regarding both as immoral. "They regard all the 'Muscovite' women as cheap and promiscuous," and so behave toward them with a "sexual vulgarity that they would never dare to do in the case of Sephardi women and, still less, of German or English Christian women."[13]

The newspaper Hed-Ha'Zman, writing from an Eastern European point of view, said that Jewish prostitution in Palestine was an Eastern European import. It was distinguished by the shamelessness of the behavior of pimps and prostitutes in the town:

Every week, more and more brothels are opened in our country, especially in the coastal city, Jaffa. And if this "business" continues to develop in this way, it is likely that the Jews will become the leaders

in this trade in our country. . . . But already today, our enemies here
are beginning to single us out with regard to this business. They disregard the Arab and Greek backstreets devoted to these "houses" and
point, like European anti-Semites, only at the "houses" belonging to
the Jews. But one must tell the truth: the Jewish prostitution, which
has brought with it European ways, is brazen and flagrant and consequently stands out.[14]

The Arab and Greek women, on the other hand, said the newspaper,
"confine their activities to their rooms, and when they go about in the
market, they are veiled like decent women."[15]

Many complaints about the spread of brothels and the moral degra-
dation it brought to the town were made to Abraham Isaac Ha-cohen
Kook, the rabbi of Jaffa. The petitioners asked the rabbi to root out
the phenomenon, which they felt brought shame to the Jewish community. Among them were some who even placed blame on the rabbi,
claiming that he did not take sufficient interest in matters relating to
the community and that he was "over-spiritual."[16] The rabbi replied
that he knew that "traders in women were becoming increasingly common in our town," and he "had begun several times to make some
attempt to repair [the situation], but I must honestly admit that to
my great regret I had little success."[17] In a port, brothels were a social
necessity. Sailors who spent weeks at sea, immigrants far from their
families, or those who were simply bachelors—all sought relief for their
desires. And where there is a demand, there is always someone who
will supply what is needed. The rabbi of Jaffa was powerless to oppose
this phenomenon.

Those who were able to fight it were the Ottoman authorities, who
sometimes turned a blind eye to the trade and at other times closed
the brothels and expelled prostitutes and their employers from the
town: "The Russian Jews who came to our town to open brothels and
trade in souls have been expelled this week by the authorities. Thanks
are due to the admirable folk who have done this, for it has removed
a great disgrace to our people."[18] Another source claimed that the authorities had closed "brothels, and all the Arab women involved in this
business have been sent away. And we now have to make an effort to
expel the women of our people who do this so that we shall not be an
object of scorn and calumny among our neighbors."[19]

Many of the brothels were opened by Jewish immigrants who had settled in the town. The clients were sailors and local people, and the question remained: Who were the prostitutes? Where did they come from, and how did they get to Jaffa?

These "Ashkenazi" Jewish prostitutes came from Eastern Europe, and they were generally supplied to brothels by white-slave traders who had enticed them by deceitful means. This was the fate of many girls in the Pale of Settlement, but instead of going to the United States or Argentina, the great centers of the white-slave trade at that period, there were some who came to Palestine. The trafficking in Jewish women in Palestine was a stage in the white-slave trading route that began in Odessa, continued in Constantinople, and ended in Alexandria, Port Said, and Jaffa. Sarah Azaryahu relates in her book of memoirs, *Pirkei Ha'im*, that in sailing with her sister, who was ill, from Palestine to Russia, she stopped on the way in Constantinople. On the quayside of the port, she met a young man who presented himself as a guide to the sisters. He offered them his help in purchasing boat tickets to Odessa and in dealing with their passports at the Russian consulate. In their wanderings around the city, the three of them passed a tall building, and the guide burst out, "Here I could have sold you!" Azaryahu relates, "I had an inner shock on hearing the tone in which he said these words, but outwardly I tried to preserve my composure."[20] Bracha Habas, in her biography of David Ben-Gurion, also describes his encounter with white-slave traders who accompanied him on the ship to Palestine. In the course of the journey, the passengers noticed that the white-slave traders were bringing a Jewish girl to Constantinople, held her passport, and did not allow her to mix with the other passengers. Ben-Gurion, together with other passengers, went to the captain and succeeded in preventing her from being taken off the ship at Constantinople, thus rescuing her from the clutches of the white-slave traders.[21] These two examples show how the journey to Palestine was very dangerous for girls. The actual experience was a far cry from the romantic ideal of returning to the land of the forefathers.

Moreover, the traders sometimes realized that if they came to one of the shtetls in the Pale of Settlement and said they wanted to marry a woman and take her to America or Buenos Aires, it would immediately arouse suspicions. This was not the case, however, if they said

they wanted to take their "wife" to Palestine. The pimps assumed that
a girl's family would not suspect that a trade in women was developing
in Palestine and even gaining momentum. Here, the Zionist ideology
was exploited for the purposes of their scheme. A young, handsome
white-slave trader would go to one of the many shtetls in the Pale
of Settlement and begin to court one of the girls in the shtetl. He
would shower her with money and jewels and capture her heart and
that of her parents. After a time, when he was convinced the girl was in
love with him, he proposed marriage and a luxurious life in a country
overseas. If he said he intended to take his fiancée to Argentina or the
United States it would give rise to suspicions and people would begin
to ask questions, but not if he told the girl he intended to go to Palestine. The accepted image of the country was one of piety and asceti-
cism, on the one hand, and pioneering Zionist activity on the other.
By means of Zionist ideology, the youth could persuade the girl to join
him on a "Zionist journey" to Palestine, where she would finally be
sold to one of the houses of prostitution in Jaffa or at one of the stops
on the way—Constantinople, Alexandria, or Port Said. As we read in
the newspaper *Ha-Zman*:

> This trade, if it is allowed to develop, will have a glorious future
> in Palestine. A young trader arrives in a town in Russia or Galicia
> and begins to look for a match among the girls of the place, but he
> puts himself in danger if he dares to tell his "fiancée" or her parents
> that he is about to travel to Argentina or to some large maritime
> city. But this does not apply to Palestine. Palestine is believed in
> the Diaspora to be all piety, asceticism and Judaism. And everyone
> knows that today Palestine is also attractive to the younger genera-
> tion. Who could object to such a journey? In whom would such a
> journey arouse suspicions?[22]

Another operational strategy of the white-slave traders was to target
girls among the immigrants already on their way to Palestine. A pimp
would arrive in Odessa—the principal port of departure for Palestine—
and put up at one of the lodging houses that received travelers sailing
to the country. He usually introduced himself as a farmer from Palestine
with a property in Petah-Tikvah or Rishon-le-Zion, and after gaining
the confidence of the travelers who were interested in hearing about the

country or who simply wanted news of their relatives, he tried to entice one of the girls to come to Palestine with him on his own passport. In this way, he said, she would be saved unnecessary expenses. The unsuspecting girl usually did not see through this "Zionist" pretense and agreed to go along with him. For example, in Zidlitz's lodging house in Odessa (where all the less-well-to-do immigrants to Palestine put up), there was a farmer from Petah-Tikvah who said wonderful things about Palestine and its inhabitants, helped the travelers and gave them advice on what to do on the journey, and casually proposed to take one of the girls on his passport.[23] But "when they got to Palestine, these people learnt that it was all nonsense, and the farmer from Petah-Tikvah" was revealed as an impostor.

In Constantinople too, white-slave traders lay in wait for female immigrants who were traveling alone and who left the ship to make an excursion into the city or get their *tazkra*. The girls who they enticed were sold to brothels. Then, the Russian consul was only able to help these girls if relatives were able to locate them or they succeeded in escaping from their place of imprisonment:

> The Society for the Protection of Women in Odessa received word from the Russian consul in Constantinople that a young woman of twenty-two wanted help in returning to Odessa. Three and a half months ago the young woman was on her way to Jaffa to a female relative who promised to find her work, but when the ship docked at Constantinople, a young man called Rizhnikov enticed her to get off at Constantinople and have a look at the city. There he sold her to a house of prostitution. The Russian consul took an interest in the young woman's situation, and on his orders Rizhnikov and his associate in the white-slave trade, Aharon Rozenkrein, were immediately arrested, and the two "traders" were sent to Odessa where they were brought to justice.[24]

The trade in women in Jaffa was practiced openly, like any other business in the town. "A band of white-slave traders," wrote the newspaper *Ha-Herut*, "which is led by a man from Jaffa, and which to our great shame is composed entirely of Jews, one of whom receives *haluka* [charitable funds sent from Jews abroad], has existed in our town for some time." The pimps rented an apartment near the shore and practiced "their disreputable trade quite openly in the sight of everyone without

any shame." The writer of the article, who signed with the letter "X,"
expressed shock at the indifference and lack of interest shown by the
Yishuv:

> If we continue to take our distance and watch all this coldly and with
> indifference as we have done until now, how will it all end? Where
> is the recently founded organization with the impressive title "The
> Society for the Protection of Women in Jaffa," and why is it sleeping?
> Why is it taking its afternoon nap when it has such enormous oppor-
> tunities for action?[25]

The pimps not only imported women into Palestine but also exported
them overseas:

> But there is an even more depressing fact: there are signs that our
> country is becoming a center for white-slave trading in general. Many
> new faces have appeared in Jaffa (and, to a lesser degree, in Haifa and
> Jerusalem). These people frequent lodging houses and taverns a great
> deal; they are to be found on the seafront and on the ships, and they
> engage in a constant exchange of correspondence with people abroad.
> The more young and handsome ones have begun to match themselves
> up with the poor girls of the country. Last month, there were two oc-
> currences, one an import and the other an export. . . . If we do not
> find a way of immediately eradicating this evil, Palestine will enter into
> competition with the great centers of prostitution in the world and
> become a sort of Buenos Aires. There are two sides to the picture: on
> the one hand Palestine can provide plenty of raw material for other
> countries because of the poverty of its inhabitants, and on the other
> hand these filthy people can find their "booty" abroad more easily if
> they are helped by Palestine.[26]

Like similar groups in Buenos Aires and Manhattan, in Palestine too
there was an organization of white-slave traders, whose innocent-looking
name "Omanim Mehagrim Tzion" (Immigrant Artists of Zion) was a
cover for illicit activities. The head of the organization was S. Lerner,
who due to the color of his hair and fictitious occupation was called the
"blond baker." Lerner placed advertisements in newspapers announcing
the founding of the organization and describing its aims:

> A new organization has been founded in Jaffa: "Omanim Mehagrim
> Tzion." The aim of the organization is to give assistance to poor im-

migrant artists who arrive in Jaffa. The organization contains artists and workers from all branches of society, and anyone who wishes to join the organization and become a member must apply to the head of the organization, S. Lerner. From the apartment of the head of the organization, Neve Shalom, Jaffa.[27]

In reality the organization was not looking for actual members. Instead its purpose was to send poor immigrants to America on tickets at specially reduced prices. These immigrants who turned to the organization for help in leaving the country were told to deposit a sum of money with the organization. In return, close to the time of sailing, they would receive tickets provided by the Russian consul himself. Suspicions against Lerner were aroused by the specially large reductions given to women who bought tickets. "We are afraid," wrote the editor of the newspaper *Ha-Hashkafa*, "that behind this there is some business of trafficking in human beings. The suspicion is all the greater because the price of the tickets is reduced even more for women."[28] The suspicions against Lerner increased when reports came from several towns in Palestine that Lerner and his agents were roaming the country seeking out women and poor immigrants: "And above all, we have a growing suspicion . . . that the agents of the 'blond baker' have gone to the towns and villages of Palestine to catch living people."[29]

The publicity against Lerner in the newspapers forced the crook to leave Jaffa, but before he left, he succeeded in cheating even more immigrants. Upon his sudden disappearance from the town, one of the travelers whose money had been stolen by Lerner published a warning in the newspapers about the doings of the "blond baker" of Jaffa, who was "of average height, with yellow hair and a husky voice," who perhaps "will go to one of the coastal cities and do more things of this kind."[30]

A warning to travelers not to fall victim to people who do you favors but who are not honest. In the last few days there was some trouble in our town, Jaffa, when some new doers-of-favors came on behalf of the "Immigrant Artists of Zion" headed by S. Lerner. He said he would try to send people to America and Russia at half price and took a deposit from all the travelers, and I, too, the undersigned, gave twenty francs on condition that he would give me two tickets to sail to Russia. But every time we asked for the tickets, he said the ship had not come in yet, and on Thursday the 25th of Iyyar he left with the money he had collected from the travelers.[31]

With the spread of this phenomenon in Palestine, the Society for the Protection of Women began to watch what was happening in the country. In May 1911, Frau Bertha Pappenheim visited Palestine. "On the termination of the Sabbath, Frau Pappenheim from Vienna spoke at the Beit Ha-Sefarim about the white-slave traffic. The hall was full. She spoke for about half an hour, and gave a somber description of this shameful traffic."[32]

Bertha Pappenheim (1859–1936) was a feminist social worker of German Jewish origin. She founded the Alliance of Jewish Women, which fought against the white-slave trade. In her lectures and writings, Pappenheim stressed the causal connection between poverty and prostitution, as well as the basic connection between prostitution and the social and religious oppression of women.[33] Her arrival in Palestine and her lecture on the subject are evidence of the growth of the phenomenon in Palestine. Her feminist approach to the white-slave traffic was adopted by labor circles in the country. It is likely that representatives of the newspaper *Ha-Ahdut* were present at her lecture, because a week later an article appeared in the paper titled "The White-Slave Trade in Our Country" that adopted Frau Pappenheim's feminist approach:

> So long as the status of women in the home, in society, and in the work-place is a low one, so long as fathers see their daughters as ne'er-do-wells and deprive them of education and the national spiritual inheritance . . . the Jewish woman in the land of national rebirth will be ensnared by the white-slave traders. . . . Only national schools and a broad and comprehensive moral and social education of girls while they are still young [combined with] massive participation of women in the aspirations of the people, in its social creativity in the present and future, can rescue the Jewish woman and our Jewish society from the white-slave trade.[34]

The white-slave trade in Palestine only came to an end when the trade as a whole came to an end. The closing of the sea routes, new socioeconomic conditions in the country and in the wider world, and immigrants' integration into their new countries finally led to the end of the phenomenon, except in Argentina. But with the renewal of waves of immigration to the State of Israel at the end of the twentieth century, the trade was renewed in all its ugliness and cruelty.

The development of prostitution and white-slave traffic in Palestine shows that this immigration, like the others, was accompanied by dubious and negative types who were part of Eastern European Jewish society at that period. They exploited the period of the great migration and the precarious situation of the immigrants in order to make a profit, and saw the country as a suitable terrain for their business. At the same time, most of the immigrants were neither pioneers nor crooks, but "ordinary" people who left Europe in the hope of finding a better future. They had no special faith in the Zionist ideology but tried to make their way in a complex and difficult reality, fighting hard for survival and incessantly struggling for sources of livelihood.

The Town and the Village

A return to the soil and working on the land were cornerstones of Zionist ideology in general and of the Labor Movement in Palestine in particular. In Palestine, it was believed, Jews could distance themselves from the exilic experience. Thus, a healthy, productive nation would come into being in the Land of Israel country. The Ha-Po'el Ha-Tza'ir Party and its spiritual leader, A. D. Gordon, were very insistent about this. The members of the movement regarded work on the land as the way to national renewal and the creation of a new and healthier life in the country. There was therefore a strong preference for village life and work on the land over town life and commercial activity in the port, thus creating a socioeconomic basis for Jewish life that differed from that in the Pale of Settlement. Joseph Aharonovitch, one of the leaders of Ha-Po'el Ha-Tza'ir, declared that "if there was not a large sector of workers close to nature and the productive materials of nature, such a people would end by degenerating physically and spiritually and would have no right to exist." Aharonovitch said he was even ready to abandon the Zionist enterprise in Palestine "if it was nothing more than a collection of tradesmen, peddlers and middlemen."[35]

This point of view dictated the norm with regard to the kind of immigrants thought to be needed in Palestine, and it created the idea that only immigrants of this kind came to the country. According to an article in the newspaper *Ha-Ahdut*:

> They did not seek satisfaction of their basic needs here; they did not aspire to life in the present. They looked ahead to the end of days and dreamed of the return to Zion; they did not think of creating their own lives but of building the nation. Immigration to the land of Israel had an ideal character and was motivated by idealistic spiritual factors. . . . The immigration was mainly directed to work on the land and only those who knew this work and wanted to devote themselves to it came to the country.[36]

The choice of immigrating to Palestine was seen as part of a change in the values of Jewish society, transforming the exilic Jew who lived in a city or shtetl in Eastern Europe, earning his living by brokerage and *Luftgeschäft* ("air business") into a Jew healthy in body and soul who worked in agriculture in the land of Israel. The standard-bearers of this vision were the *halutzim* (pioneers) of the second aliyah, who saw immigration to the country as an opportunity to shed the sicknesses of exile and create a more just and healthy society. These and similar themes recur in various forms in the rhetoric of the period.

But the reality was different from the one described in *Ha-Ahdut*. Some of those who came to the country did believe in the Zionist vision of working on the land and a few actually put it into practice, but they constituted a very small minority of those who entered Palestine during the period. Thus, not all who settled in the agricultural colonies did so out of idealism and a vision of working on the land. Many of these settlers had failed to find work in the towns, and the colonies were a last resort. "Very often," wrote Zeev Smilansky,

> one can meet professional people and skilled technicians who overseas were well-paid for their work, and who when they get to Palestine choose to go and work in the colonies simply because there is no demand for their labor. One can consequently find among agricultural workers not only weavers, brush-makers, confectioners, etc., whose professions are still unknown in Palestine, but also locksmiths, shoemakers, house-painters, bookbinders etc., for whose work there is a certain demand in the country, but a very limited one.[37]

In a census of workers for the year 1912, Smilansky wrote, it appeared that out of 378 workers employed in the Judean colonies 14 percent had work that differed from what they did in their countries of origin. He also said that these workers had not originally intended to work in the colonies. Thus the work in the colonies was not always ideologically motivated but instead was occasioned by a real existential need to gain a livelihood and survive in the new country, despite the fact that the wages of an agricultural worker "were generally lower than those of an industrial worker in Jaffa or Haifa."[38]

As discussed in chapter 3, most of those who came to Palestine did not settle in the Jewish colonies. Like their counterparts who went to America and settled in the cities, immigrants to Palestine tended to live in the towns. The impressive growth of the Jewish population of Jaffa in the years 1904–1914 supports this assertion: The number of Jews in the town rose from 5,000 in 1905 to about 15,000 on the eve of World War I.[39] There were two main reasons for this growth of population: (1) intercontinental migration and (2) internal migration from some of the settlements in Palestine to Jaffa.

Immigrants to Palestine chose to settle in towns rather than in villages for a number of reasons. First, the great majority of immigrants had lived in towns in the Pale of Settlement, and this tendency continued in Palestine. Second, immigrants had earned their living from trade and various crafts and could not conceive of raising a family solely from work on the land in harder conditions than those they had known in their countries of origin. Finally, the move to a new country was bound up with a complete change in their way of life. Living in a village would have been too drastic a change for these immigrants; they wanted to continue the traditional way of life they were used to in Palestine as well:

> Tel Aviv plays an important part in the growth of the Yishuv: it attracts new people. It makes the change of place, the move from Europe to Asia, easier for them. It makes the country attractive to them, as we know, but there is a catch. Many people see it as their resting-place and choose to settle here rather than to go out to a colony, build a two-storey house and lease it, or rather than to plant an orchard or start a business.[40]

Sources of Livelihood

Zionist historiography generally has not addressed the mass of petty tradesmen and artisans who came to the country during the period from the beginning of the twentieth century until the outbreak of World War I. Most of the books and articles on this period have been concerned with a small, idealistic, pioneering group whose members—whether of the labor movement or engaged in private enterprise—were only a small minority of those who came to Palestine during those years. There can be no doubt that this elite group was a pillar of fire and that its actions were motivated by a highly developed national and historical consciousness. But other people also came to the country in this period, including immigrants of the middle and lower classes who were petty tradesmen, artisans, and providers of services. These workers set up dozens of small workshops and factories. As these people were for years involved in a hard struggle for survival and economic viability, and did not engage much in politics and public affairs, they have been completely overlooked in the historiography of the period. The fact that this population of artisans and tradesmen did not go in for unionization or party affiliation—as the "pioneers" did, for instance—also contributed to its disappearance from collective memory.

In the remainder of this chapter, I shall attempt to examine, against the background of the economic situation in Palestine from the beginning of the century until the outbreak of World War I, the way in which the Eastern European immigrants of the lower and middle classes succeeded in integrating into the Palestinian economic environment. What economic situation did this mass of artisans and petty tradesmen find on arrival in the country? What were the possibilities of employment? Which of the groups had the best chance of finding work in the country? We shall also investigate how immigrants who found work managed in their new country. How much did they earn? How much did they pay for essential commodities and rent? What organizations did they set up to deal with the new reality they found?

From the data in chapter 2, it appears that more than 50 percent of those who turned to Sheinkin's and Ruppin's information bureaus were artisans and tradesmen, but it is difficult to determine how many of them reached Palestine. It is also difficult to gain accurate information on this from previous discussion on the profile of emigrants and the breakdown of those leaving the port of Odessa. We know that many of those who left the port of Odessa were artisans, workers, and agricultural laborers, but their relative proportions are uncertain. We also know that a high proportion of those who left the port of Odessa were tradesmen on various levels, but the distribution of these is also uncertain.

An exact profile of immigrants who arrived in Jaffa in 1905–1907 and in Haifa and Jerusalem in 1907 may be obtained from the data from Sheinkin's information bureau published in the Zionist organization's newspaper *Ha-Olam* in April 1908. The aim of the article, said Sheinkin, was "to give a correct idea of recent Jewish immigration to Palestine" and reveal the extent to which immigrants succeeded—if they did—in striking roots in the country. The information, he said, would show poor immigrants, artisans, and petty tradesmen "who think that a large number of rich people are already coming to the country . . . and that there is therefore a need for the services of lesser people" that it was still too early to come to Palestine. In this way, he said, the hope was to prevent immigrants from being "needlessly disappointed."[41]

The data provided by the information bureau showed that, according to the relation of the number of people to the number of families, only small families—Sheinkin described them as "bachelors and married men with no more than one child"—could settle in Jaffa. Almost all the families with many members "had to leave the town." Because possibilities for employment outside of Jaffa, in the agricultural colonies or in the other towns in Palestine, were even smaller, many people left the country after a short time.

Of the various types of employment, said Sheinkin, "only locksmithy, carpentry, dressmaking and cobbling, and in the liberal professions only teaching, could sustain a reasonable number of families." Those that practiced these professions, especially locksmiths, could find work owing to the industrial enterprises that were beginning to spring up in Jaffa at that time. The first and most important of them was Leon Stein's pioneering metal foundry. The factory manufactured corn-grinding machines, iron railings, iron gates, water pumps, and ice-making machines. There were about 40 workers in the enterprise, rising to 46 in 1906. In 1907, there were already about 125 workers, and in 1909 there were about 150.[42] By the standards of the Yishuv, this was a huge factory that supported many families. Its closure in 1910 as a result of losses brought about "a terrible crisis in Jaffa so that dozens of families left the country."[43] In Jaffa, there was also the Kadima workshop for metal frames, which employed dozens of workers and manufactured water pumps, iron beds, chairs, ovens, ice containers, and English locks.[44] Stein and Kadima provided employment for immigrants who had just arrived in the country and had suitable training. People in other professions, such as dentists, midwives, hairdressers, bookbinders, bakers, coopers, butchers, innkeepers, café proprietors, and ordinary laborers, had difficulty in finding work in the town.

An interesting fact published by Sheinkin's information bureau was how many tradesmen and shopkeepers came to Jaffa relative to other occupations. The large number suggests that there had been great hopes in the country of origin of finding a livelihood in trade and shopkeeping in Palestine. But retrospectively, the small number who found work there shows that these hopes were exaggerated and unrealistic. Trade in Palestine at that time was almost entirely in the hands of Muslims and Christians. The immigrants had to compete with them, and moreover they had to learn the language and familiarize themselves with the trade and currency laws prevailing in the country. Zeev Smilansky, in his article "Al dvar ha-aliyah ha-ivrit le-eretz-israel" (On the Hebrew Immigration to the Land of Israel) in the newspaper *Ha-Yom* in 1906, described the difficulties of tradesmen in finding work in Palestine as compared with the difficulties of artisans:

> We must also take note of this: that a large section of our people in
> Eastern Europe engage in trade and act as middlemen, and thus the
> latter are very prominent among the immigrants. And thus it appears
> that while craftsmen and people who can provide for themselves and
> so on can find a livelihood as soon as they arrive in the country, so
> that it sometimes seems that artisans who only yesterday came off the
> ship, are already working the next day as paid assistants, even with-
> out knowing the Arabic language . . . our brethren who in the lands
> of exile were dealers, middlemen and luftmenschen, do not find a
> place of work immediately. They must get used to the weights and
> measures accepted in the country and familiarize themselves with the

complicated values of the different currencies used here, and gain
a little knowledge of the local language, and all this takes time and
understanding.[45]

The founding of Tel Aviv in 1909 provided employment opportunities that did not exist previously. "When they came to build Tel Aviv,"
wrote Sheinkin, "and we knew there would be work for hundreds of
builders, we made this known far and wide."[46] At the same time, the
upsurge in building was not sufficient, and the replies of Sheinkin and
Ruppin in the years 1912–1914 still showed that about 60 percent of
the applications to the bureau were answered negatively, 20 percent
received a positive reply on certain conditions, and 20 percent received
a positive reply without conditions. The newspaper *Ha-Zman* in the
year 1914 made an appeal to immigrants on the lines of the immigration policies of Sheinkin and Ruppin, dissuading them from a mass
immigration to Palestine:

> The situation of the poor who have recently come to Palestine in
> such numbers is worse. The others only lost a few hundred roubles
> on the expenses of the journey, and when they return to the lands of
> exile they will still have a substantial sum to start up a business. But
> the poor who come here destitute and don't have anything, and who
> will have great difficulty in finding work, and whose wages will only
> be enough for a very meager life, and some of whom won't even find
> work, are doomed to a very bitter fate. . . . However, among the im-
> migrants of this kind there have also been a few artisans, and nearly
> all of them have found work, but if a few more artisans come, there
> will not possibly be enough work for all of them, and the artisans who
> have come so far have nearly all come without means, and as they can't
> work on their own account, they have to be employed by the local
> artisans, and they exploit this influx of craftsmen to give them a low
> wage and also lower the wages of the local assistants.[47]

The picture that emerges from the data from Sheinkin's information bureau in the years 1905–1907 and from the information bureau in
Odessa in the years 1908–1914 largely reflects the economic situation in
Palestine at that period. Trade was mainly in the hands of the local
population who knew how to take advantage of the new opportunities that had arisen in local and international commerce, which made it
difficult for the Eastern European tradesmen and shopkeepers to find

a place in the existing market.[48] In trade, wrote Sheinkin, summing up
the year 1908,

> there has not been any progress on the part of the Jews in general
> and the immigrants in particular. Most of the trade is in the hands
> of the Muslims and Christians. Those Jews who in the last ten
> years have expanded their businesses significantly have remained static
> and have not moved forward. None of the new visitors [the immi-
> grants] have founded a major enterprise.[49]

In industry, on the other hand, there was real progress, as Arabs
with capital did not invest much in this area but instead invested mainly
in the purchase of agricultural land worked by leaseholders or in construction of buildings for rent in the cities.[50] The vacuum was filled by
Jewish entrepreneurs such as Leon Stein, Shmuel Pavzner, and Nahum
Wilbushevitz, who set up the Hadid oil factory in Beit Arif, a concern that was amalgamated after a time with the Atid-Kadima company
and other small enterprises. Industry made possible the absorption of
many artisans. At the same time, the success of industry was somewhat
restricted by the lack of an infrastructure, and most of the factories
closed after a few years after incurring heavy debts. "There is no longer
room for large-scale industry in Palestine in places where there is none,
or where materials for industry have not been found," wrote the newspaper *Ha-Po'el Ha-Tza'ir*, after the closure of the Atid factory. The
absence of customs duties, fierce unregulated competition that drove
down prices to the point of loss, and rough roads that made transpor-
tation of goods difficult were factors that hindered the development of
industry in the country:

> It is also very difficult for small-scale industry, which serves local needs.
> Not having the protection of high customs duties, Palestine is a market
> for all the world's industries. This market receives the simplest goods,
> and the competition between the various countries is so great that
> the goods are sometimes sold more cheaply here than in the country
> where they are made. And it is difficult for local production to with-
> stand this competition. . . . The lack of properly maintained roads in
> the country sometimes prevents goods from reaching their destination
> on time and harms commercial relations. These also suffer from the
> lack of commercial laws and the impossibility of trusting the chief pur-
> chaser—the fellah and the rural tradesman.[51]

The chief problems, however, were a lack of capital and difficulty in obtaining credit, which is so necessary to the success of a business in its early stages. Most of those who came to the country were immigrants of the lower and middle classes, people without means or with very limited means who found it difficult to support themselves and sometimes became a burden on various institutions. "Recently," wrote Sheinkin to the Odessa Committee, "despite the rapid change for the better in the political and economic situation in Palestine, well-to-do people have stopped coming, and only a number of young people and poor people come on each ship. . . . This lowers our value in the eyes of the people of the country [who look upon us] with scorn and derision and no longer respect us at all."[52] People with capital, respectable businessmen who acted with prudence and avoided investing in the country for fear of financial loss, came to Palestine, looked around, and returned to their country of origin. "There have been men of means who came to Palestine," wrote Sheinkin, "and saw things with their own eyes, and were made good offers in settlement or other businesses—things unlikely to make a loss and likely to make a good profit—but who nevertheless 'went home' just as they came." Until some capital was brought into the country, he continued, the future of the Yishuv would be in doubt, and "if they won't begin to invest considerable sums in Palestine and if a certain number of new settlers won't begin to come, our situation here will be endangered both from within and without. We can expect a total end, a natural death from exhaustion."[53] At the same time, despite Sheinkin's pessimistic view of the future of the Yishuv, it must be pointed out that in the period of the second aliyah the economy began to grow, largely due to Zionist settlement. The Zionist movement led to the entry of private capital into the country, a tendency that only increased in the last decade of the Ottoman period.[54]

Old Professions in a New Environment

The settlement of artisans in towns gradually led to the creation of an economic infrastructure, which began to provide places of employment. In 1905, for instance, a cork-manufacturing factory was opened in Jaffa. The business was launched by two brothers who brought machines and implements for the manufacture of corks "as good as the corks of good quality in Europe" from the Pale of Settlement. This factory employed four workers who received a salary of 2 bishlik a day although they were not trained for that work.[55] In that same year, a candy-making factory was opened. The founder of the factory was a Jew from Gomel, who together with his wife had been the overseers of a similar factory there. When they arrived in Jaffa, they thought they had a good chance of succeeding, "and in their first year they began a business on a small scale, but because of a shortage of cash they were unable to purchase the machines and implements needed for this factory." After a year, they went into partnership with another man who arrived in Palestine in 1906, and with his help they expanded the business. The factory employed two salaried workers and produced "sweets of a better kind than there had been before, and the merchandise was as good as that from abroad, and was accepted by the shopkeepers of Jaffa."[56]

Thus not only were small factories founded but also dozens of small workshops were established that employed assistants and apprentices. Thus, in 1906–1907, a workshop for carpets was founded as well as a workshop for furniture and wooden toys that, according to Sheinkin, "for a small sum of money and simple work employs dozens of people, most of whom did not know any trade." A cooperative carpentry shop came into being, along with a workshop for making barrels; a shoemaker who employed nearly twenty people who made shoes "of the best kind"; the Kadima workshop for frames that produced iron bedsteads, stoves, ice containers and English locks; a workshop for cigarette cases; and workshops for "optical things and gold and silversmith's work."[57] Barbershops were also opened. "A few years ago there was not a single Jewish barber in Jaffa, and only two years ago [in 1905] an Ashkenazi barber came from Russia and opened a barber's shop, and in a short time a fair number followed." There was stiff competition between the barbers, and as a result some of them closed. Smilansky said that those that remained earned between 80 and 100 francs a month.[58]

Artisans were in a better position than tradesmen. An artisan could bring his tools with him from abroad and could easily open a workshop. Tradesmen, on the other hand, needed capital for startup, credit, and a knowledge of languages—requirements that made things difficult for them. Thus Sheinkin reported on the work of his information bureau in the year 1907:

> In trade there has not been any progress in recent years, especially as far as the new immigrants are concerned. Large-scale business is in the hands of the Christians and Muslims: none of the arrivals has begun to do business on a large scale. Generally speaking, no branch of trade in Palestine is run on European lines. They are run here by tricksters and despicable types who would disgust a European. Due to lack of capital and experience, the newcomers have been unable to compete with the Christians and the local Jews, and only two or three of the new immigrants earn their living in this way.[59]

The wave of immigration to Palestine led to the creation of sources of livelihood dependent on immigrants, such as hotels, restaurants, and other such establishments. "There has been a growing need for hotels in the last two years, after Jewish immigration has increased, and in particular, there has been an increasing number of Jewish workers from the colonies who visit the town frequently," wrote Smilansky. Before the large wave of immigration in 1905, there were three restaurants in Jaffa, but "in the two last years their number has increased, and in the summer of 1905 there were six eating-places, and there is another café belonging to two Ashkenazis who are partners, and this the first café for Ashkenazis." And, as mentioned, there was also a need for hotels in Jaffa:

> This phenomenon is due to the Ashkenazi immigration to Jaffa. . . . All Jewish hotel-proprietors are making money; nearly all the Jewish hotel-proprietors that now exist started some years ago. All of them previously had small rooms and small, cramped apartments, and now they have larger rooms and more spacious apartments. . . . The Jewish hotel-proprietors not only make money from the Jewish immigrants coming from abroad, but also from the Palestinian Jews, who often come to Jaffa on business, and especially those from the colonies who often visit the town for various purposes, and in summer many of our brethren come in from the towns and colonies to bathe in the sea. . . . Among the extra sources of income of the owners of the Jewish lodging-houses may be included taking people off the ship, transporting belongings from the customs-house, etc. This source of income used to be in the hands of middlemen who dealt with the ships; now the hotel-proprietors also do these tasks.[60]

Working Conditions and the First Strikes

The working conditions of artisans were better in Palestine than in America or in the Pale of Settlement. Although some lived in poverty and their home served as a workshop, the hours of work in Jaffa were generally shorter and the artisan ended his workday relatively early. Smilansky wrote that Jaffa had "one very commendable feature, and that is that working-hours corresponded roughly to the hours usual in most European countries." Workshops closed at sunset and did not open "before the eighth hour":

> Apart from a few factories and the shops in Jewish neighborhoods open 11–13 hours a day, the other workshops and stores are not open more than nine to ten hours a day. And when one deducts the lunch-hour, one sees that in practice all the workers in workshops and stores work seven to eight hours a day. It seems that the number of working-hours they are still fighting for in all the European countries are already usual in ours.[61]

Likewise, in the colonies, the workers did not work more than eight to eight-and-a-half hours a day, and sometimes even less.[62] This relatively short workday was characteristic of the Middle Eastern way of life, in which "the sons of the East, who like rest, tend not to be busy in the evening after sunset."[63] Because the immigrants became an inseparable part of the local population and the Middle Eastern scene, they blended into it, adopting its way of life, and after their working hours they too would "go into the cafés and sit at ease and enjoy sipping coffee and smoking a *nargileh* [hookah]."[64] In England, according to Smilansky, artisans' working conditions were much worse:

> In the small workshops, which are eighty percent of the workshops for stitching clothes, the places are crowded with occupants and workers, the hygienic conditions are very bad, and the working-hours are at least thirteen to fourteen hours a day. . . . Jewish immigrants have recently worked a great deal in the production of the simplest kinds of shoes. . . . Those who do this work fifteen to eighteen hours a day, and newcomers often work twenty hours a day.[65]

The working conditions of salaried workers in local industry in Jaffa were worse than those of self-employed artisans and of the agricultural workers in the colonies. Their working hours were twelve hours and more, and the discipline was strict:

> In that workshop there were ten to twelve workers. There were twelve working-hours, of which half an hour was given for breakfast, an hour was given for lunch, and the rest were given to work. The times of work are not fixed, and they change according to the boss's fancy. Sometimes it is from six in the morning to six in the evening and sometimes from six thirty to six thirty.[66]

The break for meals was generally only half an hour and was deducted from the workers' wages. Conditions were also hard in Stein's metal factory. In summer, they worked from six in the morning to six in the evening and in winter from seven in the morning to seven in the evening, including a half-hour break for breakfast and an hour for lunch. On busy days workers sometimes had to work for eighteen hours. Discipline was strict, and workers had to sign a pledge to fulfill all the demands of their employers:

> Article 4. All workers, without exception, must accept the discipline of their superiors and supervisors, must respect them and follow their orders with the utmost exactitude in all matters pertaining to their work and the factory, and any worker who will not accept the demands of discipline will be punished or dismissed if he misbehaves or if he returns to his evil ways.[67]

The bad conditions, strict discipline, and low wages—as compared to those of artisans' assistants, for example—caused bitterness and led to the creation of local bodies that organized strikes for the improvement of working conditions and higher wages. In H. Altman's oil factory, for instance, the workers resigned in protest against the fact that they were expected to

> work fifteen hours a day at a stretch, apart from half an hour for lunch. They worked fourteen hours a day for a salary of 2.5 francs, but the owner of the factory thought that these hours of work were insufficient and wanted to add more. That is how a miniature "sweating system" developed amongst us.[68]

The "sweating system" was common in the American garment industry. The workshop was owned by a contractor, who entered into a contract with an industrialist to stitch together garments after the pieces of material had been cut. The pieces were transferred in bundles from the industrialist to the contractor, who gave them to the tailors. The contractor provided the tailors with everything necessary for the work—sewing machines, irons, ironing boards, and other items. The accepted method of payment in the workshops was based on the sum of money a worker received for the amount of work he or she did in a day. The work was conducted at great speed and demanded much effort and dexterity from the tailors. These workers were exploited, as they were made to work long hours without suitable compensation. For immigrants who had just come to America, this was an ideal solution that spared them the language difficulties and necessity of bargaining in the new country. Though the conditions were difficult, the system enabled them to earn a living quickly without any initial expenses on their arrival in the United States.[69]

The accepted system in Palestine was not the "sweating system" but work on a daily basis in a factory, and the owner of the factory was responsible for the functioning of the factory and its workers. It would seem that the use of the term "sweating system" did not really correspond to the reality. The physical conditions and hours of work of immigrants working in industries in the United States at that time were also worse than those of industrial workers in Palestine. The immigrants to the United States generally ate and slept in the room in which they worked, and there was no separation between the "workshop" and the living quarters. Conditions were also harsh in most factories, and workshops were situated "in dark shops in rickety buildings; climbing up four, five and six flights of wooden stairs; cases full of dust and rat dirt; working under gas light from seven o'clock in the morning till six in the evening."[70] The hours of work varied in accordance with the need of the industries and cycles of booms and depressions. In times of depression the hours of work in the clothing trade were about six or seven hours a day, and in boom years they were sixteen or even nineteen hours a day.[71] Strikes in the local workshops and industries reduced working hours to twelve to fifteen hours a day, and in later years to eight to ten hours a day.

Strikes for improved working conditions and for a reduction in hours of work were also declared in Jaffa—in Altman's oil-factory mentioned previously, for instance. A strike was also called in the carpentry workshop in Jaffa. In this workshop there were about ten to twelve workers who worked twelve hours a day—sometimes from six in the morning until six in the evening, and sometimes from six-thirty in the morning to six-thirty in the evening. These irregular working hours, and especially the time that work ended—6:30 P.M.—created a situation where the workers stopped work after nightfall and had no time for rest and recreation. They asked the owner to stop work at six o'clock so that "they would have the opportunity to take in some air after a day of work."[72] The workshop owner's refusal of their request led to a thirteen-day strike, at the end of which the two sides agreed to appeal to the Va'ad ha-Shalom law court to mediate the situation. The workers asked for work to end at six in the evening, for the strike organizers not to be dismissed, and for the workshop owner to pay them compensation for lost workdays. The owner of the workshop, for his part, asked to be allowed to fix the hours of work himself, to be able to dismiss the two workers who began the strike, and to make the workers reimburse the financial losses caused by the strike out of their own pockets. The law court ruled that

> the workers must return to their work from six-thirty in the morning to six in the evening without taking a half-hour break for breakfast, and if they keep to these times exactly for two weeks, they will be able to begin to work together with having breakfast. The owner of the workshop is not allowed to dismiss the initiators of the strike. Neither side can make any monetary demands of the other.[73]

The immigrants' geographical distance from their old homes created stimuli that did not exist in the Pale of Settlement or in America. The non-Jewish businesses closed relatively early, and so the time that remained till sundown could be spent in cafés, in bathing in the sea, or in nightly walks along the shore. This form of recreation was unknown to most of the immigrants, and those who had lived close to the sea in the past had been unable to bathe in it because of the climate. This, however, was not the case in Jaffa. The pleasant climate and the Mediterranean mentality, so different from the European mindset, led immigrants to the conclusion that they too wanted to spend part of the day in recreation, whether in cafés or bathing in the sea. And in fact, much of the population of Jaffa—both Jewish and non-Jewish—went to bathe in the sea after a day's work, and there is no doubt that this had a great influence on the lifestyle of the immigrants and their leisure culture:

> Sea-bathing in Jaffa is a naked spectacle under the skies . . . and in the evening hours the Arabs flock to the seashore from all parts of the town to look at the Jewish girls bathing in the sea half naked. Every year the rabbi protests at this profanation . . . but the world does as it pleases. The Arab girls only bathe at night, with greater modesty.[74]

There were some who immediately understood the economic potential of this flocking to the sea after the hours of work and the potential for a flourishing business. They created bathing beaches and set up kiosks to sell drinks and bathing-costumes:

> Something new: this year, our brothers who came here from Russia set up wooden structures along the seashore for bathers. Each structure has a large forecourt and four small rooms. In these structures, all kinds of drinks are for sale, and also bathing-costumes. The price for bathing is one tenth [of a monetary unit] for one bathe in the large forecourt, and two tenth in the small forecourt. Notes are also printed, in each one of which there are thirty tenth. With this note, each person can bathe thirty times, and the price of the note is two *bishliks* [1.10 francs].[75]

The concentration of most of the immigrants in the town, and the fact that some of them earned their living from crafts, trade, and small-scale industry, led to fierce competition between practitioners of the various occupations and a worsening of working conditions. The workers protested against these deteriorating conditions. To this must be added the effects of the local leisure culture and the connection with the sea, which for many immigrants was an experience they had not known in the conditions of the Pale of Settlement. It is not surprising that the workers insisted that their working hours should not extend beyond six in the evening so that they could enjoy the last half-hour of daylight after their tiring day's work in the Jaffa workshop.

Living Conditions

The living conditions of immigrants in Jaffa were better than those in the Pale of Settlement or in the city of New York. In Jaffa, immigrants lived in relatively decent and well-lit apartments. They did not suffer from the problems experienced by their brethren who remained in the Pale of Settlement or who had traveled to New York. Smilansky said about a one-room apartment:

> An apartment costing 80–100 francs does not generally have more than one room, but it often has a balcony where one can eat most days of the year. . . . Among the poor families in our town, there are some who live all the year round in booths made of wooden boards and temporary structures where the wind comes through in the rainy season . . . but in a warm place like Palestine where for three-quarters of the year it is sunny and warm outside, and where even in winter, except for a few weeks during the rains, one does not feel cold, one can live in booths. . . . We should note one pleasant fact, and that is that in Jaffa no family lives in a cellar, or in a room half sunk into the ground.[76]

Because in Jaffa there were no apartments in cellars or rooms "half sunk into the ground," the rooms were better lit and ventilated than in the Pale of Settlement and New York. Smilansky wrote that the apartments in Jaffa were spacious, with high ceilings:

> The hot climate is largely responsible for the last feature, for on hot nights it is hard to breathe in an apartment with a low ceiling. For that reason, it seems that in most houses in Jaffa they add above the window, the height of which is generally 1.60 to 2 meters, other small circular or semicircular windows of a height of sixty centimeters to a meter. The local people especially build many apartments of this kind in order to reduce the heat and increase the amount of air in the apartments as much as possible.[77]

In the Jewish neighborhood in Bialistok, on the other hand, wrote Smilansky, "only in the turner's apartment are there 6.30 cubic meters of air per person, which is less than the normal amount, and among the other apartments there are none with even half the normal amount of air a person needs in order to breathe."[78] Jacob Lestschinsky gave a similar description of a one-room apartment in the Kiev region in the same year:

> The air is polluted by the dust and is stifling for the people in the room. The sun's rays do not penetrate and shine on the workers,

warm them and refresh them. . . . There are no wooden floors in the house, and there is a great deal of dust. On the eastern side, there are no windows because the house is joined to the next one, which is under the same roof. And there are no windows on the southern side either because it faces the valley which is always full of excrement. Only on the western side is there a single low window to light up the room. Seven people live in this room and breathe its stifling air.[79]

In the United States, specifically in New York, the tenements and living conditions of Jewish immigrants were not much better than in the Pale of Settlement. They lived in tenements built on the "dumb-bell" plan designed by the architect James E. Ware in 1879. Buildings of this kind were constructed in the years 1879–1901. They had a space for ventilation in the center, and the back of the apartments flanked this central space. This space was supposed to provide light and air to the rooms at the back, but in practice it gave out noise and smells, and if a fire broke out the space acted as a flue that endangered the lives of the occupants.[80] This space also served as a refuse dump and was therefore infested with rats, insects, and fleas. There were a very large number of buildings without light, ventilation, hot water, baths, or toilets. Out of 1,558 rooms, 441 (27.7%) were totally dark, and no air penetrated from outside. These difficult living conditions did not escape the notice of the New York municipality, which in 1901 published regulations obliging the building owners to place a window in every room, put lighting in the corridors, replace the public toilets with private ones, and repair the fire escapes, but the owners were slow to comply, and conditions hardly improved.[81] This is how Charles Bernheimer described the crowded living conditions of Jewish immigrants in New York in 1905:

In New York the immigrant Jew is principally a dweller in the tenement house. Although scattered all over the city, a large proportion of Russian Jews live on the East Side, South of Fourteenth street and east of the Bowery; principally in the Seventh, Tenth, Eleventh and Thirteenth wards. These wards enjoy the evil distinction of being the most densely populated spots in the United States, and probably on the earth. The Tenth ward has over 700 persons to the acre, the Thirteenth about 600.[82]

Rent was the biggest expense for an immigrant who arrived in Palestine with his family. Unlike unmarried immigrants, who did not find it difficult to look after themselves, someone caring for a family found it more complicated and expensive, especially in view of the considerations that guided him in finding suitable living-conditions for his family—the necessary basis for adaptation to the new country.

In 1907, a long article was published in the journal *Ha-Omer* on the Jewish community in Jaffa in the year 1905. The article was written by Zeev Smilansky, who immigrated to the country in 1891 and returned to Russia ten years later after a bout of malaria. He returned to Palestine in 1904, settled in Jaffa, and ran a kindergarten. Smilansky was one of the founders of the Ha-Po'el Ha-Tza'ir Party and also an editor of the party newspaper.[83] In 1905 he carried out a private census of the population in Jaffa, attaching great importance to obtaining accurate information. "As long as the figures will guide me, the 'subjective author,'" he wrote, "and every time events and items come up that contradict the author's ideas, if he is honest, he will not disregard them but will admit that this particular case contradicts his argument." Smilansky then described his methods of research. He said that questionnaires were distributed "to every family and every family member, taking care to go from house to house and from family to family and make it clear to everyone that there was no danger involved in the census."[84]

The scale of the immigration to Palestine that began to gain momentum in 1904, and the tendency of immigrants to settle in the towns, led to a significant increase in rents. "In general, one can say," wrote Smilansky, "that rents for apartments have increased, due to the rise in Jewish immigration, by a quarter or a third more than in previous years, especially in those parts of the town most populated by Jews."[85] The financial resources that immigrants to Palestine brought with them permitted them to live in an apartment with one room or two rooms at the most. Out of 1,059 Jewish families living in Jaffa, 56 percent lived in a one-room apartment and 59 percent in a two-room apartment. The remaining 15 percent lived in apartments of three rooms or more. According to table 5.1, the rent for a one-room apartment was $17 a year, and for a two-room apartment it was from $19 to $45 a year. A comparison of the rent in several countries at that period shows that, in this respect, Jaffa was the cheapest.

TABLE 5.1

Yearly rents in Jaffa compared with other countries of immigration.

Country	One-room apartment	Two-room apartment
United States	$47.50 [$969]*	$95 [$1,938]
Britain	$38 [$775]	$66.50 [$1,357]
France	$37 [$755]	$45.50 [$928]
Germany	$23 [$469]	$38 [$775]
Belgium	$19 [$387]	$38 [$775]
Jaffa	$17 [$285]	$29 [$961]

* The present value in dollars is given in square brackets.
SOURCE: Z. Smilansky, "Yehudei Yafo le-or ha-misparim al ha-dirot" (The Jews in Jaffa in Light of Numbers on the Apartments), Labor Archives, IV-104-95, file 8.

A comparison between the data provided by Smilansky and that provided by the information bureau in Saint Petersburg, as published in the booklets of guidance for immigrants to America, shows that Smilansky's data was very accurate. The rent for a one-room apartment, for example, was $48 a year, which according to rates of exchange at the time was equivalent to 96 roubles or 252 francs. The rent for a two-room apartment was between $60 and $95 a year, a sum equivalent to 120–192 roubles or 315–505 francs.[86]

Despite the rise in rents in Jaffa, which was due, as we said, to the waves of immigration to Palestine, they were still much lower than in other countries. But a comparison between rents in various countries cannot teach us anything if we do not know the proportional relationship between rents and income:

> Although [rents] have increased in Jaffa recently, they are nevertheless not high in relation to rents in the cities of Europe, and when we calculate the percentage of income spent on rent with that in other countries, it is even more evident that the cost of rent is smaller in Jaffa than in other places. A family has to spend much less on rent in Jaffa than it would in other places, and in particular in highly-populated cities.[87]

If one compares the percentage of income paid on rent by Jews in the Pale of Settlement and by Jews in Jaffa, it appears that Jaffa was "outstanding for its inexpensive, good-quality apartments." At the same time, the great difficulty for a tenant was that he had to pay the whole year's rent in advance. Immigrants had trouble in finding the initial payment:

> One other thing distinguishes the apartments in Jaffa. The owner of the place rents out the apartment or the shops for a year at a time and not for a month, and the rent for the apartment or shop must generally be paid in advance all at once for the whole year. . . . For the people in the apartments it is most disagreeable that they have to pay at the beginning of the year all the money that they could have easily paid little by little in regular installments, but for the renters of the apartments it is a very advantageous condition, because they receive all the rent early and all at once and they do not have to worry about continually asking the tenants for payment.[88]

Professional Associations as *Landsmanschaften*

Immigration to a new country was necessarily a difficult and troubling experience for an immigrant who was cut off from his familiar surroundings and came to a new environment. He had to familiarize himself with a new language and a completely different reality from that of his country of origin. The break with the family and the country of origin, and the first encounter with the new country, gave rise to confusion and perplexity and, above all, fears that the decision to come to the country had been a mistake. To overcome this initial shock, immigrants tended naturally and spontaneously to live next to one another and to set up voluntary mutual aid organizations, with the common bond among members their shared origin in the city or shtetl of their birth. These were the *landsmanschaften* organizations.

The great wave of immigration to America brought about the establishment of hundreds of such organizations. In the city of New York, for example, there were 3,000 *landsmanschaften* with 200,000 members.[89] The *landsmanschaften* had various aims, but its chief purpose was to provide an immigrant with protection and security in his unfamiliar new environment along with a warm social framework where he could find information, psychological and social support, and sometimes a source of livelihood.

The two main institutions of these organizations were the synagogue and the cemetery. The synagogue was not only a place of prayer, where immigrants congregated during the week and on Sabbath eves and festivals, but also a place where various decisions were made with regard to the aims and functions of the *landsmanschaften* and where immigrants could alleviate their loneliness and longings for home. The cemetery was also important. One of the first acts of these organizations was to buy a plot of land for their members, who spent most of their lives in the new country in the company of strangers and wished to spend eternity among their Jewish brethren.[90] Another function of the *landsmanschaften* was to send money to the families who had remained behind in the old country to help them face the difficult situation there. The immigrants felt a great responsibility for the families or the women of their town who had remained behind. The *landsmanschaften* was not limited to a socioeconomic function, however. The immigrants would attend these groups and nostalgically recall their old homeland, meet immigrants who had just arrived, and pump the new arrivals for information, thus preserving their ethno-cultural identity.

In Palestine at the beginning of the twentieth century there were no *landsmanschaften* in the accepted sense of organizations set up on the basis of towns of origin. The chief reasons for the founding of the *landsmanschaften* in America were the large numbers of immigrants who came to America and their tendency to congregate in the cities. As against this, scarcely 35,000 people came to Palestine, and many of them returned to their countries of origin after a short stay. For this reason, there was not a suitable demographic basis in Palestine for setting up such organizations. Immigrants who remained in the country found it difficult to come together, even if they wanted to, on the common basis of their town of origin. Moreover, the *landsmanschaften* were founded in consequence of a particular situation in which the immigrants were frightened of strangers and insecurity. There were fewer causes of alienation in Palestine than in America. The immigrants came to the Yishuv, whose institutions provided, or at least tried to provide, for all their needs, so there was no necessity to set up local organizations that would look after the immigrants' requirements. The Yishuv provided immigrants to Palestine with every-thing that immigrants received from the *landsmanschaften* in America. In practice, the entire Yishuv served as a *landsmanschaften*. If, for example, the *landsmanschaften* in America undertook to find work for its members, in Palestine there were two information bureaus that looked after immigrants and tried to find them work. In Jaffa there were two soup kitchens that fed poor and hungry immigrants, and there was also a committee that helped poor immigrants to find money to return to their country of origin, as it was decided that "the best way of helping those who have no hope or possibility of settling in Jaffa is to send them back to their homelands or to disperse them within the country."[91] In Jaffa there was a school of crafts for poor children. They learnt Torah and Gemara there, but also crafts like locksmith's work and carpentry. Unlike in America, there was someone in Palestine to receive the immigrants on arrival and soften the blow of their first encounter with the country. The activities of the various institutions, both of the old Yishuv and the new one, created a situation where immigrants did not feel the lack of these organizations, and so there was no need to set them up. Cases like that of the burial of a Jew in a Greek cemetery or of a sick immigrant unable to make a living did not exist in Palestine.[92] The mutual support of the various institutions in the Yishuv was greater than in America and did much to alleviate immigrants' distress.

But in addition to the small number of immigrants who came to Palestine as compared to the United States, and in addition to the institutions in the country that helped immigrants in one way or another, the expectations of immigrants also contributed to the absence of *landsmanschaften*. Immigrants had expectations that national institutions— especially Sheinkin's information bureau and, some time later, the Palestine Office headed by Ruppin—would help them in absorption, finding work, and so on. These expectations of immigrants in Palestine were infinitely greater than similar expectations of immigrants to America. Already when immigrants started out on their journey to Palestine, various institutions were at work subsidizing their boat tickets and helping immigrants to obtain the proper documents. But this was not the case with those who went to America. Their boat tickets were not subsidized and, at most, immigrants enjoyed reductions due to competition between the shipping companies. When they reached Palestine, immigrants expected the Jewish institutions—both Zionist and non-Zionist—to help in their absorption just as they helped them to come to the country:

> In addition to all this, it seems that whereas the immigrant coming to another country knows that he has to rely on his own resources, in Palestine the immigrants expect the national societies and institutions to look after them and help to prepare them for life in the country, and when the immigrant does not get the support or assistance he expected, he comes with complaints. . . . He thinks the societies are obligated to look after him, and if not, he gets angry and blames the institutions for not preparing a feast for his arrival.[93]

Although no *landsmanschaften* of the New York type existed in Palestine, various organizations were founded in the country that catered to needs similar to those provided for by the *landsmanschaften* in the United States. In the Old Yishuv, for example, the *kollel* (an institute for *study* of the *Talmud* and *rabbinic literature*) served as a *landsmanschaften* for all intents and purposes. Membership of a *kollel* was on the basis of one's country of origin, and it gave protection and economic and psychological support to its members. One's place of residence in the country was largely determined according to the distribution of the members of the Old Yishuv in Palestine. The people of the Hasidic sect *Habad* from White Russia, for example, made Hebron their permanent base. Hasidim from other areas found the towns of Galilee to be suitable places to establish their social and economic bases in the country.[94]

Among the new arrivals in the country at the beginning of the twentieth century there were also organizations that gave the immigrants psychological and material support. The difficulties of daily life gave rise to local organizations in the form of professional associations, membership of which was not determined by a common town of origin but by a common occupation. The reason for this was that in Palestine it was easier to gather seventy people who did the same work under the same roof than seventy people who came from the same town. These associations provided the immigrants with an intimate setting, a touch

of warmth, someone who would listen to them, and moral and financial assistance. They gave them a sense of security and of belonging to
the new and unfamiliar environment. Although the idea of the Yishuv
alleviated their distress to some extent, for many this was an abstract
concept with which it was hard to identify.

The professional associations the immigrants set up in Palestine and the mutual assistance in the professional and moral spheres
were modeled on their experience in Eastern Europe. There, Jewish
artisans would form professional associations for the purpose of pro-
tecting their members from the fierce competition of non-Jewish associations and from various government decrees and also to give
members moral and economic support. The idea of professional associations originated in the synagogues of poor artisans called *kabtsansk*.
Although the artisans were religious people, they had a definite class-
consciousness that developed in the synagogue, long before socialistic
ideas began to be disseminated in the Pale of Settlement. The synagogue was their main meeting place; it was there that they exchanged
ideas on Sabbath eves and festivals on how to confront difficulties
and help one another. Many houses of learning and *kloyzim* (places
of Torah study) were given the names *shneiderische* (tailors), *katsvische*
(butchers), *stallers* (carpenters), *bakkers* (bakers), and so on.[95] The associations and societies that arose in the shtetls of Eastern Europe were
mainly based on social assistance and mutual aid among the members.
Their activities included aiding the hungry, clothing the poor, providing loans, aiding sick artisans unable to provide for their families, setting up funds for widows and orphans, and caring for the education of
poor children in need. The associations' principal sources of income,
which financed their members' social activities, were the taxes that the
members paid at intervals, legacies, and fines imposed on them for
infractions. If after all the necessary financial expenses there was still
money in the kitty, it was generally devoted to the upkeep and repair of
the synagogue where the members prayed. The mutual assistance was
not only confined to the material sphere: Many associations were too
poor to help their members in need. In such cases, the assistance mainly
took a spiritual form. If one of the members fell ill, the others would
pray for him and read psalms on his behalf. The professional associa-

tions that arose in Palestine in the early twentieth century were similar in their aims to the professional associations in the Pale of Settlement.

The difficulties of life in Palestine in general and in Jaffa in particular gave rise to local organizations, such as professional associations, for the purpose of helping immigrants to cope with the harsh conditions in the country. Zalman David Levontin, the first director of the Anglo-Palestine Bank, said that thirty-four professional associations were founded in the years 1904–1910. Although most of these were organizations of farmers and vinegrowers of the period of the first aliyah, there were also organizations of artisans like the Malve association, founded in Jaffa in 1905, which comprised 172 tradesmen and artists of various kinds; the Kadima association founded in Haifa in 1908, which had 118 members; and the Yarkon association founded by workers and artists in 1909, which had twenty-two members.[96]

The *Agudat Ha-Tzayarim ve-ha-Tzovim be Yerushala'im* (Jerusalem Painters and Housepainters Association) was founded on the 28th of Tishri, 1912, in Jerusalem. Its aim, as described in its regulations, was "to improve the material and spiritual situation of painters and housepainters in Jerusalem and outside." The members of the association undertook to pay a membership fee every two months, and the association undertook to create a special kitty for "assistance in exceptional cases like a prolonged illness, etc., and assistance in times when no work is available, and so on."[97]

Another association whose aims were similar to those described in the preceding section was the *Agudat ha-pekidim* (Clerks' Association), which also sought "to improve the economic and spiritual situation and public standing" of its members.[98] The locksmiths also established associations of their own. "Two months ago," wrote the newspaper *Ha-Po'el Ha-Tza'ir*, "a professional association of locksmiths was founded in Jaffa, and on the 21st of Sivan it had its first general meeting." The aim of the association was to improve the material and spiritual situation of workers and locksmiths. The association accepted "only workers who worked on their own account and did not employ workers or assistants. Every person joining the association must pay an entrance fee of one franc and a membership fee of four tenths a month."[99] The printshop workers in Jerusalem invited all workers, "whether they are members of the association or whether they are not yet members, to come to the general meeting which shall take place on one of the intermediate days of Succot. The subject of the meeting: how and in what way to improve the material situation of printshop workers."[100] It was not only the "pioneers" who had an organizational consciousness and practiced mutual aid.

One of the professional associations that arose in Palestine and one of the few that survived World War I was the *Merkaz Ba'alei Melakha* (Artisans' Center). The artisans, like members of the other associations, brought their ideas and their forms of organization from their former place of residence and from the cultural environment in which they were reared:

> They [the founders of the center] who had been familiar, when abroad, with self-organization and with professional groups, who knew the usefulness and necessity of such groups, and who decided to remain in this country and make their lives here, could not by any means accept the miserable condition of the artisans and the way they were treated. A handful of enthusiastic young people came together at that time and decided to take on the task of uniting the artisans and creating a professional association on the lines of associations of this kind abroad.[101]

Like the artisans' "societies" in Eastern Europe, which met mainly in the synagogue, the artisans in Jaffa wished to create for themselves a synagogue that would be not only a place of prayer but also a meeting place for members: "One of the most important spiritual needs of the Jewish population is the need for a synagogue, where it spends a great deal of time. . . . The founders of the center understood this, and saw the necessity of building a special synagogue for the center which would be both a meeting-place for members and a house of prayer, and on which the whole spiritual life of the member would be centered."[102]

The aim of the Artisans' Center as described in its regulations was "to improve the material and spiritual situation of artisans through mutual assistance." The means by which this aim was accomplished was through the creation of a cooperative lending bank and cooperative shops and warehouses, raising the value and quality of work by improving the technical proficiency of members, forming a professional library, providing evening classes, and setting up a court of arbitration. When immigrant artisans came to Jaffa, the center absorbed many members, and on the eve of World War I they numbered about 150 people.[103]

The professional associations that were founded were an Eastern European "importation" that immigrants brought with them to Palestine. These groups were not *landsmanschaften* in the sense of expressing nostalgia for the country of origin or serving as a means of sending money to relatives abroad, but they provided immigrants with material and moral support and facilitated their absorption into the country. The associations had no party affiliation, and their members did not have a concrete ideal of the Yishuv that they sought to put into practice. With regard to this, it is interesting to note the place ideology assumed among the associations and their members. Among the ordinary immigrants, the Zionist ideology became part of their outlook at a later stage of their lives in the country. The ideological outlook generally only developed when material conditions improved in two ways: if immigrants established themselves economically, which enabled them to be open to other things than making a living and surviving; or if the interests of ideology and making a living coincided.

The story of the Artisans' Center provides an excellent illustration of the dialectical relationship between the labor parties. which stood for *avoda ivrit* (Jewish labor), and the Artisans' Center, which supported the Jewish labor struggle only when it clearly served the economic interests for which it was founded. The Artisans' Center was founded primarily as a result of the hard economic situation of artisans and their difficulty in making a living; Zionist ideology did not play an important part in its establishment. "We look upon this period as the period before the history of the Center," said Ruppin in a lecture:

> We don't want to overlook the negative aspects of the Center at that period, such as its attitude to the language question and so on, and it is not surprising if the commercial spirit sometimes prevailed over the basic idea of the founders of the Center. This was due to the proliferation of new members that came into the Center and who were generally far from any idealistic aspiration, and only material considerations influenced them to become members.[104]

The staff of the *Ha-Po'el Ha-Tza'ir* newspaper expressed dismay that the Artisans' Center did not adopt a position on the struggle for revival of the Hebrew language in the country. They wouldn't take part in the struggle, they said. Not only that, but they put on plays for their members in Yiddish!:

> The last attempt to put on a play in Yiddish took place four years ago. After that time, even the circles that put on these plays (such as the Artisans' Center and the like) came to the realization that to put on a play in Yiddish at a time when all efforts are directed to implanting the Hebrew language in all spheres of life is a criminal offence.[105]

Not all members of the center had a Zionist outlook. Many were "far from any idealistic aspiration, and were only influenced by material considerations." A rapprochement between this "materialism" and the Zionist ideology only took place when a collaboration began between the ideological elements in the Yishuv—that is, the labor parties, which stood for the struggle for Jewish labor—and the members of the center, who came to understand that this struggle served the interests of the members of the center above all. The members of the center knew that the success of the struggle would mean that the Arab artisan would be replaced by a Jewish one, a member of the center. This was the start of the relationship between the center and the labor parties, especially Ha-Po'el Ha-Tzavir, which helped the center to overcome the limitations of its conservative outlook:

> The influence of the labor organization and their organs, and especially "Ha-Po'el Ha-Tza'ir," and their constant struggle against the rot in the life of this country, and their call for healthy national labor, was also felt among the workers of the Center and helped it to overcome the narrowness of its naturally conservative outlook and enabled it to absorb Zionist ideas and aspirations. *Little by little*, the Center changed from being a purely professional organization to an organization with national aims and responsibilities, and as a result, the attitude of the Center on economic questions changed.[106]

The change in the Artisans' Center led to the inauguration of evening classes in the sciences and in the Hebrew language:

> They arranged popular lectures on Zionist subjects and set up libraries of professional subjects and economics, and it was nice to see old people coming after a day's work to take part in the lessons and the lectures . . . and a decision was made by "*Hovat Ha-Shekel*" that every

member of the Center would automatically be an official member of the Zionist Organization.[107]

At the beginning of the twentieth century there were groups in the Yishuv that were not motivated by the Zionist idea. Even if the idea had great influence in immigrants, the difficulties of initial absorption into the country were so great that their thoughts were centered on the struggle for survival, and ideology was set aside. The various professional associations that were founded in this period were the product of a hard economic situation that made the artisans among the new immigrants come to the conclusion that the way to overcome difficulties was to set up trade organizations similar in aim to those they had known in Eastern Europe.

The case of the Artisans' Center clearly demonstrates the meeting point between the aims of the center, which were chiefly economic, and the Zionist ideology that guided the labor parties that led the national struggle in nearly all areas in the country. It was the "conquest of labor" that linked the center to the Ha-Po'el Ha-Tza'ir Party. In the first stage, the connection between them, at least on the part of the Artisans' Center, was purely economic, without any ideological justification. The idea of "Jewish labor" strengthened Jewish artisans economically and gave them preference over Arab artisans. In the second stage, there was an ideological connection, and the center, which had been a purely professional association, became an entity with ideological objectives and a sense of national responsibility.

The private enterprise that developed in Palestine in those years not only came from capitalists within and outside of the country, who began to establish an industrial infrastructure. Neither did stock companies that purchased land and sold it at a profit, like the Geula or Neta'im companies, have exclusive domination over private enterprise. There was also the different kind of private enterprise consisting of dozens of small businesses of various kinds launched by new immigrants, artisans, and petty tradesmen. Many of them failed, but there were also some who succeeded.

One of the only leaders in the Zionist movement and in the Yishuv to recognize the importance of this group was Menahem Sheinkin, who made every effort to recognize it. With Sheinkin's premature death in a motor accident in Chicago in 1924, there was no longer any leader in the Yishuv who valued the group's contribution. In his article "Ha-po'alim u-ba'alei ha-melakha ba-aliyah" (Artisans and Workers on Aliyah), Sheinkin spoke about this:

> Where Jewish immigration to Palestine is concerned, it is wrong to identify Zionism with the labor movement or with class warfare. From the point of view of Aliyah, it is definitely a sin to give preference to the party-affiliated Jewish worker and leave the Jewish artisan who is truly productive and economically well set-up in the shade.[108]

The main purpose of aliyah, said Sheinkin, was to bring as many Jews as possible into the country. And therefore, "and especially from this point of view, Jewish artisans, particularly those with families, should be given first place in Aliyah." Bringing this group of people into the country was important on both moral-ideological and economic levels. On the first level, "the normal Jewish artisan in his middle years," wrote Sheinkin, "has his Jewish soul intact. . . . The simple family of the working artisan is the natural material for the Jewish qualities of the Jewish folksongs and legends, and that is what passes them on to the next generation. . . . From this healthy root, the new natural Jewish non-Jewishness will spring up soonest."[109] On the economic level, Sheinkin saw the artisan as "the most suitable and strongest of the immigrants." By his work, he said, he makes a significant contribution to the development of the country, and "ensures that not many different finished products will come into the country from abroad, and so diminishes the drain of capital out of the country."[110] Since according to Sheinkin the artisans' contribution to the Yishuv was so crucial, he could not understand why Zionist literature and promotional material ignored them as if they did not exist:

> Is the ordinary Jewish artisan with a family not a real "pioneer"? Does his decision to move to Palestine and his actual immigration demand less courage and national spirit than those of the young pioneers who are given preference? This approach does not correspond to the reality. A young unmarried man only has to decide for himself. He is not responsible for anyone else. He decides to go to Palestine, and he goes there immediately in the company of friends and comrades, and, lo and behold! He's a much-praised and loved "pioneer"

and he's sure of getting help on the way. When he arrives in the country, he is received in a ready-made organized group with a cadre which fixes him up with work and suitable psychological conditions. But a man with a family has to work hard to convince his wife and children of the need to go to Palestine, and he bears the responsibility for their material and spiritual requirements. On the way there he is generally on his own, without the welcoming cultural atmosphere: he's just an ordinary immigrant. It's harder for him to obtain the passport and visas, and his expenses are also greater. If a child falls ill on the way or something is lost from the "load" he is carrying, he is made to suffer by his family which brings him back home. And when he finally arrives in Palestine, he is once again alone, without any friends to help him. . . . Is his capacity for self-sacrifice not worthy of the title "pioneer"?[111]

Sheinkin, as we said, was alone in his attitude to the immigrants who were not known as "pioneers." His friends in the Zionist leadership saw work on the land as the main thing. They and their successors were lavish in their praise of the idealistic minority, and by accident or design they ignored or forgot the work of the majority.

Six Leaving Palestine

The return of immigrants to their countries of origin is an insepa-rable part of the immigration process. In every wave of immigration there is a counterstream, and in this respect Palestine was similar to other countries of destination for immigrants.[1] In every such country of destination where there are immigrants, there will be some who, for various reasons, will choose to return to their former homeland or, alternatively, move on to other destinations. Just as there were im-migrants who came to Palestine at the beginning of the twentieth cen-tury and left, so there were immigrants to the United States in the same period who tried their luck but then returned to their countries of origin. The difference in these patterns for immigrants to Palestine compared to the United States lies not in the phenomenon itself but rather in the volume of those who left and their motives.

This chapter discusses those who left Palestine at the beginning of the twentieth century. Here I will describe a further stage, expe-rienced by at least some of the immigrants, in the immigration pro-cess. This phase included sending letters to immigration bureaus, a period of hesitating about where to go to and when to leave, and fi-nally reaching a decision about staying or leaving. Unlike immigrants who found work and began a new life, those who left had once more to take up the wanderer's staff and begin the migratory process all over again.

Leaving Palestine was a sad end of the complex, difficult, and dan-gerous journey of people who left their countries of origin and mi-grated to Palestine, despite all the obstacles, in the hope and belief that they would find there the solution to their distress. This chapter will deal with four questions in particular: How many people left Palestine? Where did they go? Who were they? And why did they leave?

An examination of these questions can not only contribute to the matter under consideration but will also inform us about the drawing power of Palestine as a country of immigration and the possibilities of absorption there. Thus we will have a better idea of the role of Zionist ideology in the via dolorosa of the immigrant to Palestine from his arrival in the country, through his pains of absorption, and finally leaving the country just as he came.

The Scale of Departure

The historian Yehoshua Kaniel was one of the first scholars to try and ascertain the scale of departure from the country in the late nineteenth century and the early twentieth century.[2] In his article "Meimadei ha-yerida min ha-aretz be-tekufat ha-aliya ha-rishona ve-ha-sheniya" (Jewish Emigration from Palestine during the Period of the First and Second Aliyot [1882–1914]), Kaniel points out the methodological difficulty of arriving at exact numbers. He claims that the existing data are generally scattered and sometimes arbitrary, because there are hardly any comprehensive annual accounts. He also explains that the data we have on the scale of departure are generally taken from reports made in times of crisis, when the whole Yishuv was in a state of despair. These reports tend to exaggeration and fear for the fate of the Yishuv on the assumption that by exaggerating one could alert the Zionist institutions to the seriousness of the phenomenon. Yet, despite his many reservations, Kaniel says that one may nevertheless arrive at a true estimate of the scale of departure from the country, which according to him at the time of the second aliyah stood at an average of 40 percent.[3] The sources that Kaniel had at his disposal were articles in the journal *Ha-Po'el Ha-Tza'ir*, which provided data on the scale of departure chiefly for the years 1912–1914.

However, there are also additional sources for the scale of departure from the country in the period of the second aliyah that Kaniel did not utilize when he made his study. The data provided by Menahem Sheinkin's information bureau, for instance, and some reports by the statistician Zeev Smilansky permit us to study the scale of departure from the country in the earlier years 1905–1907, a period that Kaniel did not discuss at all. And one may also find in the Central Zionist Archives the raw material that were the basis of the articles in *Ha-Po'el Ha-Tza'ir*, from which Kaniel drew his conclusions. By combining the sources for the two periods, 1905–1907 and 1912–1914, one gains a slightly different picture from that given by Kaniel to see that the scale of departure in these years was more than 40 percent and in the initial years of immigration reached about 80 percent.

1. The Scale on Which People Left Palestine in the Years 1905–1907 and Where They Went

When Sheinkin came to Palestine and opened his information bureau in 1906, he wrote several reports on the economic situation in the country. The limited opportunities for employment in Palestine and the economic incapacity of the country to absorb the thousands of immigrants who fled from the pogroms resulted, according to Sheinkin, in many having no livelihood and moving around without an occupation. The large number of immigrants who had no work explained the strong tendency of those immigrants to leave the country. As the director of the information bureau, Sheinkin estimated the number of immigrants without work at 75 to 80 percent of those who entered the country during those years. He claimed that of all those who entered the country, only 20 to 25 percent succeeded in settling there. The difficult situation in the country created a form of "natural selection," so that only the strong and determined remained; the weak ones, many with large families, had to leave the country.

> A. The number of people who settled in Palestine after immigration was very small: only 20 to 25 percent of those who came; B. Of those with capital, only one in a hundred at the most of those who came settled in the country; C. The others who settled were workers and artisans and a few members of the liberal professions; D. Of those who settled in the country, all the weak ones and all those with large families had to leave after the natural selection. Only the younger people, those who were stronger material and stronger in spirit, and the number of whose working hands corresponded to the number of mouths

to feed, remained; E. This natural selection became more stringent
day by day. All that the local society could absorb of the European arts
and crafts as now developed had been filled.[4]

In another report, Sheinkin insisted that "these are the facts. They
cannot and should not be denied."

> Jews have left Palestine in recent months in their hundreds. Young
> people and people with families who were born here have left. *Halutzim*
> (pioneers) have left. . . . Householders who attempted to earn a living
> and even to save money have left. In short, they flee and go to where the
> dollars come from, and even go back to Poland, Rumania and Russia.[5]

Despite Kaniel's general estimate, it appears that at least in the initial years of the twentieth century, far more than 40 percent of the
immigrants left Palestine. Sheinkin's assessments correspond to Zeev
Smilansky's findings in his article "Al dvar ha-aliyah ha-ivrit le-Eretz-
Israel" (On the Hebrew Immigration to the Land of Israel). Although
he does not give exact information about the scale of the departures,
we see from his descriptions that a large number left and only a few
succeeded in settling in the country:

> The Jews leaving it have reached horrific numbers one could not have
> imagined in previous years. . . . When we try to estimate the number
> of Jews who have been added to the Yishuv in the last three years, we
> are very surprised to find that not only were there not ten thousand,
> but their numbers hardly attained a few thousand. Although more
> than ten thousand Jews undoubtedly immigrated to Palestine in the
> last three years, the number of Jews who remained and settled in the
> country was very small.[6]

From Smilansky's lists we can also see where those that left the country chose to go to. Egypt and the United States were the chief countries they went to, and a small minority chose to go to South Africa,
Australia, and the countries of Western Europe. The Sephardic community, unused to intercontinental migration, chose Egypt as its favor-
ite destination, closer and cheaper than Jaffa. The Ashkenazis, on the
other hand, went to their relatives in the United States after they were
sent money, or they returned to their countries of origin.

> The Ashkenazi community is used to migrating to distant countries
> overseas in every part of the world. . . . Foremost among the coun-

tries that have absorbed most of those who have left Jaffa are Egypt and the United States. People from the Sephardic and Yemenite communities do not go far from Jaffa, and apart from a few exceptions who went to western Europe and America, they all chose to settle in countries close to Jaffa. As Egypt has undergone a renewal in the last ten years and has made great progress in comparison with other counties of the East, many have decided—let's go to Egypt. Most of the Ashkenazis have migrated to the United States because they already have relatives there, and they only have to read a few letters concerning the number of dollars for the thought to work on their minds and give them no rest, so that they will be influenced by the slightest thing.[7]

A few of the emigrants traveled to South Africa. Smilansky claimed that unlike in the United States, where in a short time the emigrants find themselves "in a large Jewish community, and they are involved in the life of a Jewish population with all its characteristics," in Australia and South Africa "they do not have a Jewish community such as they are used to. They feel lonely, frustrated and abandoned without a Jewish community life, which makes them long to return to Palestine."[8]

2. The Scale on Which People Left Palestine in the Years 1912–1913 and Where They Went

We have no data on the scale of departures from Palestine in the years 1908–1911, but we do have data on the years 1912–1913. The founding of the Palestine Office in 1908 somewhat institutionalized the work of gathering information on immigration to Palestine, ordering the process of recording data on both those entering the country and those leaving it. This task was undertaken by Haim Ridnik, an immigration official at the Palestine Office and the representative of the office at the port of Jaffa. Ridnik registered the immigrants who arrived at the port of Jaffa, debriefed those who left, and drew up final reports on the scale of immigration to and emigration from the country. A few of these reports were published in the newspaper *Ha-Po'el Ha-Tza'ir*, others, which were not published, were preserved in the Central Zionist Archives in a section devoted to the Palestine Office.

TABLE 6.1

Emigration from Palestine, 1912, in absolute numbers and percentages.

Month	Immigrants	Emigrants	Ratio of no. emigrants to no. immigrants in the same month	Emigrants			Destination (815 people asked)			
				men	women	children	Russia	US	Africa	Australia
	(1)	(2)	(2:1)	(a)	(b)	(c)	(a)	(b)	(c)	(d)
January	92	82	89.0	50	18	14	20	10	6	3
February	163	98	60.0	56	22	10	22	14	25	2
March	222	185	83.3	147	28	10	50	21	5	1
April	234	188	80.3	142	39	17	91	17	7	12
May	246	101	41.0	74	20	7	45	21	2	—
June	220	105	47.7	73	20	12	58	11	3	4
July	225	123	54.6	96	19	8	51	23	2	5
August	250	69	27.6	61	6	2	23	12	5	—
September	228	173	75.8	149	18	6	107	26	—	2
October	128	68	53.1	61	5	2	28	7	2	—
November	129	68	52.7	51	10	7	25	9	3	2
December	143	64	44.7	57	7	—	23	10	—	—
Total	2,280	1,324	58.0	1,017	212	95	543	181	60	31

SOURCE: Haim Ridnik, "Ha-hagira ha-ivrit derech hof Yafo be-shenat 1912" (The Hebrew Immigration through Jaffa Port in 1912), CZA, L2, file 75/2.

In an article in *Ha-Po'el Ha-Tza'ir* on the scale of emigration from Palestine, Ridnik spoke of his methods of gathering information and how he had trouble applying them in Jaffa:

> For about three years I have been dealing as an official with the Jewish immigrants who have come to Jaffa. During that time, I have seen many decreases in the stream of incomers, and the same applies to the stream of those leaving the country. Reading many newspapers, both here and abroad, I saw how little idea our journalists and communal workers have of the growth and shrinkage of our numbers in this country. . . . They have no true, or even approximately true idea of the numbers of those entering and leaving, or of their age, occupation, capital, etc. . . . but obtaining this information in our local conditions requires a great deal of time and work, which is beyond the capacity of the private individual. Rousing myself, I nevertheless decided to fulfill some small part of the task I have referred to.[9]

To illustrate Ridnik's point, data in Table 6.1 show that in 1912 about 2,280 immigrants entered Palestine, but 1,324 people left—58 percent of those who entered the country in that year. According to the table, 66 percent of those who left returned to Russia, their country of origin, 22.2 percent went to America, 4.6 percent went to South Africa, and 2.3 percent went to Australia.

The data in Table 6.2 relate to the Hebrew months Shevat 5673 to Adar 5674 (5673 was a leap year and therefore had 13 months), corresponding to 9 January 1913–27 March 1914. I could not find figures for Sivan, Tammuz, Av, or Elul 5673 (6 June–1 October 1913).

The data in table 6.2 show that in 1913 and in the three months of 1914 the volume of those leaving the country reached 43.6 percent of the total population entering the country in that year. Fifty percent of these immigrants returned to their country of origin, 15.7 percent went to America, and 4.5 percent went to South Africa.

According to table 6.3 the percentage of those leaving Palestine and the percentage of Jewish immigrants who left the United States during the same years shows that a much higher proportion of Jews left Palestine than left the United States. Relative to other peoples, it appears that those Jews who went to Palestine, at least at the beginning of the period, left the country at an extraordinary rate. The high rate

TABLE 6.2

Emigration from Palestine, 1913 (8 months) and 1914 (3 months).

Month	Immigrants	Emigrants	Ratio of no. emigrants to no. immigrants in the same month	Emigrants			Destination (1,418 people asked)					
				men	women	children	Russia	US	Australia	Africa	Egypt	Europe
	(1)	(2)	(2:1)	(a)	(b)	(c)	(a)	(b)	(c)	(d)	(e)	(f)
9 January–7 February 1913	166	106	40.7	62	26	18	31	20	5	7	27	16
8 February–9 March 1913	249	112	45.0	65	26	21	27	35	15	6	12	17
10 March–7 April 1913	271	122	45.0	70	29	23	58	19	5	5	11	24
8 April–7 May 1913	234	65	27.7	43	13	9	38	11	8	4	2	2
8 May–5 June 1913	327	269	82.2	139	67	68	93	73	32	22	21	28
October 1913	264	45	17.0	28	11	6	23	7	—	—	10	5
December 1913	274	124	45.2	83	26	15	60	17	10	—	15	22
January 1914	265	113	42.6	75	30	8	83	6	1	5	6	122
February 1914	330	176	53.3	119	40	17	108	14	12	2	19	21
March 1914	395	201	50.8	149	37	15	127	8	19	14	3	30
Total	3,261	1,423	43.6	891	325	212	710	224	107	65	134	493

SOURCE: Haim Ridnik, "Ha-hagira ha-ivrit derech hof Yafo be-shenat 1912" (The Hebrew Immigration through Jaffa Port in 1912), CZA, L2, file 75/2.

TABLE 6.3

The volume of emigrants from Palestine relative to the volume of emigrants from the United States.

People	Country of departure	Percentage of emigrants according to year
Jews	United States	5.2 (1908–1924)
Italians	United States	54.7 (1908–1924)
Poles	United States	39.7 (1908–1924)
Rumanians	United States	65.9 (1908–1924
Russians	United States	65.9 (1908–1924)
Jews	Palestine	75–80 (1905–1907) 51 (1912–1914)

SOURCE: Liebman Hersch, "International Migration of the Jews," in W. Willcox, ed., *International Migration* (New York: n.p., 1931), 2:488.

of emigration of Italians, Poles, Russians, and Rumanians from the United States may be explained by the fact that it was an emigration of unmarried men who did not intend to settle. Many of them only emigrated in order to send money home, and as soon as their families' economic situation improved, they returned. Jewish emigration to the United States, on the other hand, consisted of families who wished to settle, and this explains the low rate of departure. But what applied to the United States did not apply to Palestine. The immigration to Palestine was also one of families and not of individuals, but the proportion of those who left Palestine was especially high, which shows that the immigration of families does not necessarily indicate a desire to settle. Where Palestine was concerned, it may be that the push factors that caused emigrants to leave their countries of origin were much more powerful than the pull factors that drew them to Palestine. Many saw Palestine as only a temporary refuge and left it at the earliest opportunity either for the United States or for their countries of origin.

The Emigrants' Profile

An analysis of the profile of those who left Palestine in the years 1905–1914 shows a change in the composition of those who left at the end of the period, during the years 1912–1914, as compared to the beginning of the period in the years 1905–1907.

At the beginning of the period, most of those who left Palestine consisted of entire families who found the country too small to absorb them. Reasons for their departure included an inability to obtain a livelihood or, alternatively, the problem of low wages that were not enough for families to live on. In his article "Misparim makhkimim—le-matzav ha-yishuv be-Eretz Israel" (Instructive Numbers: On the State of the Yishuv in Palestine), Sheinkin wrote that "only small families—that is to say, bachelors or married couples with no more than one child—are able to settle in Jaffa. Nearly all the families with many members have had to leave the town."[10] He did not say where they went to. But as the situation in Jerusalem, Haifa, and the agricultural colonies was no better, it may be assumed that in a short time these families understood that they could not continue in Palestine and once again would have to migrate to countries overseas.

These families were joined by young unmarried workers who found that, as soon as their work ended in the Jewish colonies, they were in a similar situation to those with families. Being unable to support themselves, they had to leave the country:

> At the end of the previous year [1906], many people began to leave the country. During the winter, nearly all those left who had come to the country without money or without a profession. There were also some artisans who left because they earned hardly enough to cover the bare necessities (four shoemakers and tailors), and finally a few who were looking for wages on which they could support their families. In the months of Kheshvan, Kislev and Tevet, that is to say when the work ended in the colonies in the season between harvest and the onset of the rains, there was a crisis among the agricultural workers and dozens of them left the country (especially members of Po'alei Tzion).[11]

In his article "Al dvar ha-aliya ha-ivrit le-Eretz-Israel" (On Hebrew Immigration to the Land of Israel), concerning the years 1905–1906, Smilansky gave a similar account to Sheinkin's, stating that a good number of those leaving were families who had come with the intention of settling in the country but had to leave because there was no way of subsisting there:

> The celebrated days of October gave birth to a new current of Jewish immigration to Palestine, and this time many Jews came with

their families and possessions, and others brought their families later on, and only a few came in order to examine the conditions in the country. On the very day they arrived in Jaffa, we learned that only a small number of those who had come to our land in recent years had prepared themselves, and most of them left the country . . . and even among those who had come with their families and had definitely decided to remain in our country, there was always a large number who soon left and chose to return to its land of exile or looked for a new country because they saw that others also left and did not want to remain in our country.[12]

In the second period, the years 1912–1914, there was also a significant change. Many of those who left the country were young people of less than 20 years of age. We learn from Ridnik's reports that, in 1912, 30 percent of the people who entered the country were less than 30 years old, and about 60 percent of those who left also belonged to this group. Ridkin wrote it appeared, "from the numbers," that

> 2,280 Ashkenazis entered the country and 1,324 left, which leaves a remainder of 956. But if we take into account that 30 percent of those who entered and 60 percent of those who left were young people, we will realize that this tiny number has little significance as most of those who remained were old people going to Jerusalem.[13]

According to table 6.4, for 1913 and for the three months of 1914, the data on the emigration are similar to those for 1912. In January 1913, 68 percent of the emigrants were young people of less than 30 years of age, and 8 percent were artisans; in February, 56 percent of the emigrants were young people of less than 30 years of age and 6 percent were artisans; in March, 66 percent were young people and 6 percent were artisans; and in May, 53 percent were young people and 7 percent were artisans. During 1913, an average of nearly 62 percent of those who left were young people of less than 30 years of age, and only 6.5 percent were artisans.

What made all these emigrants leave? And why was it that young people especially, who belonged to the pioneering society and came to Palestine with a clear ideology and national aspirations, were the first among those who left?

TABLE 6.4

Profile of those who left in 1913 (8 months) and 1914 (3 months).

Month	No. of emigrants (A)	Profile of emigrants (B)							
		Young people		Elderly		Skilled		Families	
—	—	No (1)	% 1:A	No (3)	% 3:A	No (5)	% 5:A	No (7)	% 7:A
9 January – 7 February 1913	106	72	68	n/a		9	8	n/a	—
8 February– 9 March 1913	112	67	59.8	24	21.4	6	5.3	n/a	—
10 March– 7 April 1913	122	66	54.0	33	27.0	9	7.3	n/a	—
8 April– 7 May 1913	65	43	65.1	13	20.0	4	6.1	n/a	—
8 May– 5 June 1913	269	144	53.5	57	21.1	20	7.4	n/a	—
October 1913	45	34	75.5	5	11.1	3	6.6	3	6.6
November 1913	90	66	73.3	12	13.3	10	11.1	5	5.5
December 1913	124	94	75.8	15	12.0	0	0	9	7.2
January 1914	113	83	73.4	22	19.4	6	5.3	5	4.4
February 1914	176	131	74.4	28	15.9	13	7.3	8	4.5
March 1914	201	153	76.1	33	21.5	15	7.4	12	5.6
Total	1,423	881	61.9	242	18.3	86	6.5	42	5.6

SOURCE: Haim Ridnik, "Ha-hagira ha-ivrit derech hof Yafo 1912" (The Hebrew Immigration through Jaffa Port in 1912), CZA, L2, file 75/2.

The Reasons for Emigration

There were five main reasons for emigration from Palestine in the early twentieth century: economic factors; cost of sailing from Jaffa to Eastern Europe; the encounter between newcomers and old-timers; and the encounter with the Palestinian landscape and Zionist ideology.

1. Economic Factors: Demand and the Search for Sources of Livelihood

The main reason for leaving Palestine in the period of the second aliyah (1904–1914) was the difficult economic situation that existed in the country, which was incapable of absorbing the thousands of immigrants that streamed into it. The constant search for work, hunger, and low wages led many to the conclusion that there was little possibility of subsisting in the country and they would have to look elsewhere:

> The number of Jews leaving Palestine increases from day to day, and the reason is known, which is that there is no work or trade here. The question of "What shall we eat?" forces them to leave our country for America and Australia and for countries where our fathers and forefathers have never set foot. Nearly every week, many families sail by ship from Jaffa and go wherever the wind takes them.[14]

The profile of those leaving confirms this view. Those who found work in Palestine and were able to support their families remained in the country and became a part of it. Those who did not succeed in finding a satisfactory source of livelihood had to try their luck somewhere else. That is why only a few of the artisans who came to Palestine left the country; a larger number of tradesmen and middlemen left, at least at the start of the period, in 1905–1907. In these early years, the immigrants, and especially the petty tradesmen and middlemen, had many difficulties in adapting as they had to compete with their colleagues, the Arab tradesmen. In addition, they had to learn the languages spoken in the country and know the rates of exchange. Because of the slow process of absorption, they used up the little money they possessed and in a short time found themselves in a situation where they were without money, without work, and, above all, without hope:

> On the other hand, our brethren who in the lands of exile were dealers, middlemen and *luftmenschen* and do not immediately find work, must familiarize themselves with the weights and measures prevailing in this country and get to know the complicated rates of exchange of the various currencies used here and get some small idea of the common language, and all this takes time and knowledge. . . . And so many days pass and they cannot reach a clear decision, and meanwhile their money runs out from day to day and tears and doubts prevent them from making a definite decision about what to do or whom to turn to. In such a situation, it is easy to understand how the slightest thing can persuade these people to leave the country.[15]

The percentage of artisan-immigrants who left the country, on the other hand, was small—an average of 6.5 percent of those who left in the years 1912–1914. The fact that the artisans created their own professional associations to support them and give them moral and economic assistance facilitated their absorption into the country and helped them to remain there. Many of these artisans felt secure and protected, and they knew that in an hour of need there would be someone to help them and look after them. These professional associations accepted into their ranks new members: immigrants and their relatives who had recently arrived in the country. Thus, there was less probability that an artisan, unlike a tradesman or a middleman, would waste his time and money until he found work and thus increase the chance he would leave the country. Joseph Nahmani, in his article "Yishuv yashan and yishuv hadash li-fnei ha-mashber ha-olami" (The Old Yishuv and the New Yishuv before the World Crisis [the First World War])," discussed the question of leaving the country. This is what he said:

> Most of the artisans here are truly connected to the country. When an artisan comes here, he does not find all the obstacles that the Jewish worker finds on his path . . . and when a new artist comes, he also immediately finds work in his profession. And after a certain time, he knows and becomes used to his environment and begins to love the place. He saves up some money, buys a plot of land for building and builds a house. When he becomes a householder in the land of Israel he is already connected to the country and nothing on earth will take him away from here.[16]

The Merkaz Ba'alei Melacha (Artisans' Center) in Jaffa, for instance, the largest and most important professional association in the country at that time, was interested in absorbing new members and including in its ranks "a huge number of varied elements, especially new immigrants who were not yet used to conditions in the country."[17] The center found work for these newcomers and supported them until they were fully acclimatized to the country. At the time of the great crisis that overtook the Yishuv during World War I, the artisans were in a good economic position in comparison with other groups of workers. When the question of whether to accept Ottoman citizenship came up, the center decided in favor without any difficulty, and "very few members left the country willingly. . . . The center participated in the process of Ottomanization as a whole, and, apart from that, took upon itself the Ottomanization of all the artisans in Jaffa, including those who were not members of the Center,"[18] in order to avoid expulsion by the Ottoman authorities.

For these reasons, few artisans left the country. This fact bolsters the argument that the main factor in their decision to leave or stay was based on economic considerations, that is, the ability to earn a living.

2. The Cost of Sailing

The low cost of sailing to and from Palestine enabled many migrants, even if they were poor, to easily find the money to buy tickets. Unlike sailing from Palestine to America, South Africa, or Australia, which was very expensive (for some of the migrants, the sum represented a large part of their capital), sailing between Jaffa and Russia was much cheaper. The low cost of boat tickets made it much easier for many migrants to decide whether to remain in Palestine or leave it. The cost of sailing to the United States, for instance, was much higher, and if there was a decision to return home it was extremely difficult to find the money to cover the expenses of the voyage:

> The cost of the journey is so low that anyone who has fifteen to twenty roubles in his pocket can easily return to Russia, and anyone who has just twenty francs can travel to Egypt. New Jewish immigrants to our country always know that for a small sum they can return to Russia, and even if they do not have this small sum, they can easily obtain it from relatives and friends. They consequently make no attempt to stay in our country and they especially avoid making a decision to settle in our country if they see they have to suffer for a certain time while they set themselves up.[19]

This claim is supported from a slightly different angle by reports of the JCA information bureaus. The officials in the local bureaus scattered throughout the Pale of Settlement came into daily contact with immigrants. As a result of these meetings, the officials wrote reports providing information of particular interest on Jewish immigration in general and Jewish immigration to Palestine in particular. The local official in the bureau at Berdichev in the region of Kiev, for example, reported that he had recently found (in 1909) that the number of people who turned to the information bureau had increased. Most of them had gone to the United States and some to Argentina and Palestine. Their reason for going to Palestine, wrote the official, was their poverty and inability to find the money necessary for a boat ticket to the United States. Because many of these emigrants wanted to escape from their home country, they decided on Palestine for lack of an alternative because it was near and cheap relative to other countries of immigration.[20] The fact that immigrants could reach the country without resources allowed them to return to their countries of origin without difficulty. Thus the economic risk of sailing to Palestine was lower than that of sailing to America—just as it was easy to reach the country, it was easy to leave it.

3. Old-Timers versus Newcomers

The cold relations between the old, established inhabitants of the country and new immigrants, especially of hotel proprietors and the people of the colonies, was already evident upon their first encounters in Jaffa. Old-timers discouraged the new arrivals about their chances of gaining a foothold in the country; their advice was that they should return just as they came, by the very next ship. This initial meeting sowed confusion and dismay among the immigrants: They had only just arrived, had not yet seen Jaffa, and were not yet acquainted with the way of life, but already they were hearing stories about the country from people who had failed.

The hotels were the immigrants' first real encounter with Palestine and its inhabitants. Most of the immigrants spent at least their first days in the country in one of the hotels in Jaffa, where they met Jewish guests. The clientele included people from the colonies, who had come to Jaffa on business; and Jewish families who had decided to leave the country and were waiting in the hotel till their ship departed. This meeting created an interesting dynamic between those who were coming to the country, and who had only just arrived with expectations of a new beginning in the country, and cynical old-timers and people leaving in despair. The encounter soon extinguished the little hope that immigrants brought with them from overseas. "At one of the hotels in Jaffa one of the guests who had come off the ship and people from the colonies who had come dozens of years ago were sitting round a table," wrote Zeev Smilansky in *Ha-Yom*. During their conversation, the old-timer asked the new immigrant why he had come to the country, and "the guest answered that in his opinion, with money one can find a place in the country. The colonist replied, 'I've been here for more than twenty years, and I promise you that there's nothing to be done here even with a lot of money.' Another guest came forward and answered that they had run away from the pogroms. A second colonist butted in and asked: 'What makes you sure that here in Palestine there won't be pogroms?'. . . . Some of the immigrants sighed, and one woman was in tears." And then the colonists continued to disillusion the newcomers. Don't be sorry about the expenses of the journey, they told them: "Leave the country quickly while you still have some money, or you won't have any even for the journey!"[21] Smilansky's account continued:

> When they [the colonists] come across a Jewish immigrant, they see fit to immediately pour cold water over him and dash his hopes with all kinds of mockery and sarcasm. One can easily understand the situation of an immigrant who comes to a foreign country and finds a new environment. The conditions are unknown to him, and apart from the fact that he lacks reliable information, he meets with indifference from his brethren who live here, who pour scorn on his aspirations to set himself up in his country. All this weakens his resolution, until even the most energetic and strong-willed of them regret their decision to come to Palestine, and they no longer think they can survive and make a decent living in our land.[22]

Apart from the points discussed earlier, there were two other reasons why pioneers left the country that explain why the percentage of leavers among the laborers of the second aliyah was particularly high. They not only had to grapple with difficulties that faced other immigrants, such as searching for work, low wages, and alienating attitudes. In addition, the pioneers' youth and search for excitement and distractions that were lacking in their home countries, along with their ideology, posed stumbling blocks for them when they could not find what they were looking for immediately. All this led many of the pioneers to the conclusion that while the place of the Jewish people was in the land of Israel, perhaps it was not to be at this particular time nor at any price.

4. "Like a Savage on a Distant Island": The Search for Distraction

The stimulation to which the young immigrants had been accustomed in the big cities of the Pale of Settlement was not to be found in Palestine, which was only a remote province on the edge of the Ottoman Empire. Although Jaffa was an important local center, it was not a great city, and it was therefore unable to satisfy the pioneers' cultural and spiritual requirements. In the newspaper *La-Yehudim*, a journal of a humorous nature published during the time of the second aliyah, a man called "Paul" described his feelings of boredom and being condemned to a life of dullness and monotony in Palestine:

> I'm miserable; what a huge gap there is between my wants and the reality! . . . I'm made miserable by a life which is like nothing else. I go to bed at nine; on the Sabbath I sleep all day. . . . How nice it was in Berdichev to doze off on a bench, and there was suddenly a noise, and the sound of applause would wake you up! What an agreeable sensation would go through you on feeling that you too were part of the meetings! And here? I'm not included in anything, I'm a sacrifice! I'm a dreadful sacrifice on the altar of my love for my homeland! Others left the country—not me! Here I shall remain, here I will live and here I'll die. I'm a sacrifice, I shall remain a sacrifice. They speak of workers who are among the fallen: I too am one of the fallen.[23]

The sacrifice, according to Paul, was leaving a place that was full of cultural and spiritual life for a place that was empty and boring. The price he paid, he said, was not different from that of the guardians in the Jewish colonies. The author saw his article as "a work of literature which for some unknown reason was not published in *Yizkor*"—a book commemorating the members of the "ha-Shomer" organization, who fell in performance of their duty and became a legend in their death.[24]

The shepherd Alexander Brockner in Kinneret, for example, described in a letter to Eliyahu Oilitzky a sense of loneliness similar to that of Paul. Brockner came to Palestine from Russia in 1906. After staying a few days in Jaffa, he went to the colony Zikhron Yaakov and then from there went to Shfeya, which was nearby. In July 1911 he moved to Kinneret, and two months later committed suicide after he had an epileptic fit that confined him to his bed. In his letter to

Oilitzky, Brockner described his feeling of loneliness and his longing for "a printed word in Hebrew":

> I'm weak and overcome with sadness. . . . The days of joy and hap-
> piness of former years have gone and my courage has disappeared. I
> feel quite numb, as if my blood had stopped flowing. I'm in a helpless
> state and can't see a way ahead. A silent grief has spread over me and
> I've lost all sense of happiness. It's as if I'm on a far-away island. I'm
> far away from any book or newspaper, like a savage on a distant is-
> land. . . . My heart simply cries out with longing for a printed word in
> Hebrew and some news of the Jewish world.[25]

The letter reveals a strong desire for a link with civilization, and this sense of disconnection depresses the writer. The "printed word in Hebrew" represents for him what he has left behind: company, cul-ture, and perhaps even his former identity, all of which he longs for. Brockner's loneliness is due to his distance from the world of the living. He sees himself as a kind of Robinson Crusoe—a civilized man who to his misfortune has been abandoned on the far-away island of Kinneret.

For the pioneers, who were young, Palestine was a depressing place, different from what they had known in Europe. The release from the bonds of ideology and obligation and the search for the "good life" caused many of them to leave the country and go to big, populous centers. Cairo was such a destination, an important central city close to Palestine, so that the cost of the journey was small and affordable by all. "In recent years, young people and intellectuals have proliferated here [Cairo], people from Russia who stayed for a few years in Pales-tine and then migrated to a place where one can live a little more eas-ily," we read in the newspaper *Ha-Po'el Ha-Tza'ir*. Many of those who come to the city, according to the article, "put their whole past behind them and change completely from head to foot, and begin to frequent the coffee-house instead of the club, and play dominoes instead of going to meetings."[26] But it was not only the young agricultural work-ers who left the country because of its lack of cultural interest. The sons of the colonists of the first aliyah also did not find their place in the colonies and left the country for a similar reason:

> The Palestinian colonies are almost empty of young people. Not only
> colonies like Rishon-le-Zion and Petah-Tikvah, but Rehovot and

Zichron Yaakov as well have already begun to provide material for emigration. Only about ten young people have remained in Rishon-le-Zion with its twenty-five years of existence. I do not wish to slander the sons of the colonies by saying this: they are not guilty of anything. They are leaving the country because there is nothing to do at their parents' place. There is nothing to put their youthful strength and energy into. At home they suffer in body and soul and do not see any future ahead of them.[27]

For many of the immigrants, leaving the country was a relief, a kind of liberation from a burden—a heavy burden of lofty self-sacrifice that few people could bear. Leaving was not, in some cases at least, accompanied by a feeling of regret but rather of joy and a sense of "thank heavens it's over." This is how one of the workers in the year 1911 described the moment of leaving and entering the ship:

Before leaving the land of Israel I was sick with malaria for about a month. So I said: the land of Israel has given me the blessing of departure. My desire to leave the country grew from day to day, and my distress greatly increased because I could not believe that happy moment would ever come. When the moment arrived, I was filled with a boundless joy, and I did not feel any sadness of farewell whatsoever. On the contrary: my last glance at Jaffa was full of superciliousness and rejection. To hell with Jaffa, I'm on the ship, on the sea!

When the ship reached Italy, he said:

Italy, Italy makes me want to sing! I had come from the land of Israel, from a warm country, but I was nevertheless surprised to feel as if I had come from the cold of Siberia. . . . I don't know how or when the land of Israel suddenly came into my mind. I immediately began to cry out in my soul: your Palestine does not have air like this; it is warm there too, but the warmth is dried-up and not fragrant![28]

5. Ideology

There was also another aspect to the phenomenon of workers leaving the country. These pioneers who came to Palestine with fully formed national ideals, and an honest desire to build the country and be built by it through changing the old social order and transforming the Jewish people, were among the first to leave the country. The very ideology that was their main reason for coming also caused them to leave Palestine. The greater their expectation for a new life in the country, full of satisfaction and fulfillment, the greater their disappointment—which was bitter and grievous. Many of the young pioneers imagined life in the new country would be heroic and full of valor, but the reality turned out to be totally different: humdrum, enfeebling, and boring. Many began to feel that the price they had to pay was much higher than what they had expected, and they were gnawed by doubts as to whether realization of their vision was possible. Aliza Shidlovsky gave a good description of this feeling at a cemetery at Kinneret, thirty days after the death of Berl Katznelson, one of the most important leaders of the labor movement in Palestine, when she tried to explain the reasons why many of her friends committed suicide. This is what she said:

> There were those who imagined life in the country to be different, who envisaged a rich life of heroism and poetry, and did not have the imagination to clothe the sight of the bare hills in poetry, or to see heroism in driving the plough on a long, scorching day in the Jordan Valley, and they were consumed by doubts about the realization of their vision and about their ability to carry the burden.[29]

The many suicides among pioneers of the second aliyah offer an extreme and tragic illustration of the reasons why people left Palestine.[30] Many of those who came, full of hopes and good intentions, were unable to bear the disappointment and especially the sense of personal failure when their world collapsed upon their arrival in the new country. They felt lonely and were immersed in a daily reality that was grey and tiring. Thus the "Zionist dream" of a life of satisfaction failed to come to pass. The following two examples, that of Rachel Mayzel and Tamar Berstein, exemplify the magnitude of the pioneers' sense of rupture and disappointment with the new country. Unlike their friends, these young women did not put on a brave face—they just chose not to live. This is what was written by Rachel Maisel, a pioneer who killed herself in the month of Adar bet 1910: "May those close to me forgive me, but when there's no God one can't take a single step forward. Life is beautiful from a distance, but I've lost all distance. At close quarters, life is coarse and unbeautiful, and I'm going. I'm at peace with myself and I feel good. Shalom, Rachel."[31]

The routine, grey reality made it difficult for Rachel to look at the country with the eyes of a dreamer from afar. She realized to her disappointment that life in the land of Israel looked fine from a distance, from abroad, but once there it was revealed as coarse and ugly. In Tamar Berstein's obituary published by her brother in *Ha-Po'el Ha-Tza'ir*, he said:

> Not a year has passed since she set foot in our land in the hope of finding satisfaction for her soul thirsting for a life of plenitude and freedom. But here too her hopes were disappointed, and instead of light and splendor she found only shadows and darkness, and instead of a life of creativity she saw only pain and suffering around her. . . . May you rest in peace, good sister! May your soul be bound up in the bond of everlasting life. Your mourning brother, Abraham-Yitzhak.[32]

✳

Emigration from Palestine back to the country of origin or other destinations was the main (and sensitive) issue for understanding migration to Palestine at the beginning of the twentieth century. The proportion of those leaving the country was high in comparison with that of Jewish migrants leaving the United States or other countries to which Jews had arrived in those years. About 75 percent of the migrants left the land of Israel during the years 1905–1909, and when Tel Aviv was founded, the rate of emigration decreased to about 50 percent. These rates were more than ten times higher than those for the United States in those years. The causes for emigration included the harsh climate of the country, its poverty, limited opportunities for employment, encounters with local inhabitants, and disappointment with the Zionist idea because of an unrealized expectation that Zionist institutions would extend a hand to new immigrants.

An analysis of the profile of those who left shows that pioneers who came to Palestine out of ideology and belief in the Zionist idea were those who left it soonest. It appears that the ideology that directly or indirectly brought them to the country also took them out of it. The ideological rupture that took place following the first encounter with the country set a large question mark over their endeavors and created doubts concerning their capacity to achieve their objectives and respond to the challenge they had set for themselves. Many left the country for that reason, crestfallen and with a sense of failure, but also with a certain sense of relief at returning to "normal" life and the surroundings they had left, and for which it is reasonable to suppose they felt a longing.

It is an interesting fact that it was precisely those immigrants for whom ideology was not a central consideration in their decision to immigrate who, at least at the end of the period of the second aliyah, remained in the country and became part of it. Perhaps this was because their expectations were not high compared with those of the agricultural workers. Those who did not try to create an image of a "new Jew" ex nihilo, and whose expectations were confined to improving their economic and financial situation, were not disappointed in the country. Those who found work did not have to worry about taking their family on a further journey and remained in the country. Their concern for their families was perhaps the main reason for their staying in the country—that and the desire for permanence and a normal life.

Despite the high percentage of those who left the country, there were hardly any value judgments on the leavers that condemned them or saw them as traitors who abandoned the Yishuv in a time of trouble. The term yerida, for example, which has a moral significance and tarnishes the reputation of leavers, hardly existed as yet in the terminology of the period, which used the words "emigrants" and "leavers"—terms of a more neutral character—when describing those who left the country. The reports were mostly factual, attempting to analyze the phenomenon and explain it without any commentary or apportioning of blame. Immigration to Palestine in the period before World War I, then, was mainly a normal immigration and not an ideological one. It was primarily an immigration of dealers, petty tradesmen, artisans, and members of the liberal professions who sought to improve their lives by coming to the country. But the Yishuv was too small to absorb them all, and many realized that they would not find salvation there, and so they decided to leave. Moreover, the policy of Sheinkin's and Ruppin's information bureaus clearly gave preference to people with capital over immigrants of the lower middle class, who were constantly dissuaded from coming to the country both by the local press and by letters sent by the bureaus. When they came nevertheless, but their mistake became clear to them and they then left, it was seen as perfectly natural and not a cause for shame.

Conclusion

The Jewish migration at the end of the nineteenth and beginning of the twentieth century was a dramatic event that changed the Jewish people in modern times beyond recognition. Millions of Jews sought to escape the stressful conditions of their daily lives in Eastern Europe and to find a better future for themselves and their families in one of the countries of immigration overseas. The vast majority of the Jewish migrants went to the United States; others, in much smaller numbers, reached Argentina, Canada, Australia, and South Africa. From the beginning of the twentieth century until World War I, about 35,000 Jews reached Palestine. Because of this difference in scale, and also because of the place the land of Israel holds in Jewish thought, historians and social scientists have tended to apply different criteria to the Palestine immigration than those usually applied in the study of immigration. They have stressed the uniqueness of Jewish immigration to Palestine and the importance of Zionist ideology as a central factor in that immigration.

This book has sought to question this assumption and present a more complex picture both of the causes of immigration to Palestine and of the mass of immigrants who reached the Jaffa Port in the years 1904–1914. The focus on these people, who were not motivated by the idea of return to the land of Israel and were not part of the Zionist project, enables one to see the immigration to Palestine in a much broader historical context. This historical approach removes Jewish immigration to Palestine from long-held ideological trappings that prevented examination of its other aspects, which are perhaps less flattering to the Zionist project in its early stages but were undoubtedly an inseparable part of the Palestinian reality at the beginning of the twentieth century.

233

The comparative viewpoint of this book and its use of primary sources that can generally be found in works dealing with immigration—immigrants' letters, passenger records, statistics, reports of information bureaus, and so on—permit us to gain a better understanding of the characteristics of the mass of immigrants to the country, their motivations in coming, their patterns of absorption in the towns of Palestine, and their similarities and differences to Jewish immigrants to the United States.

In my analysis in this volume, I have arrived at a number of conclusions regarding the following issues:

The place of Zionist ideology in the decision to immigrate to Palestine.

The causes of immigration to Palestine were not different from the causes of immigration to the United States. A comparison between letters sent to the Zionist information bureaus and those sent to the general information bureaus shows that in both cases the emigrants sought precise information about the economic situation in their country of destination and attendant economic opportunities. From these letters sent to the information bureaus, we see that Zionist ideology played a very limited role in immigration to Palestine. Only in a few letters did the potential immigrants refer to Zionism or a return to the historical homeland of the Jewish people. Many of them may have recognized the importance of the land of Israel and the return, but this was not expressed in the letters. Those who turned to the bureaus asked practical questions about the chances of succeeding or failing, and in general they showed no interest in being part of the social experiment undertaken by Zionism at the start of the twentieth century. Those interested in Palestine as a destination wanted to go there not because of a wish to create an ideal society or become tillers of the soil, but because they thought it might be easier to find work and begin a new life there. In addition to questions of livelihood and security, more prosaic considerations also played a part in the decision to go to Palestine: obtaining boat tickets at reduced prices, the lower cost of traveling to Palestine in comparison to the United States (which considerably reduced the danger of the immigration process), and recommendations from relatives. The society of the Yishuv was an immigrant society in all respects. Even prostitution and the white-slave trade—two phenomena that were a direct result of the great migration—were an inseparable part of life in Palestine at the beginning of the twentieth century.

The sociodemographic profile of the immigrants.

An examination of the sociodemographic profile of immigrants to Palestine supports the assertion that Zionist ideology did not play a central role in their decision to go there. It also reveals points of similarity (and also points of difference) between the demographic character of immigrants to Palestine and that of Jewish immigrants to the United States. About 40 percent of immigrants to the United States and Palestine were women, of which about a quarter were children 15 or younger. On the other hand, a larger percentage of people aged 50 and above came to Palestine: 22 percent of those who came to Palestine were over 50 years old; of those who went to the United States, only 6 percent were over 44. This difference was a major factor in the high percentage of immigrants without an occupation who came to Palestine compared to those who went to America (65 percent versus 43 percent). Another significant difference between the two groups of immigrants was the high percentage of members of the liberal professions who came to Palestine (19 percent) compared to those who went to America (4.5 percent). At the same time, we see from reports of the information bureaus and statistics that the great majority of the immigrants both to Palestine and to the United States were artisans or petty tradesmen who preferred cities to country life. Reports of the information bureaus in Palestine show that the economic situation of immigrants to Palestine was inferior to that of immigrants to the United States. It should also be pointed out that in some cases immigrants with eye diseases came to Palestine because they were unable to enter the United States due to the medical inspections at Ellis Island. Because the cost of the journey to the United States was beyond their means and the journey to Palestine was easier and less expensive, there was a large number of poor immigrants who came to Palestine. For this same reason, the percentage of Jews leaving Palestine was significantly higher than that of Jews leaving the United States. It was easy and cheap to get to Palestine and equally easy and cheap to leave it.

The emigration from Palestine.

The proportion of those leaving Palestine was significantly higher than that of Jewish migrants who left other countries of destination. If the rate of those leaving the United States in the years 1908–1914 was estimated at about 5 percent, the rate of those leaving Palestine was ten times greater—estimated in 1909 at 50 percent and in earlier years at over 75 percent. The causes for emigration were the country's harsh climate, its poverty, limited opportunities for employment, the encounter with local inhabitants, the proximity of the country to the land of origin and nostalgia for it, and disappointment with the Zionist idea because of unrealized expectations that Zionist institutions would extend a hand to new immigrants. In spite of the high rate of emigration, the attitude of Zionist institutions and the Jewish Yishuv in Palestine toward emigrants was not negative and was accepted with understanding. Since Menachem Sheinkin and Arthur Ruppin had recommended to poorer families that they should not come, it was only natural that as soon as these families came and found no work they would leave. Only in the years after World War I did the desertion of the land become a dishonorable phenomenon. The terms "aliyah" (ascent) and "yerida" (descent) were the epithets used, and those who left—the *yordim*—were considered by many in the Yishuv as betrayers who had turned their backs on their friends during the struggle to conquer the land and settle it.

The regional distribution of the immigration to Palestine.

The pattern of immigration to Palestine was different from that of immigration to America. People went to Palestine chiefly from areas in the Pale of Settlement hit by pogroms, while those who went to the United States came from the poverty-stricken industrial areas in the northwest of the Pale of Settlement. This conclusion is supported by examining the influence of the pogroms on the immigrants to Palestine and the United States. In the peak years of the pogroms, the percentage of immigrants to Palestine grew by 180 percent, while that of immigrants to the United States grew by only 18 percent. It thus appears that the immigration to Palestine in those years was caused by fright and panic and was generally less selective than the immigration to the United States in those times.

The immigration experience.

The experience of immigration to Palestine was not different from that of immigration to the United States, and the hardships endured by immigrants to Palestine were similar to those of Jewish immigrants to the United States. The difficulties in reaching the decision to immigrate to Palestine, setting out on their way, making the train journey to the port of Odessa, waiting for the ship, sailing in steerage, and encountering the new society were all things they shared with immigrants to the United States. The encounters with crooks, swindlers, and highway robbers was also an inseparable part of the journey to Palestine. It was not a return to the ancestral land after an exile of two thousand years but a prosaic journey in search of sources of income and a better life.

The formation of Zionist immigration policy.

The profile of immigrants to Palestine led to the formation of a Zionist immigration policy. In the immigrants' letters to the information bureaus, and especially in the letters written in reply, one sees the discrepancy between the type of immigrants that the heads of the information bureaus in Palestine wanted to bring to the country and those immigrants who actually came. Menahem Sheinkin and Arthur Ruppin—the two men who were responsible for migration to Palestine and for the absorption of immigrants—preferred people with capital to poor immigrants. This immigration policy was motivated by the fear that the country would be unable to absorb the thousands of immigrants who wanted to come, and they therefore gave preference to the wealthy and those with economic capabilities who would create an infrastructure for the masses who would come later. Between "the good of the country" and "the good of the people," Sheinkin and Ruppin chose "the good of the country." They warned those who turned to them of the economic dangers that awaited them in Palestine and advised them to go to the United States. The reality, however, was quite different from Sheinkin and Ruppin's aspirations, and those who came to Palestine were primarily the poor and those unable to reach the United States.

The encounter with the majority society.

The Jewish society that came into being in Palestine was an immigrant society in all respects. The immigrants who came to Palestine with their families did not drain marshes on the borders of the country—Galilee and the Jordan Valley—nor did they struggle with exotic Mediterranean diseases like typhoid fever and malaria. Work on the land did not suit them, and thus they settled in the towns and not in the villages. Likewise, the "new Hebrew man"—who had cast off the shackles of the exile and the limiting exilic ways of making a living and who came to the land of Israel to till the soil and "make the desert bloom"—was not their chief concern. These immigrants were ordinary Eastern European Jews who wanted to begin a new life, and so they came to a new country whose ways they were unfamiliar with and whose language they did not know. Their modest aspirations to a life of contentment and security were not different from those of Jewish immigrants to other countries. They also set up dozens of workshops of various kinds and founded professional associations to protect their occupations and ensure their livelihood. Their main concern was to protect their economic security.

At the same time, immigrants to Palestine never wanted to be part of the surrounding society. In this respect, immigration to Palestine was different from Jewish immigration to any other country. If in the other countries Jewish immigrants did all they could to fit into the surrounding society, to succeed economically, and to become citizens with equal rights, in Palestine the opposite process took place. Jewish immigrants had no interest in becoming part of the majority Arab society and made no attempt to adopt the Middle Eastern lifestyle. They isolated themselves from Arab society economically and culturally and formed separate ethnic enclaves that were cut off from the majority society. In this situation, it was easy for the Zionist-pioneering element to influence the mass of immigrants and bring them close to the national idea. This was a unique case of a country of immigration in which a minority succeeded in influencing and molding the consciousness of the majority and imposing on it ideas and an ideology that had been alien to it. We witness a process whereby the Jewish immigrants of the beginning of the twentieth century became impregnated with the Zionist mission. This was a gradual process and did not happen overnight. If in the United States the Jews sought to adopt the values of the majority society and to become Americans in every way, in Palestine they adopted the values of the Zionist minority and became part of that element. One could say that the Eastern European Jews came to Palestine as immigrants and became olim. Thus, paradoxically, this book ascribes much greater power and significance to the pioneers and Zionists than previous historians who have represented immigration to Palestine as something unique and unparalleled in history. The pioneers were a minority that formed the consciousness of the majority and thus succeeded in harnessing it to the national enterprise.

✳

The immigration to Palestine and the United States at the beginning of the twentieth century led to the emergence of two Jewish entities of importance in the Jewish world: the State of Israel and the Jewish community in the United States. Despite the differences that can be found today between these two great Jewish communities, the historical circumstances that led to their formation were similar. The attempt to create two different historiographies and two different scales of values for them not only falsifies the past: It also falsifies our understanding of the great Jewish migration from Eastern Europe at the end of the nineteenth century and the beginning of the twentieth.

Thus the Zionist claim that migration to Palestine should be regarded as a migration of greater value than Jewish migration to the United States and other countries appears to be inaccurate and flawed. Zionist historiography overlooked the story of the ordinary Jewish migrant to Palestine and stressed that of the pioneer—the one who dried the marshes and made the desert bloom. By doing so it created a false portrayal in which the olim—the immigrants to the land of Israel—were of a higher ethical standard than the migrants to the United States. This narrative was accepted without question among thousands of Jews all around the world and became an efficient tool of the Zionist movement and the Israeli leadership to receive moral and financial support from World Jewry for the State of Israel.

This book does not seek to destroy the myth of aliyah to the land of Israel or to diminish the role of the pioneers and the Zionist movements in building the Yishuv and in laying the foundations of the state-in-the-making. Many studies and biographies have already fixed the historical status of this unique group of people, but a historiography of an ideological-romantic nature can only be partial and cannot possibly provide a complete picture.

The case of the immigration to Palestine at the beginning of the twentieth century also exemplifies the waves of immigration to Palestine and the State of Israel in later years. If one examines the motivations and the demographic profile of immigrants who came to Palestine from the 1920s until the present, one will find them very similar to those of immigrants to Palestine at the beginning of the twentieth century. In nearly all the waves of immigration to Palestine, the forces driving the emigrants out of their countries of origin were much stronger than the power of attraction of the Zionist ideology and the land of Israel. The waves of immigration to Palestine in the 1920s were the outcome of Ukrainian pogroms in which 60,000 Jews were murdered, a worsening of the economic situation of the Jews of Poland—the largest of the Jewish communities—and the law of quotas that led to the closing of the gates of the United States in 1924. In 1925, for the first time, after the issuing of the strict quota laws, more immigrants came to Palestine than to the United States. The Nazis' rise to power in the 1930s and anti-Semitism in Poland resulted in another significant wave of a quarter of a million Jews in less than ten years. In the 1950s—the period of the great immigration to the young State of Israel—immigrants from the Arab countries came after their political and economic situation had been undermined with the founding of the State of Israel. And in the 1990s, about a million Jews came from the Commonwealth of Independent States after the breakup of the communist bloc and the uprooting of the old social order.

Although in every wave of immigration there was a minority that cherished the Zionist idea and dreamed of return to the ancestral land, the great majority were immigrants for whom the land was not an ideal. This was the case at the beginning of the twentieth century, and so it was in the other waves of immigration to Palestine and the State of Israel.

Notes

Introduction

1. An exceptional and untypical case was that of Aryeh Gartner. In 1980 a collection of articles edited by Avigdor Shinan was published, titled *Hagirah ve-hityashvut be-israel u-ba'amim* (Emigration and Settlement in Jewish and General History). The introduction to the work was written by Shmuel Ettinger, who emphasized the central place of immigration in the history of nations in general and in that of the Jewish people in particular. Among the articles in the collection there is a long article by Aryeh Gartner on the great Jewish migration in the years 1881–1914. This article is the only one in Hebrew dealing with the great Jewish migration from Eastern Europe to the West. Moreover, Gartner, although he taught at Tel Aviv University, had very great difficulty in getting his study of immigration to the United States published in Hebrew. For more on Jewish emigration also see Eli Ledenhendler, *Le'an Zramim hadashim be-kerev yehudei mizrah europah* (Concerning New Trends among East European Jews) (Tel Aviv: Open University of Israel, 2000). It would seem that the involvement of these scholars with Jewish migration was due to the fact that none of them grew up amid the pioneering Israeli experience of the 1950s and 1960s. Perhaps they were drawn to this field of research precisely because they were children of Jewish immigrants to the United States. On the other hand, a number of books by American scholars were translated into Hebrew. See Salo Baron, *Be-mivhan ha-herut, prakim be-toldot ya-hadut amerikah* (Steeled by Adversity) (Jerusalem and Tel Aviv: Shoken, 1977); Arthur Hertzberg, *Ha-yehudim be-amerikah: mifgash rav tahpukhot ben 400 shanah* (The Jews in America: Four Centuries of an Uneasy Encounter) (Jerusalem and Tel Aviv: Shoken, 1994); Aryeh Gartner and Jonathan Sarna, eds., *Yehudei artzot ha-brit* (The Jews of the United States) (Jerusalem: Merkaz Shazar, 1992); and also Paula Hyman, *Ha-isha ha-yehudiya be-svach ha-kidma* (Gender and Assimilation in Modern Jewish History: The Roles and Representation of Women) (Jerusalem: Merkaz Shazar, 1997). While all these scholars dealt with immigration, none of them focused on it as the main subject of research.

2. See for example, Gerald Sorin, *A Time for Building: The Third Migration 1880–1920* (Baltimore and London: Johns Hopkins University Press, 1992), 38; 220–

243

221; and Ronald Sanders, *Shores of Refuge: A Hundred Years of Jewish Emigration* (New York: Henry Holt, 1988), 116–127; 216–217.

3. *Kitvei Moshe Smilansky—Zikhronot, Kerekh aleph* (Writings of Moshe Smilansky—Memoirs) (Tel Aviv: Mosad Bialik, 1934), 75.

4. Menahem Sheinkin to Otto Warburg (1908?), Central Zionist Archives (hereafter CZA), A24, file 52.

5. Arthur Ruppin, *ha-Sotziologia shel ha-yehudim* (The Sociology of the Jews) vol. 1 (Berlin and Tel Aviv: Shtibel Press, 1931), 8.

6. Ibid., 112–113.

7. See Mitchell Hart, *Social Science and the Politics of Modern Jewish Identity* (Stanford: Stanford University Press, 2000). On Jacob Lestschinsky as a pioneer of Jewish immigration research, see Gur Alroey, "Demographer in the Service of the Nation; Liebman Hersch, Jacob Lestschinsky and the Start of Jewish Migration Research," *Jewish History* 20 (2006): 265–282.

8. In 1927 Lestschinsky published the book *Die Yiddishe Wanderung far die Letzte 25 Yor*. A year later, there appeared the first volume of *Shriften far Ekonomik un Statistik*, which was a sequel to *Blettter far Yiddishe Demografia, Statistik un Economik*. At the beginning of the 1930s, he published another book on Jewish migration, *Die Anhoiven fun der Emigratzia un Colonizatzia bay Yidden in Neuntenhundert*. After World War II, he published *Wohin Geyen Mir? Yiddishe Wanderung Amol un Heint*, which was translated into Hebrew a year later by Yehuda Azaria under the title *Neidudei israel* (Israel Wandering).

9. On Lestschinsky's research activities, see Alexander Manor, *Ha-hoge ve-ha-hoker* (Jerusalem: Hakongres Ha-olami Ha-yehudi Press, 1961), 55.

10. Jacob Lestschinsky, *Nedudei israel* (Israel Wandering) (Tel Aviv: Am Oved, 1945), 62.

11. See obituary notice of David Gurevich, *Statistical Bulletin*, January–June 1947, pamphlet 1–6 (unpaginated).

12. David Gurevich, Aaron Gertz, and Roberto Bachi, *Ha-aliyah, ha-yishuv ve ha-tenua ha-tivit shel ha-ukhlusiya be eretz israel* (The Jewish Population of Palestine: Immigration, Demographic Structure and Natural Growth) (Jerusalem: Ha-makhlaka le-Statistika shel ha-sokhnut ha-yehudit le-eretz israel, 1944), 19–20.

13. Ibid., 21.

14. See Roberto Bachi, "Mah bein hagirah ve-aliyah?" (Between Immigration and Aliyah), *Ahdut Ha-Avodah* 4 (1946): 27.

15. Aryeh Tartakower, *Nedudei ha-yehudim ba-olam* (Jewish Wanderings in the World) (Jerusalem: Tzionit, 1947), 99.

16. Ibid., 21.

17. Aryeh Tartakower, *Ha-adam ha-noded: Al ha-hagirah ve-al ha-aliyah ba-avar u-beyamenu* (Wandering Man) (Tel Aviv: Newman Press, 1954), 79–81.

18. Tartakower mentions the immigration of Puritans to the American colonies in the 1630s as an example of non-Jewish aliyah. This immigration to America was primarily due to a desire to create a new society there, different from the one

they knew in Europe. Tartakower claims that there was a concept and a plan of action, the plan was carried out, and the immigration was for the good of the community. In addition to the Puritans, Tartakower mentioned the attempts of various European groups to set up socialist villages in the United States. America was seen by them as a free and open land in which a more just and egalitarian society could be created than the one they left behind in Europe. Ibid., 99–100. See also M. Tugan Baranovsky, *Moshavot Socialistiyot* (Socialists Colonies) (Ein Harod: Ha-kibutz Hameuhad, 1946), 57–72. On the question of whether there could be a Jewish aliyah to a place other than Palestine, see Gur Alroey, "Aliya to America? A Comparative Look at Jewish Mass-Migration, 1881–1914," *Modern Judaism* 28, no. 2 (May 2008): 109–133.

19. Shmuel N. Eisenstadt, "Aliyah ve-hagirah, kavim le-tipologia sotziologit (Aliyah and Hagirah: The Outline of a Sociological Typology)," *Metzudah* 7 (1954): 83. See also Shmuel Eisenstadt, *Klitat ha-aliyah: mehkar sotziologi* (Immigration Absorption: Sociology Research) (Jerusalem: n.p., 1952), 9–33.

20. Ibid., 84.

21. Ibid., 85.

22. This assertion is in agreement with the conclusions of Joseph Gorny, who investigated the changes in the social structure of the pioneers of the second aliyah. See Gorny, "Ha-shinu'im be-mivne ha-hevrati ve ha—politi shel aliyah ha-sheniyah be-shanim 1904–1914," (Changes in the Social and Political Structure of the Second Aliya between 1904 and 1940), *Ha-Tzionut* I (1970): 204–246.

23. Ibid., 86. See also R. Bachi, "Ma bein hagirah ve-aliyah?" (Between Immigration and Aliyah), *Ahdut Ha-Avodah* 4 (1946): 269–271. Bachi thought that aliyah to Palestine was different because, unlike other kinds of immigration, the waves of immigration to Palestine were not motivated by economic necessity but were the result of social changes in the countries of origin. Another distinction that Bachi made between aliyah and immigration was that the purpose of immigration was to restore an economic and demographic balance that had been upset in the country of origin. The waves of aliyah, on the other hand, had the opposite effect: They upset the economic equilibrium in Palestine. Therefore, after every wave of aliyah, an economic revolution must be carried out adapting the economy to the new situation, for the Zionist economy is essentially dynamic. Ibid., 271.

24. Eisenstadt, *Aliyah ve-hagirah*, 91. He repeated this assertion in his book *Ha-hevra ha-yisraelit* (Israeli Society) (Jerusalem: Magnes Press, 1967), 44–45.

25. Ben Zion Dinur, *Yesodoteha ha-histori'im shel tekumat israel* (The Historical Foundations of the Establishment of Israel) (New York: Beit Midrash le-rabanim be-amrikah, 1955), 4.

26. Ibid., 5.

27. Ibid., 6.

28. Ibid., 2.

29. Shmuel Ettinger, *Toldot israel ba-et ha-hadasha* (History of the Jewish People in Modern Times) (Tel Aviv: Dvir Press, 1969), 148–157.

30. Ibid., 203.

31. See Yehuda Slutzky, *Mavo le-toldot tenu'at ha-avodah ha-israelit* (Introduction to the History of the Labour Movement in Israel) (Tel Aviv: Am Oved, 1973), 146.

32. Mordechai Eliav, ed., *Sefer ha-aliyah ha-rishonah* vol. 2 (Jerusalem: Yad Yitzchak Ben Zvi Press, 1981), 400–401.

33. We do not have exact numbers for the pioneers who came to Palestine in the years 1904–1914. Zvi Even-Shoshan claims that in 1906 there were no more than 350 workers and at the end of the period there were between 1,500 and 1,600, of whom 300 were Yemenites, and more than 300 hundred born in the country or oriental Jews. See Even-Shoshan, *Toldot ten'uat ha-po'alim be-eretz israel* (The History of the Labor Movement in Eretz Yisrael) (Tel Aviv: Am Oved, 1963), 266–267. Moshe Barslavski wrote that at its end, just before World War I, the second aliyah numbered over 1,200 male and female workers in the colonies, farms, and *kvutzot*. See Barslavski, *Tenuat ha-po'alim ha-eretz israelit* (The Israeli Labor Movement), vol. 1 (Tel Aviv: Ha-kibutz Hameuhad, 1966), 82. Yehuda Slutzky gave the number as 2,500 workers, 759 in the years 1904–1908, and 1,760 in the years 1909–1914. See Slutzky, *Mavo le-toldot tenuat ha-avodah ha-yisraelit* (Introduction to the History of the Labour Movement in Israel) (Tel Aviv: Am Oved, 1973), 162.

34. See Jonathan Frankel, *Prophecy and Politics: Socialism, Nationalism and the Russian Jews, 1862–1917* (New York: Cambridge University Press, 1981).

35. On the encounter of the pioneers of the second aliyah with the colonists of the first aliyah, see Zeev Zahor, "Ha-imut bein ha-aliyah ha-rishonah ve-ha-aliyah ha-sheniyah" (The Conflict between Ha-aliyot ha-rishonah ve-hashinya), in *Hagirah ve-hityashvut be-yisra'el u-ve-amim* (Emigration and Settlement in Jewish and General History), ed. Avigdor Shinan (Jerusalem: Merkaz Shazar, 1982), 233–248. See also Gur Alroey, "The Russian Terror in Palestine: The Bar-Giora and Ha-shomer Associations, 1907–1920," in *Uneasy Inheritance: Russia and Israel 1880–2010*, ed. Brian Horowitz and Shai Ginsburg (Bloomington, IN: Slavica, 2013): 31–60.

36. On the acquisition of the land at Umm Juni, see Margalit Shilo, *Nisiyonot be-hityashvut: ha-misrad ha-eretz-israeli 1908–1914* (Experiments in Settlement: The Palestine Office 1908–1914) (Jerusalem: Yad Yitzchak Ben Zvi Press, 1998).

37. Zeev Zahor, "Tzmihat ha-zramim ha-politi'im ve-irgunei ha-po'alim" (The Growth of Political Factions and Workers' Organizations), in *Ha-aliyah ha-sheniyah*, ed. Israel Bartal, vol. 1 (Jerusalem: Yitzhak Ben Zvi Press, 1997), 215–234.

38. Ibid., 222.

39. From the "Ramle Program," in Yehoshua Kaniel, ed., *Ha-aliyah ha-sheniyah*—Mekorort (The Second Aliya—Sources) (Jerusalem: Yad Yitzhak Ben Zvi Press, 1997), 48-49.

40. See n. 36 above.

41. On the Bar-Giora and Ha-shomer associations, see Y. N. Goldstein, *From Fighters to Soldiers: How the Israel Defense Forces Began* (Brighton, UK: Sussex Academic Press, 1998).

42. See Deborah Bernstein, *The Struggle for Equality: Urban Women Workers in Pre-State Israeli Society* (New York: Praeger, 1986); and see also Margalit Shilo, "The Women's Farm at Kinneret, 1911–1917: A Solution to the Problem of the Working Woman in the Second Aliya," in *The Jerusalem Cathedra*, vol. 1 (Jerusalem: Yad Yitzhak Ben Zvi Press, 1981), 246–283.

43. See Margalit Shilo, "Mabat hadash al ha-aliyah ha-sheniyah" (New Outlook on the Second Aliyah), *Kivunim* 11–12 (1998): 117–140.

44. Yossi Katz, *Ha-yozma ha-pratit be-binyan eretz-israel be-tekufat ha-aliyah ha-sheniyah* (Zionist Private Enterprise in the Building of Eretz-Israel during the Second Aliyah, 1904–1914) (Jerusalem: Bar Ilan University Press, 1989).

45. Yaakov Zerubavel, "Im hitgabrut ha-hagirah," *Ha-Ahdut* 34 (19 June 1914): 1.

Chapter One

1. We do not know how many Jews there were in Zakharino at the beginning of the twentieth century. At the same time, the town nearest the shtetl was Mstislawl in the district of Mogilev. According to the 1897 census, it had a population of 8,515, of whom 5,076 (59.6%) were Jews. It is reasonable to suppose that the number of Jews in the shtetl was much smaller than the number of people in the nearby town. See Jakob Segall, *Internationale Konfessionsstatistik* (Berlin: Veroeffentlichung des Bureaus fuer Statistik der Juden, Internationale Konfessionsstatistik, 1914).

2. Letter of David Kohelet to Arthur Ruppin, 11 November 1913, CZA, L2, file 133/3.

3. On the natural increase in the Russian Empire, see Barbara Anderson, *Human Fertility in Russia since the Nineteenth Century* (Princeton, NJ: Princeton University Press, 1979), 3–14.

4. See Simon Kuznets, "Immigration of Russian Jews to the United States: Background and Structure," *Perspectives in American History* 9 (1975): 63–64. It should be pointed out that Kuznets used Lestschinsky's data. He saw Lestschinsky as the scholar who contributed most to founding demographic economic research.

5. Jacob Lestschinsky, *Dos Yiddishe Folk in Tzifferen* (The Jewish People in Numbers) (Berlin: Klal Farlag, 1924), 31.

6. Ibid.

7. On the internal migration of the Jewish population in the Russian Empire, see Saul Stampfer, "Patterns of Internal Jewish Migration in the Russian Empire," in *Jews and Jewish Life in Russia and the Soviet Union*, ed. Yaacov Ro'i (Portland: Frank Cass, 1995), 25–50. On the migration from the northwest of the Pale of Settlement southward, see Yossi Goldstein, "Hagirat yehudim le-russia ha-hadasha [new Russia] ve ha-ma'apecha ha-hevratit-calcalit be'kirbam be-mahalach ha-mea ha-19 (The Migration of Jews to the New Russia and the Socioeconomic Revolution They Underwent in the Nineteenth Century)," *Shevut* 12, no. 28 (2004–2005): 7–8. Goldstein maintains that more than 700,000 Jews migrated to southern

248 Notes to Chapter One

Russia, and there are some who have compared this migration to the transatlantic migration of the end of the nineteenth century and the beginning of the twentieth.

8. Lestschinsky, *Dos Yiddishe Volk in Tzifferen* (The Jewish People in Numbers), 33.

9. Ben-Zion Rubstein, *Galitzia un Ihr Bafelkerung* (Galicia and Its Population) (Warsaw: Die Welt, 1923), 18.

10. Gretchen A. Condran and Ellen A. Kramarow, "Child Mortality among Jewish Immigrants to the United States," *Journal of Interdisciplinary History* 22, no. 2 (Autumn 1991): 225. This pattern of low infant mortality among the Jews in comparison with that of the general society existed almost everywhere the Jews lived except for Galicia in the mid-nineteenth century and Vilna and Lvov (Lemberg) at the beginning of the twentieth century. In those places, infant mortality was 15% higher than that of the general population. See ibid.

11. See Isaac Rubinow, "Economic Condition of the Jews in Russia," *Bulletin of the Bureau of Labor* 72 (September 1907): 577; reprint, 1970. See also Arcadius Kahan, *Essays in Jewish Social and Economic History* (Chicago and London: University of Chicago Press, 1985), 5–6.

12. Letter of Zalman Lifchitz to Ruppin, 17 July 1912, CZA, file 137/2.

13. Letter of the Alterman family to Arthur Ruppin, 5 February 1914, CZA L2, file 133/1.

14. See n. 2.

15. On the industrial revolution in Europe, see Thomas Ashton, *The Industrial Revolution, 1760–1830* (London: Oxford University Press, 1961); on the industrialization process in Russia, see Malcolm E. Falkus, *The Industrialisation of Russia 1700–1914* (London: Macmillan, 1972); Peter Gatrell, *The Tsarist Economy: 1850–1917* (New York: Batsford, 1987); Hans Rogger, *Russia in the Age of Modernisation and Revolution: 1881–1917* (New York: Longman, 1985), esp. chap. 6.

16. Falkus, *Industrialisation of Russia*, 51.

17. Ibid., 65–66; and see also Gattrell, *Tsarist Economy*, 150–154.

18. Falkus, *Industrialisation of Russia*, 65.

19. B. R. Mitchell, *European Historical Statistics 1750–1975* (London: Macmillan, 1975), 75.

20. Gatrell, *Tsarist Economy*, 67–69.

21. Lestschinsky, *Dos Yiddishe Folk in Tzifferen*, 25.

22. Letter of Zalman Lifschitz to Arthur Ruppin, 17 July 1912, CZA, L2, file 137/2.

23. Letter of Yitzhak to Arthur Ruppin, 26 March 1913, CZA, L2, file 137/2.

24. Letter of Z. Kurtzbach to Arthur Ruppin, 16 June 1911, CZA, L2, file 131/6.

25. See n. 2.

26. Rubinow, "Economic Condition of the Jews in Russia," 500.

27. On the idea of the nonproletarization of Jewish society in Eastern Europe, see Daniel Gutwein, "Proletarizatzia ve-politizatzia: Borochov u-megamot be-hitpathut shel teoriat ha-i-proletarizatzia," *Shevut* 14 (1991): 141–186.

28. In 1884, in the wake of the pogroms in Russia and the resultant shock to Jewish society, the Jewish businessman Jan Bloch in Warsaw established a statistical bureau to gather material on the difficult integration of the Jews into the Russian Empire. At Bloch's behest, researchers scattered throughout the Pale of Settlement and Poland collected material about the Jewish financial and social status in Russia, which Bloch published, in 1891, in a five-volume, 1,800-page study titled *A Comparison of the Physical Subsistence and Moral Condition of the Population in the Jewish Pale of Settlement and Elsewhere*. One of Bloch's top researchers was the economist Andrei Palovich Subotin, who was particularly interested in the Jewish question. On Bloch's initiative, see Matitiahu Minc, "Ve-eino tsofah al beit yisrael: Jan G. Bloch u-maavak yehudei Polin ve-Russia neged aflayatam, "Gal-Ed: me'asef le-toldot yahadut," *Polin* 19 (2004): 13–27.

29. Haim Dov Horowitz, "She'elat ha-calcala u'mekoma be'tenuatenu ha'leumit," *Hashiloah* 9 (1902): 17–32, 130–149, 330–305; *Hashiloah* 10 (1902–1903): 57–72, 110–127, 328–337, 400–412.

30. Ibid., 60.

31. Ibid., 113.

32. Ibid.

33. Ibid.

34. Ibid., 118.

35. Daniel Gutwein described the displacement of the non-Jewish population as "horizontal displacement" and the displacement of the Jewish population as "vertical displacement." It naturally had a far-reaching influence on Jewish society. See Gutwein, "Proletarizatzia ve-politizatzia," 150.

36. Letter of Shlomo Kaplan to Arthur Ruppin, 2 September 1912, CZA, L2, file 131/6.

37. Jaccob Lestschinsky, *Der yiddisher arbeiter in Russland* (The Jewish Worker in Russia) (Vilna: Tzukunft, 1906), 31–37.

38. Ezra Mendelsohn, *Class Struggle in the Pale: The Formative Years of the Jewish Workers' Movement in Tsarist Russia* (Cambridge: Cambridge University Press, 1970), 20–22.

39. Lestschinsky, *Der yiddisher arbeiter in Russland*, 94.

40. Rubinow, *Economic Condition of the Jews in Russia*, 526.

41. Ibid., 527–528. For more on the working conditions of the Jews in the Pale of Settlement, see Mendelsohn, *Class Struggle in the Pale*, 1–26.

42. Andrei Palovich Subotin, *Be-thum ha moshav ha yehudi* (In the Jewish Pale of Settlement) (Saint Petersburg: n.p., 1890), 31.

43. Ibid., 32.

44. Ibid., 100.

45. Ibid., 125–126.

46. Ibid.

47. Jacob Lestschinsky, "Statistika shel ayara ehat," *Hashiloah* 12 (1903–1904): 92. Lestschinsky's description of the shtetl clearly reveals the influence of Subotin.

On this, see Gur Alroey, "Demographers in the Service of the Nation: Liebman Hersch, Jacob Lestschinsky and the Start of Jewish Migration Reserarch," *Jewish History* 56, nos. 1–2 (2004): 129–150.

48. See n. 2.

49. On the infrastructure of the railways in the southwestern part of the czarist empire in 1860 and 1890, see John Norton Westwood, *A History of Russian Railways* (London: G. Allen & Unwin, 1964), 59. On the effect of the railways on Jewish society, see Israel Bartal, "Ha-rakevet magia la-ayara," in *Zman yehudi hadash: tarbut yehudit be-zman ha-hilon*, ed. Yermiyahu Yovel, vol. 1 (Jerusalem: Keter, 2007), 287–290.

50. Westwood, *History of Russian Railways*, 59.

51. Ibid., 60–100.

52. On the stops on the railway from the towns in the Pale of Settlement and Poland to the frontier, and on the cost of the journey, see *Korrespondenzblatt des Centralbureaus für Jüdische Auswanderungsangelegenheiten* (Berlin, 23.9.1909), CZA, A36, file b95.

53. Philip Taylor, *The Distant Magnet: European Emigration to the U.S.A.* (London: Harper & Row, 1971), 133.

54. Rowland, *Steam at Sea: A History of Steam Navigation* (New York: Praeger, 1970), 131.

55. See Hendrik Willem Van Loon, *Ships and How They Sailed the Seven Seas* (New York: G. G. Harrap, 1935).

56. Kurt Himer, *Geschichte Der Hamburg Amerika Linie* (Hamburg: Gustav Petermann, 1914), 147.

57. On the HAPAG shipping company, see Lamar Cecil, *Alfred Ballin: Business and Politics in Imperial Germany—1888–1918* (Princeton, NJ: Princeton University Press, 1967); Kurt Himer, *Die Hamburg Amerika Linie: Im Sechsten Jahrzeit Ihrer Entwicklung, 1897–1907* (Hamburg: n.p., 1907); Kurt Himer, *75 Jahrigen Jubilaum Der Hamburg Amerika Linie* (Hamburg: Gustav Petermann, 1913).

58. On the Dutch shipping company, see Ger H. Knap, *A Century of Shipping: The History of the Royal Netherlands Steamship Company 1856–1956* (Amsterdam: De Bussy, n.d.). On the Cunard Steamship Company, see Francis E. Hyde, *Cunard and the North Atlantic, 1840–1973: A History of Shipping and Financial Management* (London: Macmillan, 1975).

59. Cecil, *Albert Ballin*, 18.

60. Himer, *Die Hamburg Amerika Linie*, 52.

61. Shmuel Avitzur, *Namal Yafo be-ge'uto u-be-shkiato 1865–1965* (Tel Aviv: Milo Press, 1972).

62. On the Kishenev Pogrom, see Dov Valhonsky, "*Pogrom ha-petiha shel ha-me'a ha-esrim*," *He-Avar* 20 (August: n.p., 1973), 176–194; Jonathan Frankel, *Prophecy and Politics: Socialism, Nationalism, and the Russian Jews, 1862–1917* (New York: Cambridge University Press, 1981); Edward Judge, *Easter in Kishenev: Anatomy of a Pogrom* (New York: New York University Press, 1992). On the pogroms of the

1880s and the beginning of the twentieth century, see John D. Klier and Shlomo Lambroza, "Pogroms: Anti-Jewish Violence in Modern Russia History," in *Modern Russian History* (New York: Cambridge University Press, 1992); Abraham Ascher, "Anti-Jewish Pogroms in the First Russian Revolution, 1905–1907," in *Jews and Jewish Life in Russia and the Soviet Union*, ed. Yaakov Ro'i (Tel Aviv: Frank Cass, 1995), 127–145.

63. Lambroza, *Pogroms*, 228.

64. Moshe Rosenblatt was a well-known Jewish communal worker and member of the Mizrahi movement who did a great deal of work for the Jewish community in Kiev. On Rosenblatt, see *A Tekufe fun 60 yor: a Zamelbuch in Idish un Hebreish Likhvod dem 60 yorigen Yuvileum fun Ha-Rav Moshe Rosenblatt* (A Period of 60 Years: Anthology in Yiddish and Hebrew for the 60-Year Jubilee of Rebai *Moshe Rosenblatt)* (New York: Yubileum Komitat, 1936).

65. Letter of Moshe Rosenblatt to Israel Zangwill, 6 November 1905, CZA, A36, file 53b. In the archives of the Jewish Territorial Organization there are many letters of this kind from other places in the Pale of Settlement describing the terrible suffering of the Jews in the Pale at the beginning of the twentieth century.

66. Letter of Moshe Rosenblatt to Israel Zangwill, 6 December 1905, CZA, A36, file 53a.

67. Ibid., file 53b.

68. Kalarash was a shtetl in Bessarabia. According to the census of 1897, it had a population of 5,153, of whom 4,594 (89.1%) were Jews. See *Sefer Kalarash le-hantshat zikhram shel yehidei ha-ayara sh-nekhreva bi-yemei hashoa* (Kalarash: A yizkor [memorial] book for the Jewish community of Kalarash, Moldova), ed. Noah Tamir (Tel Aviv: Arieli Press, 1966), 37. Letter of the committee of support for those hurt by the disturbances in Kalarash to Israel Zangwill (October–November 1906), CZA, A36, file 53b.

69. See Joseph Samuel, *Jewish Immigration to the United States from 1881–1910* (New York: Arno and the New York Times, 1914), 93; reprint, 1961. On the pogroms of the year 1881–1882, see Michael I. Aronson, *Troubled Waters: The Origins of the 1881 Anti-Jewish Pogroms in Russia* (Pittsburgh: University of Pittsburgh Press, 1990), 108–124; John Doyle Klier, *Russian, Jews and the Pogroms of 1881–1882* (New York: Cambridge University Press, 2011). For more on the pogroms of the beginning of the 1880s, see Stephen M. Berk, *Year of Crisis, Year of Hope: Russian Jewry and the Pogroms of 1881–1882* (Westport, CT: Greenwood Press 1985).

70. Zosa Szajkowski, "The European Attitude to East European Jewish Immigration (1881–1893)," *American Jewish Historical Quarterly* 41, no. 2 (1951): 127–162.

71. According to the census of 1897, there were 11,933 people in the shtetl, of whom 5,388 (45%) were Jews. See Jakob Segal, *Internationale Konfessionsstatistik* (Berlin: Veroeffentlichung des Bureaus fuer Statistik der Juden, 1914), 78.

72. David Cohen, *Schpola, masekhet hayei yehudim be-ayara* (Schpola: Jewish Life in Ukrainian Town) (Haifa: Yirgon Yotzei Schpola Be-israel, 1965), 194–195.

73. See Saul Stampfer, "The Geographic Background of Eastern European Jewish Migration to the United States before World War I," in *Migration across Time and Nation*, ed. Ira Glazier and Luigi De Rosa (New York: Holmes & Meir, 1985), 220–230.

74. Recently, Joel Perlman reached a similar conclusion. In his study, he based himself on the lists of Jewish immigrants who entered the United States through Ellis Island. See Joel Perlman, "The Local Geographic Origins of Russian-Jewish Immigrants circa 1900," Levy Economics Institute of Bard College, August 2006, working paper no. 465, 1–41.

Chapter Two

1. Irving Howe, *World of Our Fathers* (New York: Touchstone, 1977), 57.

2. Haim Avni, *Mi-bitul ha-inkvizitsya ve-ad hok ha-shevut: Toledot ha-hagira ha-yehudit le-argentina* (The History of Jewish Immigration to Argentina, 1810–1950) (Jerusalem: Magnes Press, 1982), 106.

3. Philip Taylor, *The Distant Magnet: European Emigration to the USA* (London: Harper & Row, 1971), 27.

4. Samuel Baily, *Immigrants in the Land of Promise: Italians in Buenos Aires and New York City, 1870–1914* (Ithaca, NY, and London: Cornell University Press, 1999), 35.

5. Dudley Baines, *Emigration from Europe, 1815–1930* (New York: Cambridge University Press, 1995), 26.

6. Ibid., 11; 12; 25.

7. Ibid., 9

8. Ibid., 9; 13.

9. "Ha-nedida ha-yehudit ve-temikha la-nodedim," *Hed ha-Zman* 169 (2 August 1908): 1. See also Mark Wischnitzer, *To Dwell in Safety: The Story of Jewish Migration since 1800* (Philadelphia: Jewish Publication Society of America, 1948), 100–105.

10. "Ha-nedida ha-yehudit ve-temikha la-nodedim."

11. Janovsky Archive, CZA, A156, Emigration, file 26, 4.

12. Ibid., 6.

13. I. L. Kahanowitz, "Mitokh ha-thum," *Hed ha-Zman* 143 (16.7.1907), 2–3.

14. See the budget of the information bureau, Central Archives for the History of the Jewish People (henceforth CAHJP), JCA section, files 34, 38b, 37b, 36b, 35c, 34c.

15. Ibid.

16. Shmuel Janovsky, *Divrei ha-arakha, Zikhronot, Ktavim Nivharim* (Appreciation, Memoirs and Selected Writing) (Tel Aviv: Brit Rishonim, 1947), 15.

17. Ibid., 20.

18. Ibid.,14.

19. Ibid.

20. Ibid.

21. "Oberatung fun die murshim," *Der Jüdische Emigrant* 3 (9 Adar 1909), 13.

22. "Mitokh ha-thum: rishmei masa," *Ha-Zman* 143 (16.7.1907), 3.

23. "Der Libauer Zuzamanfahr," *Der Jüdische Emigrant*, 18 (8 Tishri 1911), 1–14. On the conference in Vilna, see "Der Vilner Zuzamanfahr," *Der Jüdische Emigrant* 10, (3 Sivan 1913), 1–16.

24. "Ha-emigratzia derekh hof Libau," *Ha-Zman* 56 (9.3.1907), 3.

25. CAHJP, JCA section, file 36a, 1–3. See also "Die badaitung fun der arbeit fun informatzyones biro," *Der Jüdische Emigrant* (23 Tevet 1908), 13.

26. Janovsky Archive, CZA, A156, Emigration, file 26, 10.

27. Ibid., 13.

28. "The Objects of the 'Jewish Immigrant,'" *Jewish Immigrant* 1 (August 1908): 2. See also Wischnitzer, *Visas to Freedom: The History of HIAS* (Cleveland and New York: World, 1956), 42–43.

29. See, e.g., Alexander Harkavi, *Etses far emigrant velche fohrn keyn amerike—faraynigte staaten* (Minsk: Kultur, 1905). On Harkavi's visit to the ports of Europe and his conclusions, see the next chapter. On his visit to the ports of Europe, see also Alexander Harkavy, "Diary of a Visit to Europe in the Interests of Jewish Emigration, 1906–1907," AJHS, Harkavy papers.

30. *Emigranten un agenten: Nit keyn oysgetrakhte mayses* (Saint Petersburg: Yosef Luria Druk, 1912).

31. Ibid., 20.

32. Meir Diezengoff, "Me-et ha-vaad ha-palestinai be-odessa," *Ha-Tzofei* 658 (13 Adar 1905), 3.

33. Ibid.

34. "Ha-nedida ha-yehudit ve-ha-temicha ha-nodedim," *Hed ha-Zman* 169 (2 August 1908), 2.

35. Menahem Sheinkin, *Yedies vegen eretz yisroel* (Vilna: Kadimd, 1908), 1; and see also Margalit Shilo, "Lishkat ha-modiin shel Sheinkin be-yafo" (The Information Bureau of Mernahem Sheinkin in Jaffa during the Second Aliya Period), *Ha-Tzionut* 17 (1993): 39–70.

36. Menahem Sheinkin, *Lishkat ha-modiim be-eretz israel*, 1907, Labor Archives, IV-108–12a.

37. Sheinkin's lecture on 26 Tevet 1913, CZA, A24, file, 52/2.

38. Hadash, "Mosdotenu ha tzionim," *Ha-Po'el Ha-Tza'ir* 6 (15 Tevet 1910), 10.

39. From a letter of complaint sent to the Odessa Committee by the "Beit Ha-Am" in Jaffa, 27 July 1906, CZA, A24, file 60/6, 1.

40. Ibid., 2.

41. Ibid.

42. Afdi, "Hed eretz-israel," *Ha-Yom* 88 (26 Heshvan 1907), 1.

43. Menahem Usishkin, "Mo'ed ha-hevra ha-palestina'it," *Hed ha-Zman* 32 (13 Heshvan 1908), 3.

44. For an example of such a booklet, see Sheinkin, *Yedies vegen eretz yisroel* (Vilna: Kadimd, 1908).

45. Z. Rubashov, "Nehutza Avoda," *Ha-Olam* 43 (27 November 1911), 4–5.

46. Menahem Sheinkin, "Avoda nehutza," *Ha-Olam* 46 (18 December 1911), 5–6.

47. Janovsky, *Divrei ha-arakha, Zikhronot, Ktavim Nivharim*, 22.

48. Margalit Shilo, "Lishkat Ha-modi'in shel Sheinkin be Yaffo," 58–59.

49. Letter of Eisenstadt to Ruppin, 14 June 1914, CZA, L2, file 138.

50. Letter of B. A. Goldberg to Ruppin, 23 April 1913, CZA, L2, file 133/1.

51. Letter of Haim Levinsky to Ruppin, 28 April 1914, CZA, L2, file 131/1.

52. Letter of [name unclear] to Arthur Ruppin, 23 February 1913, CZA, L2, file 135/5.

53. Letter of B. A. Goldberg to Ruppin, 25 May 1913, CZA, L2, file 133/1.

54. See Moyshe Zelnik's letter to the IRO, 12 January 1913, AJHS, I-90 (IRO), Box 122. On this letter and others, see Gur Alroey, *Bread to Eat and Clothes to Wear: Letters from Jewish Migrants in the Early Twentieth Century* (Detroit: Wayne State University Press, 2011).

55. Letter of Moshe Borgin to the IRO, 6 July [year unknown], AJHS, I–91 (IRO), Box 122.

56. Letter of Ayzik Blum to the IRO, undated [1905], AJHS, I–91 (IRO), Box 122.

57. Letter of [name of writer unknown] to the IRO, undated [1905], AJHS, I–91, (IRO), Box 122.

58. Letter of Ben-Zion Lansky to Arthur Ruppin, 13 Shvat 1914, CZA, L2, file 133 VI.

59. Letter of N. Shmuglin to Arthur Ruppin, 32 Adar 1914, CZA, L2, file 137/2.

60. Letter of Moshe Mordechai to Arthur Ruppin, 25 Adar 1912, CZA, L2, file 138.

61. See the letter of Lipa Herzberg to Arthur Ruppin, 20 April 1914, CZA L2, file III/133.

62. Letter of Israel Nevelstein to Arthur Ruppin, 12 May 1914, CZA, L2, file 138.

63. Letter of Rabinowitz to Ruppin, 26 February 1914, CZA, L2, file 135/1.

64. See A. B. Goldberg, representative of the Hevrat Hachsharat Ha-Yishuv in Vilna, to Ruppin and Thon, 19 January 1914, CZA, L2, file 133/1.

65. Ibid.

66. I. Litvak to Ruppin and Thon, 6 Shevat 1914, CZA, L2, file 133/3.

67. Malka Kroll-Alexandrovitch, *Tsabaei ha-ir* (Tel Aviv: Bnei Shaul, 1989), 69.

68. Ibid., 10.

69. Ibid., 17

70. T. Kardash to Ruppin, 16 March 1914, CZA, L2, file 133/3.

71. Ibid.

72. Sheinkin to R. Stein, 26 March 1907, Labor Archives, IV-104–118, file 2.

73. Moshe Lieb Lilienblum, *Ketavim Autobiografi'im*, vol. 3 (Jerusalem: Mosad Bialik, 1970), 14.

74. Theodor Herzl, "The Jewish State," in Arthur Herzberg, *The Zionist Idea* (New York: Doubleday, 1966), 221.

75. On the immigration policy of the Zionist movement with regard to Palestine, see Margalit Shilo, "Tovat Ha-Am o Tovat Ha-aretz: Yahasa shel ha-tnua ha-tsiyonit la-aliyah be'tkufat ha-aliyah hashniya," *Cathedra* 46 (1988): 119–121.

76. Yediot from Eretz Israel, *Ha-Yom* 89 (28 Heshvan 1907), 2.

77. Letter of Sheinkin to Otto Warburg [1908?], CZA, A24, file 52.

78. Sheinkin's lecture, 21 Tevet 1913, CZA, A24, file 52/2.

79. Letter of Sheinkin to Mr. S. Weisfeld, of the 4 Iyyar 1907, Labor archives, IV-114–118, file 2.

80. Ibid.

81. Letter of Arthur Ruppin to Mr. Abraham Persov, 29 July 1914, CZA, L2, file 138.

82. The information bureau's answer to Eisenstadt, 25 June 1914, CZA, L2, 138.

83. Letter of Ruppin to Shalom Man, 22 Iyyar 1913, CZA, L2, 138.

84. Letter of Ruppin to Rosenboim, 23 March 1914, CZA, L2, 138.

85. Letter in reply, 22 April 1914, CZA, L2, 138.

86. Yitzhak Ben-Zvi, "Ha-hagira ve-tafkidenu," *Ha-Ahdut*, 2 Av 1910, 1–2.

87. Ibid.

88. "Le-ahar ha-congres," *Ha-Po'el Ha-Tza'ir*, 10 (4 Adar 1910), 1.

89. Ibid.

90. Bracha Habas, *Ha-Aliya Ha-Sheniya* (Tel Aviv: Am Oved, 1947), 217.

91. Menahem Sheinkin, "Dvarim ke-havayatam," *Ha-Po'el Ha-Tza'ir* 4 (28 Heshvan 1910), 3.

Chapter Three

1. "Ha-yetsia me-russia le-eretz israel" (The Departure from Russia to Eretz Israel), *Ha-Olam* 17 (12 May 1910), 14–15; "Ha-yetsia me-russia le-eretz israel," *Ha-Olam* 5 (15 February 1911), 17–18; "Ha-yetsia me-russia le-eretz israel," *Ha-Olam* 15 (6 May 1913), 9–10; "Ha-yetsia me-russia le-eretz israel," *Ha-Olam* 9 (21 Adar 1914), 15. In 1910, *Ha-Olam* for the first time published the data for 1905–1909, and from 1910 onward it published data regularly each year. *Ha-Olam* did not publish the data for 1914, but they can be found in the lists of the Odessa information bureau in the CZA, Ussishkin's personal archive, A24, file 54/2. These lists only reveal the number of immigrants who left Odessa for Palestine and their distribution according to age and sex.

2. See, for example, "Die Einvanderung Kein Palestina," *Der Jüdische Emigrant* 3 (1 Adar 1911), 10.

3. Letter of B. Spielberg to Menahem Ussishkin [1911?], CZA, A24, 54/1.

4. "Ha-yetzia me-russia le-eretz israel," *Ha-Olam*, 17 (May 1910), 4.

5. Letter of Menahem Sheinkin to A. S. Ostolvsky in Alexandria (2 Sivan 1907), Labor archives, IV-104–118, file 2.

6. CZA, L2, file 75/2. See also H. Ridkink, "Ha-hagira ha-ivrit derekh hof Yafo be-shanat 1912," *Ha-Po'el Ha-Tza'ir* (23 Shevat 1913), 11–12.

7. Ibid., 11.

8. Haim Ridnik's report, CZA, L2, file 75/2.

9. Mark Wischnitzer, *To Dwell in Safety: The Story of Jewish Migration since 1800* (Philadelphia: Jewish Publication Society of America, 1948), 133.

10. Tartakower, *Nedudei ha-yehudim ba-olam* (Jerusalem: Ha-makhon le haskala tzionit, 1947), 15.

11. David Gurevich, Aaron Gertz, and Roberto Bachi, *Ha-Aliyah, ha-yishuv ve ha-tenua ha-tivit shel ha-ukhlusia be-eretz israel* (Jerusalem: Ha-makhlaka le-Statistika shel he-sokhnut ha-yehudit le-eretz israel 1944), 21.

12. On those sailing from Trieste, see CZA, L2, file 141 and file 84. It should be pointed out that these numbers do not include the immigrants from Yemen and Salonika, who did not come to Palestine for the same reasons, and who should not be seen in the historical context of the mass migration of the Jews of Eastern Europe. For this reason, we have not discussed them in this work.

13. R. Katznelson was the first scholar to examine the immigrants to Palestine from Odessa in the years 1905–1909 according to the three criteria of sex, age, and occupation. See R. Katznelson, *L'Immigrazione Degli Ebrei in Palestina Nei Tempi Moderni* (Napoli: Studio Statistico Demografico, 1930).

14. Yosef Gorny, "Ha-Shinu'im Bamivne ha-hevrati ve ha-politi shel ha-aliya ha-sheniyah bashanim 1904–1940" (Changes in the Social and Political Structure of the Second Aliya between 1904 and 1940), *Ha-Tziyonut* 1 (1970): 204–246.

15. Letter of B. Spielberg to Ussishkin, 5 July 1913, list of passengers No. 51, CZA, A24, 1152.

16. On the negative image of the United States, see Kimmy Kaplan, *Ortodoxia ba-olam he-hadash* (Jerusalem: Merkaz Shazar, 2002), 195–209.

17. Me-hayei Yafo, *Ha-Po'el Ha-Tza'ir*, 1 (7 Tishrei 1913), 20.

18. See "Men Schreibt Unz," *Der Jüdische Emigrant*, vol. 8 (23 May 1909), 9.

19. Menahem Sheinkin, *Ha-modi'im be-eretz israel*, 1907, Labor Archives, IV-108–12.

20. Ben-Horin, "Mikhtavim mi-eretz israel," *Ha-Zman* 69 (10 Nisan 1906), 2.

21. Ben-Horin, "Mikhtavim mi-eretz israel," *Ha-Zman* 166 (22 Av 1906), 2.

22. Afdi, "Hed eretz isra'el," *Ha-Yom* 102 (15 Kislev 1907), 1.

23. Ben-Horin, "Mikhtavim me-eretz isra'el," 1.

24. "Reshimot Eretz Israel," *Ha-Yom*, 7 Heshvan 1906, 1.

25. Labor Archives, 1V-108–12b, 1.

26. "Me-hayei Yafo," *Ha-Po'el Ha-Tza'ir* (19 Iyyar 1914), 13.

27. Letter of Sheinkin to Warburg [1908?], CZA, A24, 52.

28. Yehuda Slutzky, Introduction to *Toldot tenu'at ha-avoda ha-yisraelit* (Tel Aviv: Am Oved, 1973), 146. See also Yosef Gorny, "Ha-shinu'im ba-mivne ha-hevrati ve ha—politi shel aliyah ha-shniah ba-shanim 1904–1914," 205–206.

Chapter Four

1. See CAHJP, JCA section, file 34a; and see also "Vi Azui Bakomt Men In Auslandishen Pas?" *Der Jüdische Emigrant* 3 (9 Tevet 1908), 8. The practice described here applied to the northwestern part of the Pale of Settlement, but conclusions may be drawn from it concerning other areas.

2. "Vi Azui Bakomt Men In Auslandishen Pas?" 8.

3. Ibid., 10.

4. Sheinkin, *Yedies Vegen Eretz Yisroel*, 3–4.

5. The rouble is subdivided into 100 *kopeks*. In 1900 one rouble was equivalent to a half-dollar, which is 11 dollars today. In the early twentieth century 50 kopeks would be equivalent to about 5.5 dollars today.

6. Ibid. See also David Kushnir, *Moshel Ha'iti Be-Yeushala'im: Ha-Ir Ve-Ha-Mahoz Be-Einei Ali Ekrem Bey, 1906–1908* (A Governor in Jerusalem: The City and Province in the Eyes of Ali Ekrem Bey, 1906–1908) (Jerusalem: Yad Yitzhak Ben Zvi, 1995), 62.

7. For a typical example, see Shimon Kushnir, *Anshei nevo: pirkei alila shel anshei ha-aliya ha-sheniya* (Tel Aviv: Am Oved, 1968), 27–28. Kushnir relates that Noah Naftolsky, one of the outstanding figures among the pioneers of the second aliyah, was arrested by the police at one of the underground meetings of the Po-alei Tzion Party on an evening when there was a dispute in the city park with their "treacherous" rival. See also Shimon Kushnir, *Ha-roeh le–me-rahok* (Tel Aviv: Am Oved, 1972), 18. Kushnir relates that Shemuel Yavneli left Russia disguised as an old man after he had criticized the negligence of the police during the pogroms against the Jews.

8. Sheinkin, *Yedies Vegen Eretz Yisroel*, 10.

9. M. Sheinkin, letter to the Odessa information bureau of the 28 of Tammuz 1907, CZA, A24, file 51 II, 4.

10. Kushnir, *Moshel Ha–iti Be-Yerushala'im*, 37.

11. Ibid., 55.

12. On the value of the dollar at the beginning of the twentieth century in terms of today's value, see *http://oregonstate.edu/cla/polisci/individual-year-conversion-factor-tables* (accessed 1 November 2013).

13. See *Die Faraynigte Shtaten fun Amerika—Algemeine Yedies Far Die Vos Villen Forn in Dem Land* (Saint Petersburg: Yosef Luria Druk, 1908), 6. And also *Algemeine Yedies: Yedies Far Die Vos Villen Forn in Fremde Lender* (Saint Petersburg: Yosef Luria Druk, 1906), 54. In comparing the prices of boat tickets in 1908 with those in later years, I find that they did not change significantly. See, for example, *Der Jüdische Emigrant* 15 (21 Elul 1904): 8–9.

14. See *Algemeine Yedies*, 14. The director of the JCA information bureau in Saint Petersburg pointed out in his booklet *Emigration* that half of the tickets with which the emigrants sailed were prepaid. See the Janovsky Archive, CZA, A 156, Emigration, file 26, 30.

15. Ibid.

16. *Die Faraynigte Shtaten fun Amerika*, 11–12.

17. Sheinkin, *Yedies Vegen Eretz Yisroel*, 6. On the sailing route from Trieste, see CZA, L2, file 84.

18. See Zosa Szajkowski, "Suffering of Jewish Emigrants to America in Transit through Germany," *Jewish Social Studies* 13 (1951): 106–107.

19. *Die Faraynigte Shtaten*, 16–17.

20. "Ha-emigratzia derech hof Libau," *Ha-Zman* 123 (6 June 1907), 3. See also "Reise Notiszen von Ostreichishen Granitz," *Der Jüdische Emigrant* 2 (12 Kislev 1908), 13; and Pamela Nadell, "From Shtetl to Border: East European Jewish Emigrants and the Agents System, 1868–1914," in *Studies in the American Jewish Archives*, ed. Jacob R. Marcus and Abraham J. Peck (Cincinnati: American Jewish Archives, 1984), 51–52; and Tobias Brinkman, "Managing Mass Migration Jewish Philanthropic Organizations and Jewish Mass Migration from Eastern Europe, 1868/1869–1914," *Leidschrift* 22, no. 1 (2007): 71–90.

21. "Ha-emigratzia derech hof Libau," *Ha-Zman* 121, (4 June 1907), 3.

22. Ibid.

23. Ibid.

24. Ibid. For other cases, see CAHJP, JCA section, file 34a.

25. "Ha-emigratzia derech hof Libau," *Ha-Zman* 55 (8.3.1907), 3.

26. Ibid.

27. Ibid.

28. "Agenten-shwindler," *Der Jüdische Emigrant* 1 (1 Shevat 1909), 14.

29. Ibid.

30. Sheinkin, *Yedies Vegen Eretz Yisroel*, 5.

31. From a letter of complaint sent to the Odessa Committee by Beit Ha-Am in Jaffa, 10 Av 1906, CZA, 60/6, 24A, 1.

32. Ibid.

33. Afdi, "Hed Eretz-Israel," *Ha-Yom* (4 Tishri 1906), 1–2.

34. Haim Ridnik, "Le-she'elat ha-hagira be-eretz-israel" [1912?], CZA, L2, file 179.

35. Sfog (Shmuel Tchernowitz), "Halelei ha-emigratzia," *Ha-Zman* 144 (1 Av 1907), 2.

36. "Lishkat modi'in la-nodedim," *Ha-Yom*, 139 (27 Tevet 1907), 2.

37. For the price of the boat ticket from Hamburg to New York, see *Der Jüdische Emigrant* 6 (13 Nisan 1908), 30. A boat ticket to Boston cost 75 roubles; tickets to Philadelphia and Baltimore cost 79 roubles; to Galveston, 110 roubles; to Canada, 70 roubles; and to Palestine, only 12.5 roubles. Ibid. For the prices of train journeys in the Pale of Settlement, see *Centralbureaus für jüdische Auswanderungsangelegenheiten* (September 1909): 9. Because the cost of the train journey changed in accordance with the distance from the shtetl or town to the frontier station, an average was made of the prices from various areas in the Pale of Settlement to the frontier. For the prices of the train journeys from the frontier stations

to the port, see CZA, A36, file 95b. For the cost of the medical examination, see CAHJP, JCA section, J. Teplitzki, file, 34c; *Reisebericht*, January 1907, 6, CAHJP, JCA section, file 34c.

38. On the value of the dollar at the beginning of the twentieth century in terms of today's value, see: *http://oregonstate.edu/cla/polisci/individual-year-con version-factor-tables* (accessed 1 November 2013).

39. Report on the Condition of the Immigrants in Jaffa, 1906, Labor Archives, IV-108–12b, 1.

40. Zeev Smilansky, "Al dvar ha-aliya ha-ivrit be-eretz israel," *Ha-Yom* 117 (30 Kislev 1907), 2.

41. Kurt Himer, *Die Hamburg-Amerika Linie Im Sechsten Jahrzehnt Ihrer Ent-wicklung, 1897–1907* (Hamburg: n.p., 1907), 53–56.

42. *Der Jüdische Emigrant* 21 (16 December 1910), 19.

43. *Durch Bremen Keyn Amerika mit den Dampf Shifen fun Nord-deutscher Lloyd* (Bremen: n.p., n.d.), 5–8.

44. Kurt Himer, *Geschichte Der Hamburg-Amerika Linie* (Hamburg: Gustav Petermanm, 1914), 147.

45. *Durch Bremen Kein Amerika*, 10.

46. On the Poor Jews' Temporary Shelter, see Aubrey Newman and W. Massil, *Pattern of Migration, 1850–1914* (London: University College of London, 1996), 175–186.

47. Edward Steiner, *On the Trail of the Immigrants* (New York: Fleming H. Revell, 1906), 43.

48. Ibid., 45.

49. "Oyfen Yom," *Der Jüdische Emigrant* 8 (28 April 1909), 7–8.

50. S. Bloch, "Fun Bremen kein Argentina," *Der Jüdische Emigrant* 21 (28 November 1909), 6.

51. Ibid., 3.

52. "Die libauyer Shifen," *Der Jüdische Emigrant* 8 (14 May 1909), 12.

53. See Hamburg Staatsarchiv, Auswanderungsmat 1, IIA IVc Nr 5.

54. *Durkh Bremen Keyn Amerika mit den Dampf Shifen fun Nord-deutscher Lloyd*, 38–41.

55. Alexander Harkavy, "Diary of a Visit to Europe in the Interests of Jewish Emigration," 1906–1907, 5, AJHS, Harkavy Papers.

56. *Reports of the Immigration Commission Steerage Conditions*, 61st Congress, 3rd Session, Doc. 753, Washington, DC, 1911.

57. *Steerage Conditions*, 14. See also S. Bloch, "Fun Bremen keyn Argentina," *Der Jüdische Emigrant* 21 (16 Kislev 1910), 3.

58. *Steerage Conditions*, 14.

59. Ibid., 7.

60. Ibid., 18.

61. For the route taken from Trieste to Jaffa, see CZA, L2, file 84.

62. For the route taken from Odessa to Jaffa, see ibid., A9, file 28.

63. Y. Y. Halperin, "Mehayei ha-yehudim be-arei ha-sadeh," *Ha-Zman* 12 (14 January 1910), 3.

64. "Le-to'elet ha-nos'im le-eretz ha-kedosha," *Ha-Herut* 59 (20 Tevet 1911), 3.

65. Em Kol Hai, "Reshimot me-masai le-eretz-yisrael," *Hed Ha-Zman* 107 (28 Adar 1911), 1.

66. A. Yaffe, "El ha-Gola," *Hapo'el Ha-Tza'ir* (20 Av 1911): 20.

67. Haya Rotberg, *Sefer Me'uhar* (Tel Aviv: Am Oved, 1987), 115.

68. Dvid Smilansky, *Ir Noledet* (A Town is Born) (Tel Aviv: Misrad Ha-bita-hon, 1981), 22.

69. Ibid., 24.

70. Afdi, "Hed eretz-israel," *Ha-Yom* 47 (4 Tishri 1905), 2.

71. Letter of Sheinkin to the Odessa information bureau, 28 Tammuz 1907, CZA, A24, file 51/2, 4.

72. Letter of Abraham Yitzhak Neustein to Arthur Ruppin, 27 March 1908, ibid., L2, file 131/5, 1.

73. Letter of the Palestine Office to David Yudilevitz, 26 January 1912, ibid., A192, file 1231.

74. Letter from Carmel Hotel to Ruppin, 9 February 1912, ibid., L2, file 79/2

75. Ibid.

76. On the first encounter with New York, see Irving Howe and Kenneth Libo, *How We Lived* (New York: Plume, 1979), 25–42.

77. Yitzhak Ben-Zvi, *Masaot* (Journeys) (Jerusalem: Ha-machon le-hotsaa laor be-israel, 1960), 10.

78. Em Kol Hai, "Reshimot me-masaei eretz-israel," *Hed ha-Zman* 107 (28 Iyyar 1911), 1.

79. Smilansky, *Ir Noledet*, 27.

80. "Yafo," *Ha-Herut*, 47 (8 February 1911), 2.

81. Letter of Aharon Shahak to David Yudilevitz, 22 April 1910, CZA, A192, file 1259.

82. Ben-Zvi, *Masa'ot* (Journeys), 11.

83. Shlomo Tzemach, *Shana Rishona* (First Year) (Tel Aviv: Am Oved, 1965), 58–64. Rachel Yannait described a similar impression in her book *Anu Olim* (We Immigrate) (Tel Aviv: Am Oved, 1961), 3.

84. Letter of Sheinkin to the Odessa information bureau, 28 Tammuz 1907, CZA, A24, file 51/2, 5.

85. Ibid.

86. Haim Hissin, *Ha-havatzelet* 37 (23 Tammuz 1907), 297.

87. Ibid.

88. H. Aronov, *Ha-Hashkafa*, year 5, 15 (4 Kislev 1908), 4–5.

89. Letter of Sheinkin to the Odessa Information Bureau, 28 Tammuz 1907, CZA, A24, file 51/2, 4.

Chapter Five

1. Zeev Smilansky, "Ha-Yishuv ha-Yehudi be-Yafo—al pi reshimot statistiot she na'asu bi-shnat 1905," *Ha-Omer* 1 (1907), 66

2. Haim Ridnik, *Doch al she'elat ha-hagira be-eretz israel* (1912?), CZA, L2, 79/1, 1.

3. "Me-Hayei Yafo," *Ha-Po'el Ha-Tza'ir*, 30 (19 Iyyar 1914), 13.

4. Letter of Sheinkin to the Odessa information bureau, 18 Tammuz 1907, CZA, A24, file 51/2, 5.

5. Haim Ridnik, *Doch al she'elat ha-hagira be-eretz israel*, 1–2.

6. Ibid.

7. Lecture of Menahem Sheinkin on 26 Tevet 1913, CZA, A24, file 52/2.

8. Ridnik, *Doch al she'elat ha-hagira be-eretz israel*, 3.

9. "Me-Hayei Yafo," *Ha-Po'el Ha-Tza'ir*, 30 (19 Iyyar 1914), 13.

10. "Letter From Palestine'" *Hed ha-Zman*, 50, (3 Av 1909), 2.

11. Zeev Smilansky's archive, Labor Archives, IV-104–95, file 10.

12. Libertus, "Me-hodesh le-hodesh": *Ha-Me'ir*, (Iyyar 1912), 138.

13. Ibid.

14. See "Me-eretz israel," *Hed ha-Zman*, 114 (10 Sivan 1911), 1.

15. Ibid.

16. Ben-Avraham, "Yafo," *Ha-Herut*, 25 (12 Kislev 1911), 3.

17. Ibid.

18. M. Kremer, "Ha-shavu'a," *Ha-Herut*, 23 (3 Av 1909), 3.

19. Ben-Avraham, "Yafo," *Ha-Herut*, 100 (27 Sivan 1911), 2.

20. Sarah Azaryahu, *Pirkei Ha'im*, (Tel Aviv: Am Oved, 1957), 30–31.

21. Bracha Habas, *David Ben Gurion ve-doro* (Tel Aviv: Am Oved, 1952), 60.

22. Ha-Ro'eh, "Mikhtav me-eretz israel," *Ha-Zman*, 150 (3 Av 1909), 2.

23. Ha-Roeh, "Me-eretz israel," ibid., 114 (10 Sivan 1911), 1.

24. "Hadashot be-isra'el," *Ha-Herut*, 14 (23 Heshvan 1911), 3.

25. X, "Al dvar mishar be-nefashot be-yafo," ibid., 150 (18 Elul 1911), 3.

26. Ha-Ro'eh, "Me-eretz isra'el," *Hed ha-Zman*, 114 (10 Sivan 1911), 1.

27. S. Lerner, "Moda'a," *Ha-havatzelet*, 250 (5 Iyyar 1907), 203.

28. "Azhara nehutza," *Ha-hashkafa*, 62 (26 Iyyar 1907), 4.

29. Ibid.; and see also Rezner, "Tzafat," ibid., 68 (18 Sivan 1907), 3.

30. Z. Israel, "Yafo," ibid., 62 (4 Sivan 1907), 4.

31. Ibid.

32. Ben-Avraham, "Yafo," *Ha-Herut*, 4 (19 Iyyar 1911), 2. On Pappenheim's voyage to the East and her talk in Beit Ha-Am in Jaffa, see also "Der kampf gegen frauen hendel be-eretz isra'el," *Unzer Leben*, 135 (13 June 1911), 3. On the growth of the phenomenon in the country, see Thon, *Avodat nashim*, 101–102. Raffi Thon, in his book *Ha-ma'avak le-shivyon Zchuyot ha-isha: sipur hayeha shel Sara Thon* (N.p.: Private publisher 1996), 33, understood the expression "foreign traffickers" used by his mother as referring to tourists who visited the country, causing prosti-

262 Notes to Chapter Five

tution to flourish. This expression in fact refers to white-slave traders, and one may presume that his mother was referring to the white-slave traffic that was prevalent at that time in the country.

33. On Pappenheim, see Marion Kaplan, *The Jewish Feminist Movement in Germany* (London: Greenwood Press, 1979), 29–57; 103–145.

34. "Ha-mishar be-nashim be-artzenu," *Ha-Ahdut*, 28–29 (28 Iyyar 1911), 4.

35. Shmuel Almog, "Ha-Aliyah ha-sheniya be-eineha u-be-einenu," *Leumiut Tzionut ve-Antishemiut*, ed. Shmuel Almog (Jerusalem: Ha-sifriya Ha-tsiyoniy, 1992), 194.

36. Zerubavel, "Im hitgabrut ha-hagira," *Ha-ahdut*, 34, (25 Sivan 1914), 1.

37. Zeev Smilansky Archive, Labor Archives, IV-104–95, file 14.

38. Ibid.

39. Ruth Kark, *Yaffo, 1799–1917* (Jerusalem: Yad Yitazhak Ben Zvi, 1985), 164; see also Chana Ram, *Ha-Yishuv Ha-Yehudi be Yafo: me-kehila Sefaradit le-merkaz tzioni, 1839–1939* (Jerusalem: n.p., 1996), 164.

40. "Me-Hayei Yafo," *Ha-Po'el Ha-Tza'ir*, 1, (7 Tishrei 1912), 20.

41. M. Sheinkin, "Misparim machkimim—le-matzav ha-yishuv he-hadash be-eretz israel," *Ha-Olam*, 14 (1 April 1908), 178–179.

42. On Stein's factory, see Shmuel Avitzur, "Halutz ha-ta'asia ha-hadasha be-eretz-israel: beit haroshet L. Stein, gilgulo ve-aharito," *Chtedra* 15 (Nisan 1983), 69–94. See also Shmuel Avitzur, *Matzevet filter le-mamtzi: mifalo ha-nahshoni shel L. Stein ve-aharito* (Tel Aviv: Mozeon Haaretz, 1982); and Yossi Beilin, *Ha-ta'asia ha-ivrit—shorashim* (Jerusalem: Keter, 1987).

43. Zmani, "Le-inyanei ha-sha'a," *Ha-Po'el Ha-Tza'ir*, 2 (14 Tishrei 1913), 1.

44. M. Sheinkin, "Sikkum le-avoda shnatit," 28 June 1907, Labor Archives, IV-104–118, file 22.

45. Zeev Smilansky, "Al dvar ha-Aliyah ha-ivrit le-eretz-israel," *Ha-Yom*, 121 (6 Tevet 1907), 1.

46. Sheinkin, "Misparim machkimim," *Ha-Olam*, 14 (1 April 1908), 179.

47. Ben Yisrael, "Michtavim me-Yafo," *Ha-Zman*, 5 (4 Shvat 1914), 2.

48. Nahum Gross, *Bankai la-umma be-hitchadshuta*, vol. 1 (Ramat Gan: Masada, 1977), 53.

49. Sheinkin, *Sikkum la-avoda shnatit*, 28 June 1907, Labor Archives, IV-104–118, file 22.

50. Gross, *Bankai le-umma be'hitkhadshuta*, 1, 53.

51. Zmani, "Le-inyanei ha-sha'a," *Ha-Po'el Ha-Tza'ir*, 2 (14 Tishrei 1912), 1.

52. Letter of Sheinkin to the Odessa Committee, 18 Shvat 1909, CZA, A24, file 51/2, 2.

53. Ibid.

54. Gross, *Bankai le-umma*, 1, 60.

55. Smilansky, "Ha-yishuv ha-ivri be-Yafo," *Ha-Omer*, 1b (1907), 54.

56. Ibid., 67.

57. Sheinkin, *Sikkum la-avoda shnatit*, 28 June 1907, Labor Archives, IV-104–118, file 22.

58. Smilansky, "Ha-yishuv ha-yehudi be-yafo—al pi reshimot statistiot she na'asu be-shnat 1905," *Ha-Omer*, 1b (1907), 70–71.

59. Sheinkin, *Sikkum la-avoda shenatit*, 28 June 1907, Labor Archives, IV-104–118, file 22.

60. Smilansky, "Ha-yishuv ha-yehudi be-Yafo," 65–66.

61. Ibid., 107

62. Ibid.

63. Ibid., 108.

64. Ibid.

65. Ibid.

66. "Meoraot u-ma'asim," *Ha-Po'el Ha-Tza'ir*, 15 (17 Iyyar 1910), 14.

67. Avitzur, *Matzevet filter la mamtsi*, 127–128. In his article "Halutz ha-ta'asia," Avitzur claimed that relations between Stein and his workers were good, and that Stein had an "almost fatherly" attitude to his workers (77–78). It was only after the concern became a stock company that the regulations were written out by Stein in French but the text was falsified in the translation to Hebrew. The workers refused to sign the undertaking to observe the regulations, and in the course of the dispute, one of the workers was dismissed.

68. "Ha-shavua," *Ha-Po'el Ha-Tza'ir*, 35 (25 Sivan 1914), 18.

69. See Deborah Dwork, "Health Conditions of Jews on the Lower East Side of New York 1880–1914," *Medical Health* 25 (1981): 14–15; and also, Irving Howe, *World of Our Fathers*, 154–159.

70. Dwork, "Health Conditions of Jews," 15; and also, Charles Bernheimer, *The Russian Jew in the United States* (New York–Toronto: Young People's Missionary Movement, 1905), 125.

71. Dwork, "Health Conditions of Jews," 18.

72. "Meoraot u-ma'asim," *Ha-Po'el Ha-Tza'ir*, 15 (17 Iyyar 1910), 15.

73. Ibid.

74. I. D. Freyer, "Ha-saison ha-eretz-israeli," *Hed ha-Zman*, 229 (30 Tishrei 1910), 1–2.

75. Ha-mevaser, "Yafo," *Hashkafa*, 59 (23 Iyyar 1907), 1–2.

76. Zeev Smilansky, "Yehudei Yafo le-or ha-misparim—al ha-dirot," Labor Archives, IV-104–95, file 8, 16.

77. Ibid.

78. Ibid., 17.

79. Lestschinsky, "Statistika shel ayara ahat," *Ha-shiloach* 12 (1903–1904): 95–96.

80. Dwork, "Health Conditions of Jews," 5.

81. Ibid., 10.

82. Bernheimer, *Russian Jew in the United States*, 283–284. See also: Elizabeth C. Cromley, *Alone Together: A History of New York's Early Apartments* (Ithaca, NY,

and London: Cornell University Press, 1990); Andrew S. Dolkart, *Biography of a Tenement House in New York City* (Santa Fe, NM, and Staunton, VA: Center for American Places, 2006); Marcus T. Reynolds, *The Housing of the Poor in American Cities* (Baltimore: American Economic Association, 1893).

83. On Z. Smilansky and his long article on Jaffa, see Nurit Guvrin, *Ha-Omer: tnufato shel ktav ha-et ve-aharito* (Jerusalem: Yad Yitzhak Ben Zvi, 1980), 102.

84. Zeev Smilansky, "Ha-yishuv ha-yehudi be-Yafo—al pi reshimot statistiot she na'asu be shenat 1905," *Ha-Omer*, 1b (1907), 3–5. The data on rents in Jaffa that appear in this chapter are from Smilansky's statistical census, but they were not published in the article in *Ha-Omer*. The data given here are taken from Smilansky's personal bequest preserved in the Labor Archives, IV-104–95.

85. Zeev Smilansky, "Yehudei Yafo le-or ha-misparim al ha-dirot," Labor Archives, IV-104–95, file 8.

86. *Die Faraynigte shtaten fun Amerika*, 90.

87. Zeev Smilansky, "Yehudei Yafo le-or ha-misparim—al ha-dirot," Labor Archives, IV-104–95, file 8, 15.

88. Ibid., 3.

89. I. E. Rontch, "Der itztiger matsav fon di landsmanschaftn," *Die Idishe landsmanschaften fun New York*, ed. B. Hoffman (New York: Futuro Press, 1938), 10. Rontch said there were about 3,000 such organizations in the United States, and nearly a third of them were in New York. On the *landsmanschaften* see Howe, *World of Our Fathers*, 220–230; and also Daniel Soyer, *Jewish Associations and American Identity* (London: Harvard University Press, 1997).

90. Howe, *World of Our Fathers*, 188.

91. "Doch le-matzav ha-mehagrim be-Yafo" [1906?], Labor Archives, IV-108, 12b, 2–3.

92. Howe, *World of Our Fathers*, 184.

93. Smilansky, "Al davar ha-Aliyah ha-ivrit le-eretz-israel," *Ha-Yom*, 117 (30 Kislev 1907), 2.

94. Nahum Karlinsky, "Ha-hevra ha-hassidit shel Tzfat be-mahatzit ha-sheniya shel ha-me'a ha-tesha esrei ke-hevrat mehagrim—hebetim demografi'im ve-gibush hevrati," in Emmanuel Etkes and D. Joseph Y. Dan, eds., *Mehkarei Hassidut* (Jerusalem: Hebrew University, 1999), 151–196.

95. On these professional associations, see Mordechai Berenstein, *Dos is geven nosach ashkenaz* (Buenos Aires: Yidbuch, 1960), 287–281; Mark Wischnitzer, *Idishe ba'al-meloche tsechen in Poyln on in Litte* (Berlin: Klal 1922); S. Rombach, *Die yidische baalmeloches in Russland in der erste halft von XIX yor hundert, Zeitschrift, buch 1* (Minsk: n.p., 1926), 25–30; and Daniel Soyer, *Jewish Associations and American Identity*, 18–19.

96. Zalman David Levontin, *Agudot meshutafot be-olam u-be-olamenu* (Jaffa: Anglo-Palestine Company, 1911), 14.

97. "Agudat Ha-Tzayarim ve-ha-Tzov'im be Yerushala'im," *Ha-Or*, 74 (23 Heshvan 1911), 3.

98. "Michtav me-Yafo," ibid., year 31, 144 (1 March 1912), 2.

99. "Ha-Shavua," *Ha-Po'el Ha-Tza'ir*, 35 (25 June1914), 18.

100. *Ha-Tzvi*, year 26, 7 (14 September 1909), 2.

101. Hartza'a al hitpathuto u-pe'ulotav shel 'merkaz ba'alei melakha' be-yafo be-meshekh eser shnot kiyumo, 1907–1916, she-hugsha le Dr Arthur Ruppin, (Lecture on the Development and Activities of the Artisans' Center in the Ten Years of Its Existence, 1907–1916, given by Dr. Arthur Ruppin in the Beit Ha-Sefarim Ha-Le'umi) (Jerusalem: n.p., 1916), 2.

102. Ibid., 3.

103. Ibid., 1–2. See also Motsi La-Po'al, "Zichronot me-'merkaz ba'alei melakha' be-Yafo," *Ha-Melacha* (Sivan 1922), 16.

104. Lecture on the Development and Activities of the Artisans' Center, 6.

105. "Ha-Shavua," *Ha-Po'el Ha-Tza'ir* (25 June 1914), 18.

106. Lecture on the Development and Activities of the Artisans' Center, 7.

107. Ibid., 8.

108. Menahem Sheinkin, "Ha-poalim u-ba'alei ha-melakha ba-aliyah," *kitvei Menahem Sheinkin* (Tel-Aviv, Reuven Mas, 1935), 293.

109. Ibid., 294.

110. Ibid., 295.

111. Ibid., 296.

Chapter Six

1. S. E. Lee, "A Theory of Migration," *Demography* 6 (1996): 54–57; and also M. Wyman, "Return Migration—Old Story, New Story," *Immigrants and Minority* 1 (March 2001): 1–18.

2. Yehoshua Kaniel, "Meimadei ha-yerida min ha-aretz be-tekufat ha-aliya ha-rishona ve-ha-sheniya" (The Scope of the Emigration in the Period of the "First" and "Second" Aliyot) *Cathedra* 73 (September 1995): 115–138.

3. Ibid., 137.

4. Menahem Sheinkin, "Misparim makhkimim-le matzav ha-yishuv be eretz israel," *Ha-Olam* 14 (April 1908): 180.

5. Menahem Sheinkin, "Ma nishma sham? (le-shurat ha-ma'amarim al ha-matzav ha-nochehi be eretz-israel)" [1908?], Labor Archives, IV-104–118, file 7.

6. Zeev Smilansky, "Al davar ha-aliya ha-ivrit," *Ha-Yom*, 116 (17 December 1906), 2.

7. Smilansky Archive, Labor Archives, IV 104 95, file 10.

8. Ibid.

9. Haim Ridnik, "Ha-hagira ha-ivrit derech hof Yafo be-shenat 1912," *Ha-Po'el Ha-Tza'ir*, 18 (31 January 1913), 11–12.

10. M. Sheinkin, "Misparim makhkimim," *Ha-Olam*, 14 (1April 1908), 178.

11. Ibid. "Sikum la-avoda shenatit," 28 June 1907, Labor Archives, IV-104–118, file 22, 2.

12. Smilansky, "Al dvar ha-aliya ha-ivrit," *Ha-Yom*, 116 (17 December 1906), 2.

13. Ridnik, "Ha-hagira ha-ivrit derech hof Yafo," CZA, L2, file 75/2.

14. M. Kremer, "Ha-shavua," *Ha-Herut*, (9 November 1910), 3.

15. Smilansky, "Al dvar ha-aliya ha-ivrit," *Ha-Yom*, 121 (23 December 1906), 1.

16. I. Nahmani, "Ha-yishuv ha-hadash ve-ha-yishuv ha-yashan lifnei ha-mash-ber ha-olami," Labor Archives, IV-126–40, file 40.

17. *Lecture on the Development and Activities of the Artisans' Center in the Ten Years of Its Existence (1907–1916)*, given by Dr. Arthur Ruppin in the Beit Ha-Se-farim Ha-Le'umi (Jerusalem: n.p., 1916), 11.

18. Ibid., 14.

19. Smilansky, "Al dvar ha-aliya ha-ivrit," *Ha-Yom*, 121 (23 December 1906), 2.

20. See "Men schreibt undz," *Der Jüdische Emigrant*, 8 (1 May 1909), 9.

21. Smilansky, "Al-dvar ha-aliya ha-ivrit," *Ha-Yom*, 121 (23 December 1906), 2.

22. Ibid.

23. Paul, "Ha-korban (roman me-hayei ha-ba'im ve-ha-holchim)," *La-Yehu-dim*, 4, (14 Nisan 1912), 6.

24. Ibid.

25. Letter of Alexander Brockner to Eliyahu Oilitzky, Hanukka 1911, Labor Ar-chives, IV-104–152, file 29.

26. A. Green, "Hizuk Pnimi," *Ha-Po'el Ha-Tza'ir*, 9 (22 November 1912), 12.

27. Z. Kaharlitzky, "Palestina u-mitzra'im," *Hed ha-Zman*, 71, (25 March 1910), 2.

28. A. Yaffe, "El ha-gola," *Ha-Po'el Ha-Tza'ir*, 20 (27 June 1911), 11.

29. Bracha Habas, ed., *Ha-Aliya Ha-Sheniyah* (Tel Aviv: Am Oved, 1947), 774.

30. On the suicides among the pioneers of the second and third Aliyot, see Gur Alroey, "Halutzim ovdei derech? Sugiat ha-hitabdut al seder yoman shel ha-aliyot ha-sheniya ve-ha-slishit," *Yahadut Zmanenu* 13 (1999): 209–242.

31. "Rachel Maisel," *Ha-Po'el Ha-Tza'ir*, 10 (4 Adar bet 1910), 29.

32. "Al mot Tamar (Bilha) Berstein," *Ha-Po'el Ha-Tza'ir*, 15, (23 January 1914), 20.

Bibliography

Archival Collections

American Jewish Historical Society (AJHS)
Central Archives for the History of the Jewish People (CAHJP)
Central Zionist Archive (CZA)
Hamburg Staatsarchiv
The Pinhas Lavon Institute for Labor Movement Research (Labor Archives)

Newspapers

Ahdut Ha-Avodah (Tel Aviv)
Der Jüdische Emigrant (Saint Petersburg)
Ha-Ahdut (Jerusalem)
Ha-Hashkafa (Jerusalem)
Ha-havatzelet (Jerusalem)
Ha-Herut (Jerusalem)
Ha-Me'ir (Jaffa)
Ha-Olam (London)
Ha-Omer (Jaffa)
Ha-Or (Jerusalem)
Ha-Po'el Ha-Tza'ir (Jaffa)
Ha-Shiloah (Krakow)
Ha-Yom (Saint Petersburg)
Hed Ha-Zman (Saint Petersburg–Vilna)
Statistical Bulletin (Tel Aviv)
Unzer Leben (Odessa)

Alexandrovitch-Kroll, Malka. *Tsabaei ha-ir* (The City Painters). Tel Aviv: Bnei Shaul, 1989.

Almog, Shmuel. *Ha-Aliyah ha-sheniya be-eineha u-be-einenu* (The Second Aliya: Self-Image and Modern Interpretation). Edited by Shmuel Almog and Leumiut Tzionut ve-Antishemiut. Jerusalem: Ha-sifriya Ha-tsiyonit, 1992.

Alroey, Gur. "'Halutzim ovdei derech? Sugiat ha-hitabdut al seder yoman shel ha-aliyot ha-sheniya ve-ha-slishit" (Pioneers or Lost Souls? The Issue of Suicide in the Second and the Third Aliya). *Yahadut Zmanenu* 13 (1999): 209–242.

———. "Demographer in the Service of the Nation; Liebman Hersch, Jacob Lestschinsky and the Start of Jewish Migration Research." *Jewish History* 20 (2006): 129–150.

———. "Aliya to America? A Comparative Look at Jewish Mass-Migration, 1881–1914." *Modern Judaism* 28, no. 2 (May 2008): 109–133.

———. *Bread to Eat and Clothes to Wear: Letters from Jewish Migrants in the Early Twentieth Century*. Detroit: Wayne State University Press, 2011.

———. "The Russian Terror in Palestine: The Bar-Giora and Hashomer Associations, 1907–1920." In *Uneasy Inheritance: Russia/Israel 1880–2010*, ed. Brian Horowitz and Shai Ginsburg. Bloomington, IN: Slavica, 2013, 31–60.

Anderson, Barbara. *Human Fertility in Russia since the Nineteenth Century*. Princeton, NJ: Princeton University Press, 1979.

Aronson, I. Michael. *Troubled Waters: The Origins of the 1881 Anti-Jewish Pogroms in Russia*. Pittsburgh: University of Pittsburgh Press, 1990.

Ascher, Abraham. "Anti-Jewish Pogroms in the First Russian Revolution, 1905–1907." In *Jews and Jewish Life in Russia and the Soviet Union*, edited by Yaakov Ro'i. Tel Aviv: Frank Cass, 1995, 127–145.

Ashton, Thomas. *The Industrial Revolution, 1760–1830*. London: Oxford University Press, 1961.

Avitzur, Shmuel. *Namal Yafo be-ge'uto u-be-shkiato 1865–1965* (Jaffa Port in Its Tide and Ebb 1865–1965). Tel Aviv: Milo Press, 1972.

———. "Halutz ha-ta'asia ha-hadasha be-eretz-israel: Beit haroshet L. Stein, gilgulo ve-aharito" (A Pioneer of Modern Industry in Eretz Israel—The History of the L. Stein Factory). *Chtedra* 15 (April 1980): 69–94.

———. *Matzevet filter le-mamtzi: mifalo ha-nahshoni shel L. Stein ve-aharito* (Filter: Memorial to an Inventor). Tel Aviv: Mozeon Haaretz, 1982.

Avni, Haim. *Mi-bitul ha-inkvizitsya ve-ad hok ha-shevut: Toledot ha-hagira ha-ye-hudit le-argentina* (The History of Jewish Immigration to Argentina, 1810–1950). Jerusalem: Magnes Press, 1982.

Azaryahu, Sarah. *Pirkei Ha'im* (Life Episodes). Tel Aviv: Am Oved, 1957.

Bachi, Roberto. "Mah bein hagirah ve-aliyah?" (Between Immigration and Aliyah). *Ahdut Ha-Avodah* 4 (1946): 269–271.

Baily, Samuel. *Immigrants in the Land of Promise: Italians in Buenos Aires and New York City, 1870–1914*. Ithaca, NY, and London: Cornell University Press, 1999.

Baines, Dudley. *Emigration From Europe, 1815–1930*. New York: Cambridge University Press, 1995.

Baranovsky, M. Tugan. *Moshavot Socialistiyot* (Socialists Colonies). Ein Harod: Ha-kibutz Hameuhad, 1946.

Baron, Salo. *Be-mivhan ha-herut, prakim be-toldot yahadut amerikah* (Steeled by Adversity). Jerusalem and Tel Aviv: Shoken, 1977.

Barslavski, Moshe. *Tenuat ha-po'alim ha-eretz yisraelit* (The Israeli Labor Movement). Vol. 1. Tel Aviv: Ha-kibutz Hameuhad, 1966.

Bartal, Israel. "Ha-rakevet magia la-ayara" (The Train Arrives to Town). In *Zman yehudi hadash: tarbut yehudit be-zman ha-hilon* (New Jewish Time: Jewish Culture in a Secular Age), edited by Yermiyahu Yovel. Vol. 1. Jerusalem: Keter, 2007.

Beilin, Yossi. *Ha-ta'asia ha-ivrit—shorashim* (Roots of Israeli Industry). Jerusalem: Keter, 1987.

Ben-Zvi, Yitzhak. *Masaot* (Journeys). Jerusalem: Ha-machon le-hotsaa laor be-israel, 1960.

Berenstein, Mordechai. *Dos is geven nosach ashkenaz* (It Was the Ashkenazi Way). Buenos Aires: Yidbuch, 1960.

Berk, M. Stephe. *Year of Crisis, Year of Hope: Russian Jewry and the Pogroms of 1881–1882*. Westport, CT: Greenwood Press, 1985.

Bernheimer, Charles. *The Russian Jew in the United States*. New York and Toronto: Young People's Missionary Movement, 1905.

Bernstein, Deborah. *The Struggle for Equality: Urban Women Workers in Pre-State Israeli Society*. New York: Praeger, 1986.

Brinkman, Tobias. "Managing Mass Migration: Jewish Philanthropic Organizations and Jewish Mass Migration from Eastern Europe, 1868/1869–1914." *Leidschrift* 22, no. 1 (2007): 71–90.

Cecil, Lamar. *Alfred Ballin: Business and Politics in Imperial Germany—1888–1918*. Princeton, NJ: Princeton University Press, 1967.

Cohen, David. *Schpola, masekhet hayei yehudim be-ayara* (Schpola: Jewish Life in Ukrainian Town). Haifa: Yirgon Yotzei Schpola Be-israel, 1965.

Condran, A. Gretchen, and Ellen A. Kramarow. "Child Mortality among Jewish Immigrants to the United States." *Journal of Interdisciplinary History* 22, no. 2 (Autumn 1991): 225.

Cromley, C. Elizabeth. *Alone Together: A History of New York's Early Apartments*. Ithaca, NY, and London: Cornell University Press, 1990.

Dinur, Ben-Zion. *Yesodoteha ha-histori'im shel tekumat yisrael* (The Historical Foundations of the Establishment of Israel). New York: Beit midrash le-rabanim be-amrikah, 1955.

Dolkart, S. Andrew. *Biography of a Tenement House in New York City*. Santa Fe, NM, and Staunton, VA: Center for American Places, 2006.

Dwork, Deborah. "Health Conditions of Jews on the Lower East Side of New York 1880–1914." *Medical Health* 25 (1981): 14–15.

Eisenstadt, N. Shmuel. *Klitat ha-aliyah: mehkar sotziologi* (Immigration Absorption: Sociology Research). Jerusalem: n.p., 1952.

———. "Aliyah ve-hagirah, kavim le-tipologia sotziologit" (Aliyah and Hagirah: the Outline of a Sociological Typology). *Metzudah* 7 (1954): 83–91.

———. *A-hevra ha-yisraelit* (Israeli Society). Jerusalem: Magnes Press, 1967.

Eliav, Mordechai, ed. *Sefer ha-aliyah ha-rishonah* (The First Aliyah). Vol. 2. Jerusalem: Yad Yitzhak Ben Zvi Press, 1981.

Emigrantn un Aganten: Nit keyn oysgetrakhte mayses—nit keyn oysgetrakhte mayses (Emigrants and Agents: Not Figments of the Imagination). Saint Petersburg: Yosef Luria Druk, 1912.

Ettinger, Shmuel. *Toldot yisrael ba-et ha-hadasha* (History of the Jewish People in Modern Times). Tel Aviv: Dvir Press, 1969.

Even-Shoshan, Zvi. *Toldot ten'uat ha-po'alim be-eretz yisrael* (The History of the Labor Movement in Eretz Yisrael). Tel Aviv: Ha-kibutz ha-meuhad, 1963.

Falkus, E. Malcolm. *The Industrialisation of Russia 1700–1914*. London: Macmillan, 1972.

Faraynigte Shtaten fun Amerika—Algemeine Yedies Far Die Vos Villen Forn in Dem Land (United States of America: General Information for Those Who Will to Immigrate to the Country). Saint Petersburg: Yosef Luria Druk, 1908.

Frankel, Jonathan. *Prophecy and Politics: Socialism, Nationalism and the Russian Jews, 1862–1917*. New York: Cambridge University Press, 1981.

Gartner, Aryeh. "Ha-hagirah ha-hamonit shel yehudei eropa, 1881–1914." In *Hagirah ve-hityashvut be-yisra'el u-bamim* (Emigration and Settlement in Jewish and General History), edited by Avigdor Shinan, 233–248. Jerusalem: Merkaz Shazar, 1982.

———, and Jonathan Sarna, eds. *Yehudei artzot ha-brit* (The Jews of the United States). Jerusalem: Merkaz Shazar, 1992.

Gatrell, Peter. *The Tsarist Economy: 1850–1917*. New York: n.p., 1987.

Goldstein, Yaacov. *From Fighters to Soldiers: How the Israel Defense Forces Began.* Brighton, UK: Sussex Academic Press, 1998.

Goldstein, Yossi. "Hagirat yehudim le-russia ha-hadasha (new Russia) ve ha-ma'apecha ha-hevratit-calcalit be'kirbam be-mahalach ha-mea ha-19" (The Migration of Jews to the New Russia and the Socioeconomic Revolution They Underwent in the Nineteenth Century). *Shevut* 12, no. 28 (2004–2005): 7–29.

Gorny, Yosef. "Ha-shinu'im ba-mivne ha-hevrati ve ha—politi shel aliyah ha-sheniyah ba-shanim 1904–1914" (Changes in the Social and Political Structure of the Second Aliya between 1904 and 1940). *Ha-Tzionut* 1 (1970): 204–246.

Gross, Nahum. *Bankai le-umma be-hitchadshuta* (The History of Bank Le'umi). Vol 1. Ramat Gan: Masada, 1977.

Gurevich, David, Aaron Gertz, and Roberto Bachi. *Ha-aliyah, ha-yishuv ve ha-tenua ha-tivit shel ha-ukhlusiya be eretz-israel* (The Jewish Population of Palestine:

Immigration, Demographic Structure and Natural Growth). Jerusalem: Ha-makhlaka le-Statistika shel he-sokhnut ha-yehudit le-Eretz Israel, 1944.

Gutwein, Daniel. "Proletarizatzia ve-politizatzia: Borochov u-megamot be-hitpathut shel teoriat ha-i-proletarizatzi" (Proletarization and Politicization: Borochov and Trends in the Development of the Non-Proletarization Theory). *Shevut* 14 (1991): 141–186.

Habas, Bracha. *Ha-Aliya Ha-Sheniya* (The Second Aliyah). Tel Aviv: Am Oved, 1947.

———. *David Ben Gurion ve-doro* (David Ben Gurion and His Generation). Tel Aviv: Am Oved, 1952.

Harkavi, Alexander. *Etses far emigrant velche fahrn keyn amerike—faraynigte staaten* (Advice for Emigrants Who Travel to the United States). Minsk: Kultur, 1905.

Hart, Mitchell. *Social Science and the Politics of Modern Jewish Identity*. Stanford: Stanford University Press, 2000.

Hersch, Liebman. "International Migration of the Jews." In *International Migrations*, edited by Walter Willcox and Imre Ferenczi. New York: National Bureau of Economic Research, 1931.

Hertzberg, Arthur. *The Zionist Idea*. New York: Doubleday, 1966.

———. *Ha-yehudim be-amerikah: mifgash rav tahpukhot ben 400 shanah* (The Jews in America: Four Centuries of an Uneasy Encounter). Jerusalem and Tel Aviv: Shoken, 1994.

Himer, Kurt. *Die Hamburg Amerika Linie: Im Sechsten Jahrzeit Ihrer Entwicklung, 1897–1907*. Hamburg: n.p., 1907.

———. *75 Jahrigen Jubilaum Der Hamburg Amerika Linie*. Hamburg: Gustav Petermann, 1913.

———. *Geschichte Der Hamburg Amerika Linie*. Hamburg: Gustav Petermann, 1914.

Howe, Irving. *World of Our Fathers*. New York: Touchstone, 1977.

———, and Kenneth Libo. *How We Lived*. New York: Plume, 1979.

Hyde, E. Francis. *Cunard and the North Atlantic, 1840–1973: A History of Shipping and Financial Management*. London: Macmillan, 1975.

Hyman, Paula. *Ha-isha ha-yehudit be-svach ha-kidma* (Gender and Assimilation in Modern Jewish History: The Roles and Representation of Women). Jerusalem: Merkaz Shazar, 1997.

Janovsky, Shmuel. *Divrei ha-arakha, Zikhronot, Ktavim Nivharim* (Appreciation, Memoirs and Selected Writing). Tel Aviv: Brit Rishonim, 1947.

Judge, Edward. *Easter in Kishenev: Anatomy of a Pogrom*. New York: New York University Press, 1992.

Kahan, Arcadius. *Essays in Jewish Social and Economic History*. Chicago and London: University of Chicago Press, 1985.

Kaniel, Yehoshua. "Meimadei ha-yerida min ha-aretz be-tekufat ha-aliya ha-rishona ve-ha-sheniya" (Jewish Emigration from Palestine during the Period of the First and Second Aliyot [1882–1914]). *Cathedra* 73 (September 1995): 115–138.

Kaplan, Kimmy. *Ortodoxia ba-olam he-hadash: Rabanim ve-darshamut be-Amerika, 1881–1924* (Orthodoxy in the New World: Immigrant Rabbis and Preaching in America, 1881–1924). Jerusalem: Merkaz Shazar, 2002.

Kaplan, Marion. *The Jewish Feminist Movement in Germany.* London: Greenwood Press, 1979.

Kark, Ruth. *Yaffo, 1799–1917* (Jaffo, 1799–1917). Jerusalem: Yad Yitazhak Ben Zvi, 1985.

Karlinsky, Nahum. "Ha-hevra ha-hassidit shel Tzfat be-mahatzit ha-sheniya shel ha-me'a ha-tesha esrei ke-hevrat mehagrim—hebetim demografi'im ve-gibush hevrati"(The Hasidic Community of Safed during the Second Half of the Nineteenth Century as Immigrant Society). In *Mehkarei Hassidut* (Studies in Hasidim), ed. Emmanuel Etkes and D. Joseph Y. Dan, 151–196. Jerusalem: Hebrew University Press, 1999.

Katz, Yossi. *Ha-yozma ha-pratit be-binyan eretz-yisrael be-tekufat ha-aliyah ha-sheniyah* (Zionist Private Enterprise in the Building of Eretz-Israel during the Second Aliyah, 1904–1914). Jerusalem: Bar Ilan University Press, 1989.

Katznelson, R. *L'Immigrazione Degli Ebrei in Palestina Nei Tempi Moderni* (The Hebrew Immigration to Palestine in the Modern Time). Napoli: Studio Statistico Demografico, 1930.

Klier, D. John. *Russians, Jews and the Pogroms of 1881–1882.* New York: Cambridge University Press, 2011.

———, and Shlomo Lambroza. *Pogroms: Anti-Jewish Violence in Modern Russia History in Modern Russian History.* New York: Cambridge University Press, 1992.

Knap, H. Ger. *A Century of Shipping: The History of the Royal Netherlands Steam-ship Company 1856–1956.* Amsterdam: De Bussy, n.d.

Kushnir, David. *Moshel Ha'iti Be-Yeushala'im: Ha-Ir Ve-Ha-Mahoz Be-Einei Ali Ekrem Bey, 1906–1908* (A Governor in Jerusalem: The City and Province in the Eyes of Ali Ekrem Bey, 1906–1908). Jerusalem: Yad Yitzhak Ben Zvi, 1995.

Kushnir, Shimon. *Anshei nevo: pirkei alila shel anshei ha-aliya ha-sheniya.* Tel Aviv: Am Oved, 1968.

———. *Ha-roeh Le'me-rahok.* Tel Aviv: Am Oved, 1972.

Ledenhendler, Eli. *Le'an? Zramim hadashim be-kerev yehudei mizrah europah* (Whither? New Trends among East European Jews). Tel Aviv: Open University of Israel, 2000.

Lee, Everett. "A Theory of Migration." *Demography* 6 (1996): 54–57.

Lestschinsky, Jacob. "Statistika shel ayara ahat. (Statistics of One Town)." *Hashiloah* 12 (1903–1904): 87–137.

———. *Der yiddisher arbeiter in Russland* (The Jewish Worker in Russia). Vilna: Tzukunft, 1906.

———. *Dos Yiddishe Folk in Tzifferen* (The Jewish People in Numbers). Berlin: Klal Farlag, 1924.

———. *Nedudei yisrael* (Israel Wandering). Tel Aviv: Am Oved, 1945.

Levontin, David Zalman. *Agudot meshutafot ba-olam u-be-olamenu*. Jaffa: Anglo-Palestine Company, 1911.

Manor, Alexander. *Ha-hoge ve-ha-hoker*. Jerusalem: Hakongres Ha-olami Ha-yehudi Press, 1961.

Mendelsohn, Ezra. *Class Struggle in the Pale: The Formative Years of the Jewish Workers' Movement in Tsarist Russia*. Cambridge: Cambridge University Press, 1970.

Minc, Matitiahu. "Ve-eino tsofah al beit yisrael: Jan G. Bloch u-maavak yehudei Polin ve-Russia neged aflayatam" (I. G. Bloch and the Battle of Polish and Russian Jewry against Discrimination). *Gal-Ed: me'asef le-toldot yahadut Polin* 19 (2004): 13–27.

Mitchell, R. B. *European Historical Statistics 1750–1975*. London: Macmillan, 1975.

Nadell, Pamela. "From Shtetl to Border: East European Jewish Emigrants and the Agents System, 1868–1914." In *Studies in the American Jewish Archives*, ed. Jacob R. Marcus and Abraham J. Peck, 49–78. Cincinnati: American Jewish Archives, 1984.

Newman, Aubrey, and W. Massil. *Pattern of Migration, 1850–1914*. London: University College of London, 1996.

Perlman, Joel. "The Local Geographic Origins of Russian-Jewish Immigrants circa 1900." Working Paper no. 465, Levy Economics Institute of Bard College, August 2006, 1–41.

Ram, Chana. *Ha-Yishiv Ha-Yehudi be Yafo: me-kehila Sefaradit le-merkaz tzioni, 1839–1939* (The Jewish Community in Jaffa from Sephardic Community to Zionist Center). Jerusalem: n.p., 1996.

Reynolds, T. Marcus. *The Housing of the Poor in American Cities*. Baltimore: American Economic Association, 1893.

Rogger, Hans. *Russia in the Age of Modernisation and Revolution: 1881–1917*. New York: Longman, 1985.

Rombach, S. *Die yidische baalmeloches in Russland in der erste halft von XIX yor hundert* (The Jewish Craftsmen in Russia in the First Half of the Nineteenth Century). In *Zeitschrift*. Vol. 1. Minsk: n.p., 1926.

Rontch, E. I. "Der itztiger matsav fon di landsmanschaften" (The Present Situation of the Landsmanschaften). In *Die Idishe landsmanschaften fun New York* (The Jewish Landsmanschaften of New York), ed. B. Hoffman, 9–23. New York: Futuro Press, 1938.

Rosenblatt, Moshe. *A Tekufe fun 60 yor; a Zamelbuch in Idish un Hebreish Likhvod dem 60 yorigen Yuvileum fun Ha-Moshe Rosenblatt* (A Period of 60 Years: Anthology in Yiddish and Hebrew for the 60 Years Jubilee of Rebai *Moshe Rosenblatt*). New York: Yubileum Komitat, 1936.

Rotberg, Haya. *Sefer Me'uhar* (A Late Book). Tel Aviv: Am Oved, 1987.

Rowland, K. T. *Steam at Sea: A History of Steam Navigation*. New York: Praeger, 1970.

Rubinow, Isaac. "Economic Condition of the Jews in Russia." *Bulletin of the Bureau of Labor* 72 (September 1907): n.p.; reprint, 1970.

Rubstein, Ben-Zion. *Galitzia un Ihr Bafelkerung* (Galicia and Its Population). Warsaw: Die Welt, 1923.

Ruppin, Arthur. *Sotziologia shel ha-yehudim* (The Sociology of the Jews). Vol. 1. Berlin and Tel Aviv: Shtibel Press, 1931.

Samuel, Joseph. *Jewish Immigration to the United States from 1881–1910.* New York: Arno and the New York Times, 1914; reprint, 1961.

Sanders, Ronald. *Shores of Refuge: A Hundred Years of Jewish Emigration.* New York: Henry Holt, 1988.

Sefer Kalarash le-hantshat zikhram shel yehidei ha-ayara sh-nekhreva bi-yemei hashoa (Kalarash: A Yizkor [Memorial] Book for the Jewish community of Kalarash, Moldova). Edited by Noah Tamir. Tel Aviv: Arieli Press, 1966.

Segall, Jakob. *Internationale Konfessionsstatistik. Berlin, Veroeffentlichung des Bureaus fuer Statistik desr Juden.* N.p.: Internationale Konfessionsstatistik, 1914.

Sheinkin, Menahem. *Yedies vegen eretz yisroel* (Information on the Land of Israel). Vilna: Kadima, 1908.

———. "Ha-po'alim u-ba'alei ha-melakha ba-aliyan." In *kitvei Menahem Sheinkin*, 292–297. Tel Aviv: Reuven Mas, 1935.

Shilo, Margalit. "The Women's Farm at Kinneret, 1911–1917: A Solution to the Problem of the Working Woman in the Second Aliya." *Jerusalem Cathedra* 1 (1981): 246–283.

———. "Tovat Ha-Am o Tovat Haaretz: Yahasa shel ha-tnua ha-tsiyonit la-aliyah be'tkufat ha-aliyah hashniya" (Changing Attitudes in the Zionist Movement Towards Immigration to Eretz Israel [1904–1914]). *Cathedra* 46 (1988): 119–121.

———. "Lishkat ha-modiin shel Sheinkin be-yafo" (The Information Bureau of Mernahem Sheinkin in Jaffa during the Second Aliya Period). *Ha-Tzionut* 17 (1993): 39–70.

———. "Mabat hadash al ha-aliyah ha-sheniyah." (New Outlook on the Second Aliyah). *Kivunim* 11–12 (1998): 117–140.

———. *Nisiyonot be-hityashvut: ha-misrad ha-eretz-yisra'eli 1908–1914.* (Experiments in Settlement: The Palestine Office 1908-1914). Jerusalem: Yad Yitzchak Ben Zvi Press, 1998.

Slutzky, Yehuda. *Mavo le-toldot tenu'at ha-avodah ha-yisraelit* (Introduction to the History of the Labour Movement in Israel). Tel Aviv: Am Oved, 1973.

Smilansky, David. *Ir Noledet* (A Town is Born). Tel Aviv: Misrad Ha-bitahon, 1981.

Smilansky, Moshe. *Kitvei Moshe Smilansky—Zikhronot* (Writings of Moshe Smilansky—Memoirs). Vol 1. Tel Aviv: Mosad Bialik, 1934.

Sorin, Gerald. *A Time for Building: The Third Migration 1880–1920.* Baltimore and London: Johns Hopkins University Press, 1992.

Soyer, Daniel. *Jewish Associations and American Identity*. London: Harvard University Press, 1997.

Stampfer, Saul. "The Geographic Background of Eastern European Jewish Migration to the United States before World War I." In *Migration across Time and Nation*, edited by Ira Glazier and Luigi De Rosa, 220–230. New York: Holmes & Meir, 1985.

———. "Patterns of Internal Jewish Migration in the Russian Empire." In *Jews and Jewish Life in Russia and the Soviet Union*, edited by Y. Ro'I, 25–50. Portland: Frank Cass, 1995.

Steiner, Edward. *On the Trail of the Immigrants*. New York: Fleming H. Revell, 1906.

Subotin, P. Andrei. *Be-thum ha-moshav ha-yehudi* (In the Jewish Pale of Settlement). Saint Petersburg: n.p., 1890.

Szajkowski, Zosa. "The European Attitude to East European Jewish Immigration (1881–1893)." *American Jewish Historical Quarterly* 41, no. 2 (1951): 127–162.

———. "Suffering of Jewish Emigrants to America in Transit through Germany." *Jewish Social Studies* 13 (1951): 106–107.

Tartakower, Aryeh. *Nedudei ha-yehudim ba-olam* (Jewish Wanderings in the World). Jerusalem: Ha-makhon le haskala tzionit, 1947.

———. *Ha-adam Hanoded: Al ha-hagirah ve-al ha-aliyah be-avar u-yamenu* (Wandering Man). Tel Aviv: Newman Press, 1954.

Taylor, Philip. *The Distant Magnet: European Emigration to the U.S.A*. London: Harper & Row, 1971.

Thon, Raffi. *Ha-ma'avak le-shivyon Zchuyot ha-isha: sipur hayeha shel Sara Thon*. Tel Aviv: Privately published, 1996.

Tzemach, Shlomo. *Shana Rishona* (First Year). Tel Aviv: Am Oved, 1965.

Valhonsky, Dov. "Pogrom ha-petiha shel ha-me'a ha-esrim." *He-Avar* 20 (Elul 1973): 176–194.

Van Loon, W. Hendrik. *Ships and How They Sailed the Seven Seas*. New York: G. G. Harrap, 1935.

Westwood, John. *A History of Russian Railways*. London: G. Allen & Unwin, 1964.

Wischnitzer, Mark. *Idishe ba'al-meloche tsechen in Poyln on in Litte*. Berlin: Klal, 1922.

———. *To Dwell in Safety: The Story of Jewish Migration since 1800*. Philadelphia: Jewish Publication Society of America, 1948.

———. *Visas to Freedom: The History of HIAS*. Cleveland and New York: World, 1956.

Wyman, M. "Return Migration—Old Story, New Story." *Immigrants and Minority* 1 (March 2001): 1–18.

Yannait-Ben Zvi, Rachel. *Anu Olim* (We Immigrate). Tel Aviv: Am Oved, 1961.

Zahor, Zeev. *Idishe ba'al-meloche tsechen in Poyln on in Litte*. Berlin: Klal, 1922.

———. "Ha-imut bein ha-aliyah ha-rishonah ve-ha-aliyah ha-sheniyah" (The Conflict between Ha-aliyot ha-rishonah ve-hashinya). In *Hagirah ve-hityashvut be-yisra'el u-bamim*, edited by Avigdor Shenan, 233–248. Jerusalem: Merkaz Shazar, 1982.

———. "Tzmihat ha-zramim ha-politi'im ve-irgunei ha-po'alim" (The Growth of Political Factions and Workers' Organizations). In *Ha-aliyah ha-sheniyah* (Second Aliyah), edited by Israel Bartal, 215–234. Vol. 1. Jerusalem: Yad Yitzchak Ben Zvi Press, 1997.

Index

Note: Figures and tables are designated by *f* and *t*, respectively, following the page number.

277

and the white-slave trade, 171; working
conditions in, 188–92. *See also* Migration
to United States (1881–1914)
Urbanization, 40–42, 116
U.S. Congress, 148–49
Ussishkin, Menahem, 77, 106

Va'ad ha-Shalom law court, 191
Vienna, 28
Villages, settlement in, 177–79
Vitkin, Joseph, 20

Warburg, Otto, 23, 97, 124
Ware, James E., 194
Water, drinking, 147–48
Wealthy immigrants, 96–103, 121, 124, 185,
232, 237
Weiss, Akiva Aryeh, 77
White-slave trade, 167–77
Wilbushevitz, Nahum, 184
Wischnitzer, Mark, 109
Witte, Sergei, 39
Women: emigration decision-making role
of, 90–96; equality concerns of, 23–24;
as immigrants, 111, 112*f*; passports for,
129; and work, 23–24, 90–91
Work. *See* Labor and employment
Working conditions, 21, 188–92
Workshops, 43, 46, 185–86, 188
World Zionist Organization, 23, 28

Yarkon association, 202
Yemen, immigrants from, 256*n*12
Yerida (descent), 231, 236
Yiddish dictionaries, 72
Yiddish language, 140, 205
Yidisher Visnshaftlekher Institut (YIVO), 9
Yishuv: adaptation and acclimatization
of, 163–208; arrival in, 156–61, 163–67,
224–25; crisis of, 210, 222; defined, 3;

demography of, 10, 17; in early twentieth century, 20; economic situation
of, 180–208, 220–23; emigration from,
209–32; establishment of, 16; immigration needs and capacities of, 78–79,
96–103, 181–83, 185, 224–25; labor and
employment of, 163, 180–87, 220–23;
landsmanschaften compared to, 199; living condition of, 192–97, 226–28; old vs.
new members of, 21, 114, 224–25; second aliyah pioneers of, 20–21; in towns
and villages, 177–79; working conditions
of, 188–92
Yitzhaki, Solomon (Rashi), 4
Young immigrants, 18, 21, 25, 83, 113, 219,
226–28. See also Children

Zangwill, Israel, 54–55
Ze'ev-Latski-Bertoldi, 8
Zelnik, Moyshe, 84
Zionism: and agricultural labor, 177–78;
development of, among ordinary
people, 204–7, 239; and emigration
from Palestine, 228–31; exploitation of,
161, 172–73; goal of, 5; and immigration
policy, 96–103, 237–38; opposition to,
166; and Palestine immigration, 1–21,
24–25, 29–30, 79–80, 83, 203–7, 231,
234–35, 239–40; and Palestine Office, 80;
and the Uganda affair, 20
Zionist Congress, 23
Zionist Federation, 21, 23
Zionist historiography: aliyah in, 5–11; on
migration to Palestine, 1–21, 239–40;
narrow focus of, 180, 208, 239; on second aliyah, 19–25
Zionist information bureaus, 73–80;
applicants to, 81–90; criticisms of,
75–77; functions of, 75, 77; information
provided by, 73–75, 78, 139